God for a Secular Society

God for a Secular Society

The Public Relevance of Theology

Jürgen Moltmann

FORTRESS PRESS
Minneapolis

GOD FOR A SECULAR SOCIETY
The Public Relevance of Theology

First Fortress Press edition 1999

Cover design by Andrea Purdie
Cover graphic:
Lyonel Feininger, "Teltow II," © V G Bild-Kunst, Bonn, 1997

ISBN 0-8006-3184-6

Manufactured in Great Britain   AF 1-3184

03   02   01   00   2   3   4   5   6   7   8   9   10

Dedicated to
Dr Daniel Ciobotea
Metropolitan of Moldavia and Bukovina
and to the Orthodox Theological Faculty
of the Al. I. Cuza University, Iasi, Romania
in gratitude for the conferral of an honorary doctorate
and in ecumenical and European friendship

Contents

Contents

4. Dialogue or Mission? Christianity and the
   Religions in an Endangered World   226
     (i) The present state of interfaith dialogue   228
     (ii) Mission is the invitation to life   238

5. Theology for the Church and the Kingdom of
   God in the Modern University   245
     (i) From a confessionally unified state to the
         multifaith society   245
     (ii) Kingdom of God theology   251
     (iii) The theological faculties and the common
           good   254

Notes   260

Bibliographical Details of Chapters   283

Index of Names   286

Preface

My previous volume of essays, *History and the Triune God* (1991), contained 'contributions to trinitarian theology'. My concern there was the Christian identity of theology. Here I am offering 'contributions on the public relevance of theology'. There is no Christian identity without public relevance, and no public relevance without theology's Christian identity, since for Christ's sake theology is kingdom-of-God theology, while on the other hand kingdom-of-God theology gets lost in the clouds of utopia unless it is based on the person and history of Christ, and unfolded out of the experiences of his Spirit. The title, *God for a Secular Society*, indicates my belief that there is an implicit theology of modern times – a theology always already existent, but not critically thought through – and that this demands an explicit public theology. Its subject alone necessarily makes Christian theology a *theologia publica,* public theology. It gets involved in the public affairs of society. It thinks about what is of general concern in the light of hope in Christ for the kingdom of God. It becomes political in the name of the poor and the marginalized in a given society. Remembrance of the crucified Christ makes it critical towards political religions and idolatries. It thinks critically about the religious and moral values of the societies in which it exists, and presents its reflections as a reasoned position. But it refuses to fall into the modern trap of pluralism, where it is supposed to be reduced to its particular sphere and limited to its own religious society. Because today these restrictions to one's own particular reserve in Western multi-religious society can be felt everywhere, and are actually welcomed by certain church leaders and theologians, I hope that these contributions may demonstrate and reinforce the public relevance of theology.

The chapters in this book are based on lectures which I have given during the last six years, for the most part in secular institutions. In order to preserve the line of argument in the individual chapters, I have not eliminated every repetition. The occasions when the lectures were held, and in some cases the places of their first publication, are listed at the end of the book. This collection of essays does not as yet present the outline of a new public theology. They are only preliminary contributions to such an outline. But with them I should also like to repudiate the new lachrymosity of some theologians, who have fallen into the snare of self-pity.

I should like to end this preface to these contributions to an understanding of modernity by telling a little ironical story, which I have from Hans Mayer.

When the modern world was born, three good fairies came along, bringing their good wishes. The first of them wished the child individual liberty, the second wished it social justice, and the third prosperity. But then, on the evening of the same day, the wicked fairy turned up and pronounced: 'Only two of these three wishes can be fulfilled.' So the modern world of the West chose individual liberty and prosperity. The modern world of the East chose social justice and prosperity. But the philosophers and theologians – and this is my own addition to the story – chose for their ideal world individual liberty and social justice, and consequently never arrived at prosperity.

Tübingen   Jürgen Moltmann

I
Theology and Politics

I

Theology in the Project of Modernity

It is simple but true. Theology has only one problem: God. We are theologians *for God's sake*. God is our dignity. God is our suffering. God is our hope.

But *where is God*? An initial answer is to say that God is the subject of his own existence. So God is not in *our* religion, *our* culture or *our* church. God is in *his own* presence and in *his own* kingdom. Our churches, cultures and religions are then in their own truth if they are in God's presence. Theology for God's sake is always kingdom-of-God theology. Gustavo Gutiérrez maintains that 'every healthy, fruitful liberation theology is embedded in the theology of the kingdom of God',[1] and the same is true for political theology in all its different guises.

As the theology of God's kingdom, theology has to be *public* theology: public, critical and prophetic complaint to God – public, critical and prophetic hope in God. Its public character is constitutive for theology, for the kingdom of God's sake. Public theology needs institutional liberty over against the church, and a place in the open house of scholarship and the sciences. Today this liberty has to be defended against both atheists and fundamentalists.

If we want to perceive the unmistakably theological, and hence universal, task of the kingdom of God in the modern world today and tomorrow, we have to grasp the *implicit theology* of this modern world of ours, and understand why and how it was born, so that we can recognize both its vitality and its congenital defects. The modern world is a child of the Jewish and the Christian hope. So in the first part of this chapter I want to talk about *the birth of the modern world out of the spirit of the messianic hope.*

It is not just the pluralism of modern times that is the problem of post-modernity. The problem is the polarization between rich and poor which is modernity and sub-modernity. So in the second part of the chapter I should like to discuss *the contradiction between modernity and sub-modernity, or end-times of the modern world.*

Finally I shall try to define afresh the tasks of kingdom-of-God theology in the modern world, and in the third part I shall come to *the rebirth of the world from the Spirit of life.*

(i) The birth of the modern world out of the spirit of the messianic hope

There are at least two significant pre-Enlightenment sources for what English speakers describe as 'modern times' and what German speakers call 'new time' *(Neuzeit)*. The first of these sources is the *conquista*, the discovery and conquest of America from 1492 onwards. The second is the scientific and techno-logical seizure of power over nature by human beings.

In 1492 the foundation was laid for the new world order which still exists today. At that time Europe moved from a fairly peripheral existence into the centre of the world. 1492 was the beginning of the European seizure of power over the other peoples and continents, and according to Hegel this was the hour when modern times were born.[2] In America, the Spaniards and Portuguese, then the English, the Dutch and the French, and in Siberia the Russians, 'discovered' a new world, each of them for themselves. To discover something means more than simply finding something that has been hidden. It always means at the same time an appropriation of what is strange and alien. So this discovery is adorned with the name of the discoverer. America was not just identified, as it were; it was appropriated, and moulded according to the will of its 'discoverers'.[3] 'America (is) an invention of European thinking,' says the Mexican historian Edmundo O'Gorman. The conquistadores found what they were looking for because they invented it. Right down to the present day, the real individual life and real individual civilizations of the Aztecs and Incas have never been perceived for what they are; they have been repressed as something different and alien, and sacrificed to the will and vision of the conqueror.[4] Long before, the indigenous peoples had named the islands, mountains and rivers. But Columbus 'baptized' them, giving them names that were Spanish and Christian. And to give something a name is to take possession of it. The same can be said about the prohibition and suppression of the languages of 'the discovered peoples'. Not least important, the myth of 'unclaimed property', 'no man's land' and 'the wild' legalized the robbery, the colonizations and the settlements.

With the conquest of America, European Christianity also came forward with a claim to world-wide domination. It won souls, not for the gospel but for the Christian imperium. The decisive question was not belief or unbelief; it was baptism or death.[5]

② The seizure of power over nature by means of science and technology is the other foundation stone of the new world order. In the century between Copernicus and Sir Isaac Newton, the new sciences stripped nature of her magic and took from her the divine mystery which up to then had been called 'the world soul'.[6] All the taboos evoked by reverence for 'Mother Earth' and the greatness of life were then swept away. The sciences 'bring' (Bacon's word) 'Mother Nature and her daughters' to the human being, who has to be a man, so that he can be nature's 'lord and possessor', to use the sexist language of Francis Bacon and René Descartes. Here too, 'discoveries' are made, are named after the discoverers, and rewarded with Nobel prizes. And here too, this scientific process of 'discovery' doesn't just put an end to our ignorance. It also puts things in our power, and makes us their determining subjects. The *novum organon scientiarum* is the *ars inveniendi*, as Bacon said: the new scientific instrument is the art of discovery. Scientific reason is instrumentalizing reason, reason whose epistemological drive is utilization and domination.[7] This pushed out the older receptive reason, which was an organ of perception, and the earlier *phronesis*, which clothed reason in the wisdom of experience. According to Kant's *Critique of Pure Reason*, modern reason only now sees 'what it itself has brought forth according to its own design', by 'compelling nature to give an answer to its questions' (Preface to the second edition). This coercion of nature is called 'experiment', and in the eighteenth century it was often compared with inquisition under torture.

Right down to the present day Bacon's motto 'knowledge is power' holds good. And scientific knowledge is power over nature and over life. From science and technology, Europe acquired that instrumentalizing knowledge which enabled it to use the resources of the colonized world to build up a world-wide civilization, the origins of which are no longer evident, because it looks just the same in Frankfurt, Chicago and Singapore. The triumphal march of science and technology conferred on Christianity the status of being the religion of the triumphant God. Victorious, expanding Western civilization called its world 'the Christian world' and in the nineteenth century termed its age 'the Christian century'. There is still a journal with that name today.

What Christian hopes motivated the modern European discoveries of the world? The underlying motivation was the vision of *the new world*.

Columbus was evidently seeking both God's Garden of Eden and Eldorado, the city of gold.[8] God and gold were the most powerful incentives of the *conquista* and were its driving power.[9] The city of gold which Columbus and the rest were looking for was not simply intended for their personal enrichment. Columbus also legitimated his search for gold by claiming that it was a way of winning back Jerusalem, appealing to Joachim of Fiore's prophecy: 'From Spain will come the one who will bring back the Ark to Zion.' Why Jerusalem especially? Jerusalem was to be the capital of the thousand years' empire. Columbus also believed more firmly than other people in the earthly paradise. When he saw the rolling hills of what is now Venezuela, he shrank back, writing in 1498: 'There is the earthly paradise which no one can attain unless it be through God's will.' He understood his mission in both messianic and apocalyptic terms, like the many conquerors and settlers of America after him: the 'new heaven and the new earth', or – as people in the United States liked to say – 'the new world', *Novus ordo seculorum*, as we can read on the United States seal. 'America' always profoundly excited the utopian fantasy of Europe. The best known examples are Sir Thomas More's *Utopia* (1516), which drew on the travel accounts of Amerigo Vespucci, and Campanella's *Civitas Solis* (1623), which took the Inca sun state as its model.

What Christian hope motivated modern civilization? It was the vision of the new era, *the new time*.

The interpretative framework which mobilized Europe's diverse seizures of power over the world and gave them their orientation was millenarist expectation: the expectation that when Christ comes, the saints will reign with him for a thousand years, and will judge the nations, and that this empire of Christ's will be the last, golden age of humanity before the end of the world.[10] There is no need to mention particularly the degree to which the Pilgrim Fathers and the pious incomers who settled North America and wiped out the Indians as 'Amalekites' were moulded by millenarianism.[11] Through immigration, European and, more recently, Asian peoples have created the United States, put their stamp on its culture, and made it the central country of the world. The Afro-Americans contributed through their enslavement and their liberation. The country of the indigenous Americans, the Euro-Americans, Afro-Americans, Hispano-Americans and Asian-Americans has been settled by a people from many nations: *e pluribus unum* – out of many, one. The United States constitutes the unique modern experiment of a universal representation of humanity; and for that reason it is also uniquely dangerous.[12] Even today, every American president invokes in his inaugural address 'the messianic faith of our fathers'; and 'the millennial role of America' is still easily detectable in the political philosophy of the United States. It is 'the innocent nation' and hence 'the redeemer nation'.

With the beginning of modern times a wave of messianic hope swept through the whole of Europe. We find it in the Jewish messianism of Sabbatai Zvi, in the Puritan apocalypse, in seventeenth-century 'prophetic theology', and in the kingdom-of-God theology of early German pietism (Comenius, Spener, Bengel, Oetinger).[13] Christianity has always been familiar with millenarist end-time hopes. But with the beginning of the modern era, the new time signal was sounded: the time of fulfilment is *now*. This hope can be realized *today*. Secularization doesn't mean making things worldly. It means the realization of the religious. That is the reason why, following Joachim of Fiore's vision, modern times were termed in Germany *Neu-zeit* – new time. 'Ancient times' and 'mediaeval times' had now been succeeded by the 'new time', which is the end-time of history and 'the third age' of the Spirit within us, who is immediate to God. World history is being 'consummated' *now*. Humanity is being perfected *now*. Unhindered progress in every sector is beginning *now*. If there is no longer any alternative to this modern civilization of humanity, then it is 'the end of history', and an era subsequent to history and without history begins: the *posthistoire*.[14]

The lordship of the saints over the nations is going to be realized *now*; the lordship of human beings over the earth will be restored *now*. Science and technology are *now* giving back to human beings what they lost through original sin – *dominium terrae*, as Francis Bacon put it: domination over the earth. Hitherto childish human beings are coming of age *now* for, as Kant said, 'Enlightenment is the departure of human beings from their self-inflicted immaturity to the free and public use of their reason.' The human being is good, and can become morally better and better. The reason for this Enlightenment optimism about the human race is wholly and utterly millenarist: 'In this final age Satan has been bound for a thousand years', so that the Good can spread unhindered.

Lessing's 'Thoughts on the Education of the Human Race'

(Gedanken über die Erziehung des Menschengeschlechts, 1777) became the foundation document of the German Enlightenment. It is messianic through and through.[15] Lessing proclaimed nothing less than 'the third age' of the Spirit, which Joachim had promised, and with it the consummation of history. This era begins when all reasonable people pass from a merely 'historical faith in the church' to 'the general faith in reason', a faith in which all human beings recognize the True itself, without the mediation of the church, and do what is good without the church's guidance, simply because it *is* the good. Religion's 'divine plan of salvation' had turned into the advance of history. For Kant, the French Revolution, with its solemn apotheosis of humanity – 'all human beings created free and equal' – and its democracy, became the 'historical sign' *(signum rememorativum et prognosticon)* of the development of a better humanity. 'We see,' he declared, 'that the philosophers can have their chiliasm too.'[16] For Kant, this chiliasm meant the 'perfect civil union of the human race' in a 'league of nations' *(foedus amphictyonum)* which would guarantee 'eternal peace'. This is an idea which in the declarations on human rights and in the policy of the United Nations (UNO) has come to be seen as an inescapable necessity if humanity is to survive.

If we look at the messianism of modern times, we can understand why for Kant the *religious* question was no longer: What links us with the source?, or: What gives me a hold in eternity? The real question was: *What can I hope for?*[17] It is only a future which we are permitted to hope for that gives any meaning to life in history and to all historical experiences and actions. For modernity, hoped-for future became a new paradigm of transcendence for what transcends history.

(ii) The contradiction between modernity and sub-modernity, or end-times of the modern world

With our credulous faith in progress it is easy for us to throw ourselves from the pre-modern into modernity, and from modernity into 'post-modernity'; but it is realistic to pause first, and to be clear about the victims of modernity in *sub-modernity*. History's fine messianic top coat has its ugly apocalyptic underside; the victorious advance of the European nations has meant the retreat of the other nations, with all the tremendous loss involved; and the development of the culture of reason has led to the subjugation of the body, the feelings and the senses of modern men and women. The success story of 'the First World' has never gone unaccompanied by the story of the Third World's suffering. We need only compare dates and simultaneous events. When in 1517 Luther nailed up his reforming Theses on the door of the castle church in Wittenberg, and the Reformation in Germany began, Hernando Cortés was sailing to Tenochtitlán, Mexico. In 1521, when he conquered the city of the Aztecs, Luther stood before the Reichstag in Worms, under the ban of church and empire. When Lessing and Kant were publishing their Enlightenment treatises, hundreds of thousands of black African slaves were being sold out of Africa to America every year. The industrial build-up of the modern world was always at the cost of the earth's destruction, as the ravaged industrial landscapes in Germany, central England, Pennsylvania and Siberia show. So the progress of the modern world has always been acquired only at the expense of other nations, at the expense of nature, and at the expense of coming generations. If the real costs had had to be met, the actual progress made would have been negligible.

Only a third of the modern world is what we now call Western civilization – the so-called First World. Two-thirds of it are the modern Third World. Modern times – the 'new time' – have called forth both modernity and sub-modernity. But because some live in the light and others in darkness, the people in the light do not see the people who are forced to vegetate in darkness. The memories of the perpetrators are always short, while the memories of the victims are long. For the repressed people in the countries of the Third World, and for the exploited and silenced earth, the messianism of modern times has never been anything but the apocalypse of their

annihilation. But because our divided human worlds are
inextricably interwoven, and because no human civilization can
cut itself free from the ecosystems of the one earth we share, the
downfall of the Third World means the downfall of the First
World too; and the destruction of the earth will also mean the
extinction of the human race.

   ②.　*The economic end-time.* With the beginning of the modern
world the Third World also came into existence, for it was in
fact only the modern mass enslavement of Africans and the
exploitation of America's mineral resources which provided
the labour and capital for the development and advancement of
the West.[18] From the seventeenth century until well into the
nineteenth, Europe's wealth was built up on the basis of a great
transcontinental, triangular commerce: slaves from Africa to
America; gold and silver from America to Europe, followed by
sugar, cotton, coffee, tobacco and rubber; then industrial
commodities and weapons to Africa; and so on. This wholesale
transatlantic commerce produced the investment capital for the
industrialization of Western Europe. Through the slave trade it
destroyed the cultures and kingdoms of West Africa, and
through monocultures it wrecked the native subsistence
economies of Central and South America, making whole
peoples the victims of European development.

   The consequences are familiar enough. Even yesterday the
direct exploitation of labour and natural resources had already
been replaced by the burden of an enormous debt which has to
be repaid with interest. Even today, the interest flowing back to
the industrial countries exceeds the capital being invested in the
so-called developing countries. Yet nowadays the automation of
production is making industry increasingly independent of the
low wages and cheap labour in the poorer countries. More and
more countries in Africa and Latin America are ceasing to be of
any interest at all to the industrial West. The number of people
and markets that are no longer needed is steadily increasing.
The exploited Third World is being turned into a superfluous
backwoods, and its population into 'surplus people'. We see the
first sign of this road to exterminism in 'the coming anarchy' in

Africa, the forgotten continent, an anarchy which Robert D. Kaplan described so movingly in his article in the *Atlantic Monthly* of February 1994.[19] West African states are disintegrating and becoming ungovernable. Power is no longer a monopoly of the state. The ecological destruction of the countryside is driving people into the slums of the big cities. Malaria and AIDS are turning more and more people into lepers. The plagues are coming back. An enormous poverty movement is going to develop which will thrust forward into the rich countries, and these will become fortresses which protect themselves against the intrusive masses by way of new iron curtains: the fortress of Europe, the fortress of Japan, the fortress of the USA, and so on. I do not myself envisage the 'clash of civilizations' which Samuel Huntington prophesied. What I do see coming are crusades of the poor against the rich countries, and the decimation of surplus people through famine and disease.

② The ecological end-time. The beginning of the modern world is also the beginning of 'the end of nature'.[20] The modern world emerged out of the scientific discovery and technological mastery of nature, and today it is living from that more than ever before. The spread of scientific and technological civilization as we have hitherto known it is leading to the annihilation of more and more plant and animal species. Carbon dioxide and methane are producing the greenhouse effect which in the coming decades is going to change the climate of the earth, with momentous consequences. Chemical fertilizers and diverse pesticides are poisoning the soil. The rain forests are being cut down. Pastures are overgrazed. The deserts are growing. In the last sixty years the human population of the world has quadrupled, and at the beginning of the next century it will number eight to ten billion people. The foodstuffs required and the waste produced will rise accordingly. In 1950 29% of the population lived in towns. In the year 2000 it will be 46.6%. The ecosystem has lost its equilibrium and is well on the way to destroying the earth and itself.

We call this slowly spreading crisis 'environmental pollution', and search for technical solutions. But it is really a crisis of the whole major project of modern civilization. The human destruction of nature is based on a disturbed and distorted relationship between human beings and nature. Unless the fundamental values of this society of ours are given a new orientation; unless we find a new praxis of living in our dealings with nature; unless human beings arrive at a new understanding of themselves and evolve an alternative economic system; unless we arrive at these things it is not difficult to extrapolate from the facts and trends of the present crises the ecological collapse of the earth.[21]

What are the ruling concerns and values of modern civilization? It is evidently *the will to dominate* that impels modern men and women to seize power over nature – the nature of the earth and their own bodily nature. The increase of human power and the securing of that power provide the driving power of progress. This progress is still always measured quantitatively, in economic, financial and military terms, and its cost is shuffled off on to nature. The modern civilization which began in Europe is an expansionist culture in relation to other countries as well as in relation to nature. Earlier 'pre-modern' or non-European societies, which are now called 'undeveloped', cherished the wisdom of self-restraint and the preservation of equilibriums between civilization and nature, but this wisdom has been lost. Today it is also disappearing among the peoples who are striving to arrive at the West's standard of living – in Korea, for example, and China. The expansion and spread of this culture of domination is accelerating, and ecological catastrophes are increasing proportionately in all the countries of the world.

That brings us to the decisive questions of the present day. Does industrial society inescapably mean 'the end of nature', or must nature be protected against industrial society? Is the biosphere the indispensable foundation of the human technosphere, or can the technosphere be so expanded that the biosphere as we have hitherto known it becomes dispensable? Should we protect nature from us human beings for its own sake, or must we reshape the earth into an artificial world, like a space-ship, in which human beings, suitably adapted through genetic manipulations, can go on existing?

3. *The God crisis* (J. B. Metz's phrase). It is understandable that the clashes and contradictions of the modern world should have led to profound crises of confidence among modern men and women.[22] Confidence in time is lost if we don't know whether there is still any future. Confidence in the earth collapes once the earth is turned into a rubbish dump. Confidence in human beings is destroyed by our modern mass murders. By loss of confidence I don't simply mean religious uncertainties. Religious certainties are on offer in teeming abundance. What I mean is a loss of the assurance of God and the self in a profounder sense. Nietzsche made the point in 1886 with prophetic solemnity: 'The greatest new event (is) that "God is dead".' My father's generation experienced precisely this in the mass slaughter of the First World War, in which the most advanced Christian European nations mowed each other down. My generation experienced it in the unimaginable horrors and unendurable guilt of 'Auschwitz', where millions of Jews and other people were murdered in gas chambers with the methods of an industrial process. Today we are asking ourselves whether our progress is worth the sacrifice among people in the Third World. The founders of the modern age thought of a new, glorious era for the whole human race; but we are surviving on islands of prosperity planted in a sea of mass misery. Those earlier men and women believed that all human beings 'are created free and equal'; but we know that our modern life-style cannot be universalized. The growing anarchy in the Third World matches the growing apathy of the First. Our social frigidity towards the disadvantaged and the humiliated is an expression of our frigidity towards God. The cynicism of modern manipulators is an expression of our contempt for God. We have lost God, and God has left us, so we are bothered neither by the suffering of others which we have caused, nor by the debts which we are leaving behind us for coming generations. We see all this, but it doesn't touch us. We know it, but it leaves us unmoved. We are as if paralysed. Knowledge

is no longer the revelation of our power; it is the revelation of
our powerlessness. Because this growing apathy is not confined
to Protestants or Catholics, Christians or Moslems, Europeans
or non-Europeans, but is becoming more and more universal, it
has to be based on an objective alienation from God. God has
hidden his face and is far from us.

The great dreams of humanity which accompanied the 'discoveries' and the projects of modern times from their inception
were necessary dreams, but they were impossible ones. They
asked too much of human beings. Mexico was not Eldorado,
and the Garden of Eden was not to be found in Venezuela. The
United States is not 'the new world' in the messianic sense, and
the modern age never became a 'new time' in any messianic
sense at all. The scientific discovery and technical mastery of
nature did not make human beings the image of God. The
humanitarian notions of the Enlightenment neither improved
the human race morally, nor did they 'consummate' history.
These images of a 'brave new world' after the end of history
merely deepened history's wretchedness, and brought the
human race closer to its end. We no longer know where the
project of the modern world is taking us. That is the 'crisis of
orientation' which is so often invoked. And we no longer know
whether our thinking and labouring within this modern project
ministers to life or to death. That is the 'crisis of meaning' which
we hear so much about.

(iii) The rebirth of modernity out of the Spirit of life

The visions of modern times are impossible visions, but they are
none the less necessary ones. There is only one alternative to the
humanitarian ideas of human dignity and the universality of
human rights, and that alternative is barbarism. There is only
one alternative to the ideal of eternal peace, and that is a
permanent state of war. There is only one alternative to faith in
the One God and hope for his kingdom, and that is polytheism
and chaos. What must we keep, of the project of modernity, and

what must we throw out? What must we re-invent, so that the project does not founder?

① *Hope for God without triumphalism and millenarianism.* The God of modern times is 'the coming God'. The God of the Bible, according to the book of the promises and the book of the gospel, is the God 'who is and who was and *who is to come*' (Rev. 1.4). That is to say, he will appear in his full God-ness only in his kingdom. But where does God already come now? Where are we so certain of his presence that we can live and act with the assurance of God and ourselves? The messianism of modern times said: with God we will enter into lordship over the earth, and with Christ we will judge the nations. This messianic dream became a nightmare for the nations, and made an excessive demand on the people concerned, a demand which ended in cold despair: a 'God complex'.[23] But it is not in our domination that the coming God is present; it is in our suffering, in which he is present through his life-giving Spirit. It is not in our strength that the grace that raises us up is made perfect; it is in our weakness.

What, according to the book of Revelation, *precedes* the thousand years' kingdom of Christ? Resistance against 'the beast from the abyss' and the great refusal to sacrifice to the idols and laws of 'Babylon', and to make common cause with Babylon by enriching ourselves at the cost of the other peoples. The millennium is preceded by martyrdom.[24] Only 'those who endure with Christ will reign with him' (II Tim. 2.12). What the messianism of modern times has skipped over is the presence of the divine future in suffering, in resistance, in persecution and in martyrdom. The outcome was the appalling picture in which 'Babylon' was Christianized, and declared to be itself 'the thousand years' empire'. For what else did Francis Fukuyama mean, when in 1989, after the collapse of 'socialism as it really exists', he glamourized 'the global marketing of all things and liberal democracy', transfiguring these things into 'the end of history'? We must again turn back theologically from the apocalyptic Armageddon to the Christian Golgotha. It was on the historical Golgotha that Christ triumphed, not in the apocalyptic Armageddon, as Carl Schmitt's friend-foe ideology proclaimed. It is on Golgotha that the coming God is present in history.

Where is God? Where can we find God in this history of ours? Before his eternal kingdom dawns, the coming God is present in *his Shekinah*. When the first Temple was destroyed in 587 BC, and Israel was driven into Babylonian captivity, what happened then to God's special 'indwelling' in the Temple? One answer was: the Shekinah of the Lord went into captivity with the people, and suffered Israel's sufferings with her. God is the comrade on the way, and the companion in suffering of his people.[25] The gospel says that the divine Word and its eternal Wisdom became flesh in Jesus *and lived among us* (John 1.14). That is the Shekinah theology of the New Testament. If God lives among us, he journeys with us too. If he journeys with us, he also suffers with us. If he suffers with us he gives us the assurance of God and ourselves in the great exile of this world.[26]

We are always inclined to perceive God, the Absolute, only in whatever is like ourselves. What is like us endorses us, what is alien makes us unsure. That is why we love what is like ourselves, and are afraid of what is strange. That is the form which social self-righteousness takes. It is typically millenarist: God is like us – we are like God. We rule with God, and God is on our triumphant side. That is the way America was 'discovered'.

We go a step beyond this when we try to revere and perceive God as the Wholly Other (Karl Barth) in what is different from ourselves and strange (E. Lévinas). We respect and recognize other people and those who are strange to us when we stop trying to make them like ourselves, but attempt to open ourselves for *their* particular character, and to transform ourselves, together with them, into a new community of people who are different from one another. Then the form which social justice takes becomes acceptance of others. Of course this presupposes that in our relation to God we know that we are accepted by him as those who are different from him, and that as those alien to him we are justified.

We take a step further still when we try to revere and discern

God in the victims of our own violence, perceiving him as being himself the victim of human greed for world domination. God – the victim in the victims: that is 'the crucified God' who looks at us with the mute eyes of the street children. When Archbishop Oscar Arnulfo Romero discovered this, he resisted the people of power – and was murdered.[27]

'God is dead – we have killed him', maintained Nietzsche. Unfortunately he failed to see *where* we kill God. We kill God when we make his image the victim of our violence, for God is in his image. We kill God when we shut out strangers and drive them away, for God is in the stranger. We kill God when we choose death instead of life, and secure our own lives at the price of the death of countless other living things, for God is a living God. Anyone who infringes life, infringes God. Anyone who does not love life, does not love God. God is a God of the whole of life, of every life and of the shared life of us all.[28]

②. *Humanity's project of modernity began with the acknowledgment that 'all human beings are created free and equal'* and that 'liberty, equality and fraternity' (or sisterhood) belong together. In the liberal democracies of the Western world we have grasped what individual liberty means over against the power of the state. But that all human beings are free? That promise of human rights and constitutional government has certainly not been realized as yet. Many civil rights movements and many struggles for freedom will be required before that promise is fulfilled. And yet this human project does not accommodate the opposite – that some human beings have been created free, for example, while others have been created unfree. The society of the free and the unfree certainly still exists, but it no longer finds any justification.

What is still totally unrealized, on the other hand, is the truth that 'all human beings have been created equal'. Because socialism made this demand of modern times its own, and in its party dictatorships so hideously betrayed it, no one wants to talk about the equality of all human beings any more – at least not their economic equality. And yet there is no universal liberty for every individual without the fundamental equality of all human beings. Without equality, liberty cannot be universalized. Without a degree of economic equality there is no democracy. But what kind of equality?

Equality as a social concept means *justice*. Without just social and political conditions there is no peace between human beings and nations. Equality as an ethical concept means *solidarity*, brotherly and sisterly love – philadelphia, as humanism put it in so Christian a way! Is that pure idealism? I don't think so. I believe it is naked realism if humanity is to survive. Without the creation of comparable living conditions in all the countries of the world, we shall not be able to call a halt to the many refugee movements in the twenty-first century. One small example is united Germany: if hundreds of thousands of Germans are not to emigrate from the east to the west, we have to create equal living conditions in east and west. That is costly, but possible. The same is true for a united Europe: in order to stop the trek from east to west, the east must be made a place where people can live. Things will be no different in the north-south conflict: we shall not be able to withstand the pressure of millions of refugees by setting up new iron curtains. We shall only be able to do so by creating living conditions similar to our own in the countries from which the refugees come. The social task of the future is equality. It is not equality 'in our own image'; it is the equality that springs from recognition of other people and the reparation due to our victims.

(3) Not least important, we are facing an *ecological* reformation of modern society and the religion of modern men and women. The nineteenth and twentieth centuries have been called the economic age, because economics have been at the centre of every concern. But the twenty-first century will become the ecological age, because the organism of the earth will be the factor that has to be respected everywhere. Global economy will become what Ernst von Weizsäcker called earth economy, and global politics will become earth politics.[29] If humanity is to survive, the human economy will have to be aligned towards preserving life through harmony with the

earth's ecology and by righting the wrongs done to the soil, the water and the atmosphere.

For this ecological reformation of society we need a new spirituality and a new theological architecture. The dominating and exploitative mentality which has prevailed up to now will give way to a new cosmic spirituality. Ernesto Cardenal's powerful *Cantico Cosmico* marvellously opens up a new spiritual world. We shall rediscover God's hidden immanence in nature, and revere the divine presence in everything created. 'No created thing is so far from God as not to have him within itself,' said Aquinas. 'God's Spirit fills the world' (Wisdom 1.7) and holds all the living in life, fusing them into a life-enhancing fellowship.

We shall leave behind us the Western anthropocentrism which with Pico della Mirandola declared the human being to be 'the centre of the world'. It is not the human being who is the measure of all things. It is God, who has created the whole of life in order to invite everything living to the sabbath feast of creation. Once we overcome modern anthropocentrism, we shall once more set free the suppressed dimensions of human bodiliness and the senses. The human being is more than just a 'subject of understanding and will'. If we can again integrate understanding and will into our bodies and sensory perceptions, we shall then also be able to integrate human culture into the nature of the earth's organism. But not the least important thing will be to reintegrate modern instrumental rationality in the sciences into the wider cohesions of wisdom, of *sophia* and *phronesis*, so that we know what we can do and what we should do better to leave alone.

The project of Western scientific and technological civilization has become humanity's fate. We cannot go on as we have done up to now without arriving at a universal catastrophe. Yet we cannot simply withdraw from this huge project, and let the world go down to destruction without us. Consequently all that is left to us is the fundamental reformation of the modern world. So let us re-invent it!

Do we still have time? We do not know and we dare not

know. If we knew that our sands had already run out, we should do nothing further, because nothing would make sense any more. If we knew that we still had time enough, we should do nothing either, but should leave all the unsolved problems to the coming generations. But because we do not know whether time still remains to us, and if so how much, we have to act today as if the future of the whole human race depended on us. And yet we have at the same time to trust that God will remain true to his creation and will not let it go.

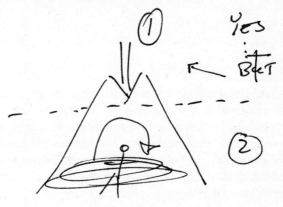

2

Covenant or Leviathan?
Political Theology at the Beginning
of Modern Times

(i) The present question

Federalism or centralism? Today that is a decisive question in
the political building up of Europe. In the Eastern European
countries, socialist centralism in a planned economy accompanied by the ideological surveillance of the people has crumbled
away. The federalist republic, with a decentralized form of communication and a multiplicity of regional, local and personal
initiatives, proved stronger.

Federalism or centralism? That is the problem of Europe's
inner unity too. Do we want a democratic Europe, in which
people are intensively involved, or do we want a smoothly running state machinery which looks after the people and incapaci-
tates them, robbing them of their responsibility?

Federalism or centralism? That is not just a question of
practical politics. It also thrusts deep into the basic trust and
basic anxieties of men and women. Don't we expect of the state
'security' and protection from our enemies first of all? Didn't
chaos break out in the Balkans after the collapse of a unified
Yugoslavia, with a cruel struggle of each against all? Doesn't
history show that without the taming of a strong hand, dog eats
dog in human society? But who can guarantee that this 'strong
state' which offers us protection and security will not itself turn
into a wolf that devours the people? Who can be sure that the
secure state will not become a 'state security' system? History

teaches us too that 'security' states have turned into dictator-ships which despise and destroy their people, dictatorships to which we have given the names of ravening beasts: the terrible Leviathan, the state Moloch and – in East Germany – the Stasi octopus. So how can we achieve pluralism in freedom without chaos, and unity in peace without dictatorship?

In trying to find an answer to these questions of our own day, I should like to offer a contribution taken from the history of political theology at the beginning of the modern era, in the sixteenth and seventeenth centuries. Perhaps we can recognize our own problems in the circumstances of that time, and at the beginning of the modern age also perceive the possibility of its end.

The word 'covenant' is used for the idea of the federalist state developed by the group of Calvinists known as monarcho-machists, as they worked out the law of resistance against the political and religious absolutism that was beginning in France. I am taking the theological and political ideas for this from the *Vindiciae contra tyrannos* (1574, printed 1579), whose most probable author was Philippe Duplessis Mornay.

The word *Leviathan* stands for the influential book of the same name published by Thomas Hobbes in 1651 (Latin 1668), on 'The Matter, Forme and Power of a Common Wealth Ecclesiasticall and Civil'. This is the utopia of the 'security' state, which unites in itself spiritual and secular, political and ideological power, and permits neither a division of powers nor a right of resistance. I am writing as a theologian, not as a political scientist, and shall look at both these treatises, the *Vindiciae* and the *Leviathan*, from the aspect of their theo-logical dimensions and their implicit theological premises. I shall then compare the two, and in doing so shall also draw on Martin Luther's 'circular disputation' of 1539 on resistance to the apocalyptic 'Werewolf'. After that I shall take a leap into the twentieth century, discussing Carl Schmitt's admiration for the *Leviathan*, and his attempted paganization of its ideas. Finally, I shall put forward a few propositions on the political theology of democracy, and the downfall of the 'Leviathan'.

Carl Schmitt's famous thesis in his political theology is as follows: 'That one is sovereign who can declare the state of emergency' (1922). My own thesis is: 'That one is free who claims the right to resist.' Resistance is the legitimate termination of lawless, tyrannical 'states of emergency' from below.

(ii) The theology of covenant and the right of resistance

Calvinism is considered to be particularly political because it is supposed to be theocratically inclined. But that is incorrect. In his letters to Huguenots, Calvin always justified political resistance only in the framework of the established law, never as natural law.[1] The established law in the France of his time was the law of the estates, which conflicted with the incipient absolutism of the French monarchy and its claim to the religion of the state: *un roi – un loi – une foi* – one king, one law, one faith. If there are estates within a commonwealth (Calvin calls them *ephori*), it is their duty to intervene on behalf of the liberty of the people against a tyrannical ruler. On the other hand, Calvin advised people without office to confine themselves to passive resistance, leaving vengeance to God (*Inst.* IV, 20, 31). Natural law and popular sovereignty play no part in Calvin's thinking. But resistance to rulers who molest and oppress faith is a religious requirement for him. For – over against the mediaeval discussion about the right of resistance – the Reformation introduced a new case: resistance, on the grounds of faith, to a change of religion ordered by the state.

In the Massacre of St Bartholomew of 1572, the French 'Rex christianissimus' had the leading Huguenots – then gathered together in Paris – murdered, among them Admiral de Coligny and the philosopher Petrus Ramus. That was the turning point, and it called into being the polemical writings of the monarchomachists.[2] In these, the point at issue was not the ancient problem of tyrannicide, but an alternative form of government to the absolutism that was beginning. The dispute with this 'modern' political form gradually brought about a transition from mediaeval government by the estates to the no less 'modern' constitutional state. The transition was effected through an increasing democratization of the right of resistance. Whereas in 1573 François Hotman could defend the estates' right to resist in the context of an aristocratically tempered monarchy, in 1574 we find Theodore Beza, Calvin's successor in Geneva, defending the same prerogative in the light of the rights of the people: 'All can resist those who, in violation of the duties of their office, arrogate to themselves a tyrannical rule over their subjects.'[3] In Presbyterian Scotland the Scots Confession was compiled in 1560. One of the 'good works' listed, following the worship of God and neighbourly love, is 'to protect the life of the innocent, to resist tyranny and to support the oppressed'. Resistance to tyrants is thus elevated to the status of a general Christian duty.[4] There is no longer any talk of restricting it to the estates or the representatives of the church. Part of the background to this astonishing generalization of the right of resistance is ancient Scottish law. In his *De jure regni apud Scotos* (1579), George Buchanan expounded it as follows: because both elective and hereditary monarchy rests on the homage of the people, once the ruler infringes the contract of rule, the people are released from their duty of obedience.

The most effective and influential exposition, however, was the famous *Vindiciae contra tyrannos*, which appeared under the pseudonym Junius Brutus, and which from 1579 onwards was frequently reprinted and widely disseminated (English translations 1648 and 1689).[5] Some people assume that the author was Hubert Languet, a pupil of Melanchthon's, who – as the diplomatic representative of the German Protestant estates – was an eye witness of the St Bartholomew massacre. It would seem more likely that the author was his pupil and friend Philippe Duplessis Mornay, one of the intellectual leaders of the Huguenots in the years of active resistance that followed the massacre. In this writing, it is no longer the estates' traditional right to resist the crown that is defended; now a new federalist, democratic idea of the state is advanced, even if there is no intention of abolishing the monarchy as such. As far as I know,

Duplessis Mornay was the first to use the theological notion of covenant as a justification for the right of resistance. Because of the interest in this aspect, it is usually only the third part of the *Vindiciae* that is read, while the preceding theological doctrine of the double covenant is overlooked. But it is with this doctrine, which he develops in the *quaestio prima*, that Mornay proposes to answer the four questions of the day:

1. Are subjects bound to obey a ruler whose commands contradict God's law? 2. Is it permissible to resist the ruler if he violates God's law? 3. Is it allowable to resist a ruler who destroys the state? 4. May neighbouring rulers help the subjects of a foreign country for religious or political reasons? The theory of contract which is used in the discussion of the right of resistance in these four cases is based, following the Old Testament, on the theology of the double covenant.[6] God himself makes the first covenant with the people of Israel on Sinai. The law of this covenant is the Decalogue. 'At the beginning the people had no king other than God.'[7] The people make the second covenant with the king 'before God' and transfer their sovereignty to him according to this contract of rule. If a ruler breaks this covenant, sovereignty reverts to the people. The king is then a tyrant whom the people must resist. But if the ruler breaks God's own covenant with the people, he is a blasphemer, whom the people are bound to resist in the interests of God's will. The people appoint rulers, confer on them the kingdom, and confirm the appointment through their voice. 'Thus kings must always remember that they are indeed kings by God's grace but that they rule through the people and for the people.'[8] That sounds like Lincoln's Gettysburg address: 'A government of the people, by the people, for the people . . .' The people make kings, not kings the people. In the contract of rule the ruler gives his promise unconditionally, the people only conditionally – if the contract is not fulfilled they are, without more ado, freed of every obligation: '*populus jure omni obligatione solutus.*' 'Popular sovereignty' is thus defined almost word for word in the way that Jean Bodin defined the absolute sovereignty of the ruler: '*Princeps legibus solutus est.*'[9]

The *Vindiciae* makes a distinction politically between *de facto* tyrants, usurpers and blasphemers. The *de facto* tyrant rules unlawfully over the kingdom conferred on him. Against him private individuals may not draw the sword, because he has been appointed not by individuals but by the people as a whole; consequently it is the representatives of the whole who have to resist him first of all. Usurpers, on the other hand, who seize the government by force, without any legal title to it, 'may be opposed by everyone without distinction, because here no contract has been made'. Finally, against the 'blasphemers', resistance in spiritual matters is actually enjoined.

For Mornay, the Old Testament lives on in the New, the people of Israel in the people of Christ, and hence the *politia Moisi* also in the kingdom of Christ. So what was required of the Jewish people is required of Christian people too. The picture Mornay draws is as follows. The people and the king answer for one another, so that neither falls away from the true God. If the king turns to strange gods, the people of God must take action against him. In the covenantal contract, God has given his people the authority and the power to adopt measures against rulers who wish to lead the people away from true faith. With powerful rhetoric Mornay enquires: why did God require the assent of the people? Why did he bind them to his law? And he appeals to the prophets, whom God appointed from among his people so that the rulers should be called to account for their sins. The people has authority *in sacris* – in sacred things – because of its covenant with God. Even if the king and a large section of the people fall away, the minority must resist, because every part of the whole has sworn obedience to God. That was the justification for resistance which Duplessis Mornay offered the Protestant Christians who in France were condemned to be a religious minority. The most moving example of that resistance was Marie Durand, who was incarcerated for thirty-eight years in the Tour de la Constance in Aigues-Mortes, and scratched into the stone there her valiant 'Récister'.

We shall pick out the following points in this concept of the state, and shall develop them a little further historically.

(1) Here the justification of the right to resist is not theo-cratically based, nor does it rest on natural law. It is founded on federal theology. Federal theology does not derive from Calvin in Geneva. It originated in Zürich, with Heinrich Bullinger's *De Testamento seu Foedere unico et aeterno* (1534). The covenant between human beings is based on, and safeguarded by, *God's* covenant with those same human beings. 'The true citizens of Christ's kingdom' are *confoederati*, fellow members of the covenant, declared Caspar Olevian, the Heidelberg federal theo-logian, in 1560. Another exponent of this tradition of Reformed federal theology was Johann Althusius. He put forward his *Politica methodice digesta* (1603) in Herborn, and out of federal theology developed not only the mutual contract of rule, but also the internal legal covenant binding society, and a social doctrine of all the different social contracts, from the family to society as a whole.

(2) The premise of federal theology is that God considers human beings to be worthy of a covenant and capable of covenant. From this trust on God's part follows the trust of human beings in their mutual capability for covenant. Men and women are symbiotic, social beings. Their social life consists of associations. Politics are symbiotic. From this the definition follows that '*politica est ars consociandi*' – politics is the art of association.[10] For this Althusius appeals, not only to the history of Israel, but to the political history of the Hanseatic and city leagues in Europe too, and to the political prototype of all federalists, the Swiss Confederation.

(3) Covenant thinking entered the political history of New England and the American Revolution by way of the Puritan emigration from the 'old world' of England into the 'new world' of America – this being interpreted as an exodus from the theo-cratic dictatorship of 'Egypt' into the covenanted community of 'the free and the equal' in the new Israel.[11] The covenant sermon which John Winthrop preached before the Massachusetts Bay Company in 1630 for the first settlers counts as the beginning of American political self-awareness: 'America: A Covenanted Nation'. The church covenant of free congregations and the

social covenant of the settlers' co-operatives strengthened one another mutually. Federalist patterns moulded the legislation of the individual states as well as their confederation, and put their stamp on the Declaration of Independence in 1776. Charles McCoy has recently shown that the famous federalist, James Madison was influenced by the federal theologian John Witherspoon, his predecessor at the College of New Jersey in Princeton.[12] The 'cause of the republic' was realized through the federal principle. Whether the word *covenant* should be used instead of constitution was also a point of discussion. That means that the constitution – in Germany it is significantly called the Basic Law *(Grundgesetz)* – is the agreement of citizens 'before God' which every government has to observe and which puts every citizen under an obligation to resist any exercise of power that is illegal, illegitimate, and that transgresses human rights. Resistance to tyrants is obedience to God, and the ultimate crisis and test of democracy.

(iii) Leviathan: the mortal God and his absolute sovereignty

Thomas Hobbes wrote and published his *Leviathan* towards the very end of the Civil War. By way of Calvinism and Puritanism, the English bourgeoisie and gentry were won for the democratic idea. On the other side, the Stuarts tried to reign in as absolute a manner as Louis XIV in France. There was no way out of the conflicts between parliament and the crown. The *Leviathan* appeared in 1651, two years after the execution of Charles I, and it is therefore also an answer to the monarchomachists' theory of the state and its political consequences.[13] But Hobbes's way of thinking is different, and devoid of concern about the position of the different estates and their traditions. In this sense it belongs as entirely to the Enlightenment as does the thinking of his contemporary, René Descartes. The state he constructs is a human artifact, *more geometrico*, 'after the fashion of geometry'. It is the a-historical utopia of a state machinery which is under the guidance of a sovereign will, and allows no room for the random contingencies of legal history. In his dispute with Sir Edward Coke (1552–1632), Hobbes rejected Common Law, and made the Common Law judges responsible for undermining royal sovereignty, and hence for the Civil War.[14] But does this mean that Hobbes's philosophy can be called 'the direct response to the civil wars of religion on both sides of the Channel', as Jacob Taubes maintains?[15] I would see it rather as an Enlightenment utopia of the state, which shows only a slight interest in tradition and religion.

Hobbes begins by assuming that the natural condition of human beings is a 'miserable' one, a war of 'every man against every man'. He sees, in the first place, 'as a general inclination of all mankind, a perpetual and restless desire of power after power, that ceaseth only in death' (Chap. XI, p.64). For that reason, 'Men have no pleasure, but on the contrary a great deal of grief, in keeping company, where there is no power able to over-awe them all' (Chap. XIII, p.81). In addition to the striving for power, however, human beings also have a drive towards 'their own preservation' and the wish to escape 'that miserable condition of war' where 'every man is enemy to every man'. People therefore make a fundamental 'covenant' in which they transfer their freedom to govern themselves to a sovereign, whether this be a person or an assembly. This is the way a state or civil society comes into being. 'This done, the multitude so united in one person, is called a COMMONWEALTH, in Latin CIVITAS. This is the generation [i.e., birth] of the great LEVIATHAN, or rather, to speak more reverently, of that *mortal god*, to which we owe under the *immortal God*, our peace and defence. For by this authority, given him by every particular man in the commonwealth, he hath the use of so much power and strength conferred on him, that by terror thereof, he is enabled to form the wills of them all, to peace at home, and mutual aid against their enemies abroad. And in him consisteth the essence of the commonwealth; which, to define it, is *one person, of whose acts a great multitude, by mutual covenants one with another, have made themselves every one the author*, to the end he may use the strength and means of *them all, as he shall think expedient, for their peace and common defence*' (Chap. XVII, p. 112). Because this state sovereignty issues from the fundamental covenant between human beings, Hobbes calls it a 'commonwealth by institution'.

Nevertheless, the political unity of the many is not vested in this fundamental covenant; it lies in the one who represents it: '*In persona una vera omnium unio.*' So out of many individuals is formed the great macranthropos, the Leviathan. The sovereign possesses all power, both worldly and spiritual. He is the head of the whole, and the subjects who have surrendered their liberty to him for the sake of their security are his body. A separation of powers would threaten the unity; the right of resistance would put an end to security. Hobbes too thinks in the categories of covenant and contract. He grew up in a Presbyterian house. However, for him there is no divine covenant with the people which sets limits to the contract of rule, but only the contract of rule made by human beings against hostile nature, as a means of ending the war of 'every man against every man'.

The sovereignty of the representative is as absolute as people can make it: *auctoritas non veritas facit legem*, authority, not truth, makes law (Chap. XXVI). The sovereign's will itself is the law, but he himself is above the law. He wields both worldly and spiritual power, so he is lord over right and truth, and thus over miracle and creed as well. He determines the political religion of the country; only the citizen's inward faith is uninfringed, inasmuch as thought is free. But politically the sovereign himself becomes the mythical hero of peace, the Leviathan, and must in the Arian way be worshipped as 'mortal god' on earth under the protection of 'the immortal God' in heaven.

Carl Schmitt and Jacob Taubes rightly pointed to the profound symbolism of the title page of the *Leviathan*. It shows a huge, giant figure, made up of many tiny human beings, in his right hand a sword and in his left the bishop's crozier. Both his hands are stretched out protectively over a peaceful city. Beneath the sword we see a castle, a crown, a cannon, lances, and finally a battlefield. Beneath the bishop's crozier is a church, a mitre, the symbol of an anathema, finally a council chamber.[16] The motto is taken from Job 41.24 [33]: 'Upon earth there is not his like.'

What did Hobbes intend to say with this picture of the 'great Leviathan'? Superficially, the canon lawyer Hans Barion will doubtless be right when he points to the mediaeval theocratic 'two swords' theory. According to the 'Dictatus Papae', secular law too is conferred by the pope; and in the same way, according to Hobbes, the political sovereign has both powers in a single hand, for the 'giant and mighty man' who provides for protection and peace wears a crown. We are reminded of portraits of Henry VIII with a sword in each hand. Jacob Taubes rightly concludes from this that the real goal of Hobbes's political theory was a theocracy.[17] This is confirmed by the *Leviathan*'s sub-title: 'The Matter, Forme and Power of a Common Wealth Ecclesiasticall and Civil.' But Hobbes is not concerned to 'draw a line between spiritual and worldly power', as Taubes thinks. On the contrary, his concern is the undivided unity of the two. The Leviathan is to be the prince of peace on earth. That is why Hobbes reiterates forty times that in his kingdom the acknowledgment is: 'Jesus is the Christ'. As far as I can see, this is only comprehensible if Hobbes's political utopia is understood chiliastically: in Christ's Thousand Years' Empire on earth (Revelation 20) spiritual and political power, state and church coincide.[18] It is only this 'Christian commonwealth' which becomes the 'mortal god on earth' or – in Hegel's phrase – 'the appearing Godhead'. But why does Hobbes call this political kingdom of peace 'Leviathan'?

This brings us to the theological discussion of Hobbes's political theology.

O. Can 'the war of every man against every man' be called the natural condition of human beings? Theologically, this is the *status corruptionis*, not the *status naturalis*. Anyone who maintains that the human being is wicked by nature blasphemes the Creator. By 'the war of every man against every man' Hobbes really means the apocalyptic end of the world, the anarchy of the End-time, the descent of the world into the chaos that was before creation. That is why he sees in the Leviathan's kingdom of peace the power to hold back this end of the world, the apocalyptic κατέχων. But the picture which Hobbes paints of nature is horrifying. For him, nature appears to be purely hostile to human beings, because it has brought them to that 'miserable condition' (p. 82). The natural state of things is merciless war; only civil society provides peace, which is the state of grace. As I see it, these ideas are based on an impaired relationship to nature. Consequently the human artefact, the Leviathan state, is an unnatural formation, destructive of nature. Carl Schmitt claimed that the human being is 'a dangerous being', driven in his reactions only by the mechanism of the will to power and the need for security. But this can be said – if at all – only of the men and women of modern European times, alienated from nature as they are; and it is a picture that is both atheistic and inhumane.

② The idea that political objectives should be formed by surrendering the individual's right to self-determination to a sovereign, who rules as he or she sees fit, is equally fictitious and counter-productive. Hobbes himself asks: 'Where, and when, has such power by subjects been acknowledged?' (Chap. XX, p. 136), and he provides no answer. Nor did he write his doctrine of the state for the citizens of the state; he wrote for the sovereign, in order to make clear to him his arbitrary power, and to show how he could subjugate men and women, and keep them subject through the terrible spectre of the struggle of 'every man against every man', and through their fear of death. The fundamental covenant which is Hobbes's point of departure is nothing other than a contract of subjugation for the purposes of survival. But it is difficult to believe that if human beings are wolves by nature they can bring about a kingdom of peace by surrendering their liberty, and subjecting themselves to a human sovereign. Does Leviathan tame the wolfish nature of human beings, or does he himself become a superwolf?[19] Why should the unquenchable will to power on the political level defer to the need for security? Why should it not rather swell to overpowering might? Is a tyranny really preferable to anarchy if, when all is said and done, tyranny is itself no more than a particularly unpleasant form of anarchy?

3. Perhaps Hobbes saw these ambiguities himself, and chose the image of the Leviathan for that reason. Let us look again at this mythical image. Is the Leviathan as prince of peace a 'Christ' figure and, as the divine human being, a reflection of the incarnate God? Or is he the Antichrist, 'the Beast from the abyss', 'the Prince of this world'? In old age Hobbes certainly contrasted with his good Leviathan the wicked Behemoth, i.e. the English parliament. But he cannot have been completely deceived about the biblical mythology. It is true that he cites only Job 41.24 [33], but he undoubtedly also knew Isa. 27.1, where Leviathan is called 'the fleeing serpent and the twisting serpent', and is put beside the dragon as the beast of chaos who is anti-God, whom 'in that day the Lord with his hard and great and strong sword will punish'. The apocalyptic writings of his time must also have made him familiar with the further development of the bibical Leviathan into dragon, devil, Satan, the god or prince of this wicked perverted world. Rev. 13.4 also says of the apocalyptic dragon from the sea – the Roman empire under Domitian – 'Who is like this beast, and who can fight against it?' Jacob Taubes illustrated his collection of essays, *Carl Schmitt und die Folgen*, with the picture of the Leviathan, mischievously entitling it 'the prince of this world'. In the Gospel of John, Satan is called 'the prince (or ruler) of this world', and his power has been broken for the first time by Christ, over whom he has no rights and no power (John 12.31; 14.30; 16.11). Paul calls him 'the god of this world' (II Cor. 4.4). It was probably the titles 'prince of this world' and 'god of this world' that gave Hobbes the phrase 'the mortal god'. In the apocalyptic picture-world of seventeenth-century England, the Leviathan is not a figure of peace. He is a power of chaos, who spreads chaos, and is the very antithesis of the acknowledgment 'Jesus is the Christ'.

If we wished to unmask the Leviathan, we might point out that dictatorships which are imposed in order to check anarchy, themselves become anarchical. Dictatorship is anarchy from above. Organized crime is certainly the end of individual crime, but it is not the end of crime as such. Organized striving for power is certainly the end of the struggle of 'every man against every man', but it is not the end of the striving for power. Hobbes's *Leviathan* can also be read as a vision of organized peacelessness. A Protestant theologian is bound to read Hobbes with this suspicion, for ever since Luther the unity of worldly and spiritual power in the hand of a single sovereign, whether it be pope or emperor, has counted as a sign of the Antichrist.

4. In the perilous year 1539, Martin Luther sent out a circular disputation about the right of resistance to the Emperor.[20] If, by waging war against the Protestant princes, the Emperor, on the Pope's behalf, should stamp out the Protestant faith, then for Luther he is not just a usurper or a ruler who is misusing his office; he is the Great Apocalyptic Tyrant. This is the *monstrum* of Daniel 11.36, who rebels against God, and the Antichrist of II Thess. 2.3. This is the *tyrannis universalis*. His principle is 'the power of the ruler is law'. He recognizes no natural law and no contract, but only the law which he himself has laid down. He himself has no legal status; he is the ἄνομος, the 'lawless one', of II Thess. 2.8. Luther says of this end-time tyrant: '*Hoc monstrum lupus est*' – this monster is a wolf – and the beast symbol he chooses to describe him is not a Leviathan or an octopus but the werewolf – a human soul with a wolf's body.

How can he be recognized? By the fact that he sets himself up over both kingdoms, the worldly and the spiritual, and plays havoc with all God's ordinances. Everyone must fight against this apocalyptic monster, rulers and ruled, rich and poor. 'This monster must in all circumstances be actively resisted by all and everyone . . . Even if in this mighty struggle judges or peasants be slain by the followers of that monster, they have by no means been wronged', says Luther in Thesis 25.[21] 'Against a lord who aids the world tyrant, the people have the right and the duty to rebel. It is a rebellion in the cause of eternal salvation, not a revolution for political purposes . . . Until the peril is past, only natural law rules . . . "*Deficiente magistratu plebs est magestratus*" '; that is the way the Lutheran lawyer Johannes Heckel explains this passage, in good federal-theological fashion: where the magistracy is deficient, the people are the magistracy.[22] Luther does not describe this monster as a 'mortal god'; he calls him the *deus infernalis*. But the essential thing here is not the apocalyptic imagery and the call to resistance. The real point at issue is the separation or the unity of spiritual and worldly power.

(iv) Covenant and Leviathan: a comparison

Let us now compare the main theses of the two political theologies that were put forward at the beginning of the modern era, not in order to harmonize them, but so as to clarify their profiles through a confrontation of the two.

The premise of the idea of the state as a Leviathan is a negative anthropology. This is required in order to legitimate a positive theology of power, authority and sovereignty. Human beings are wicked by nature, inwardly disordered and destructive, so they need a strong state to protect them from other human beings and themselves. To justify this negative anthropology, appeal is generally made to Augustine's doctrine of original sin.

The covenant idea of the state, on the other hand, presupposes a positive anthropology, so as to legitimate a critical theology of power, and democratic institutions for the control of power. 'All men are created equal [and are] endowed by their Creator with certain unalienable rights', as the American Declaration of Independence declares. This critical doctrine of the state generally draws on the doctrine of political demonism, according to which power (uncontrolled power) is evil *per se* (Jakob Burckhardt's view).

To justify the power of the state on the basis of a negative anthropology is really anarchical, for it maintains that there is no state either in paradise or in the kingdom of God; consequently the state is a phenomenon of sin.

To justify of the power of the state as deriving from a

covenant of free citizens sees the 'commonwealth' as a design created by human beings and an anticipation of 'heavenly citizenship' in the kingdom of God. The state as it is at present is certainly distorted by political demonism and human sin, but in itself it belongs to the nature of human beings, not to their estrangement.

(v) Carl Schmitt's admiration for the Leviathan and his paganization of it

In 1922 Carl Schmitt introduced the term 'political theology' for the doctrine of political sovereignty, which meant a fateful narrowing down of the ancient concept. Schmitt never made any secret of his admiration for the 'philosopher of Malmesbury' and concerned himself with the *Leviathan* throughout his life. In our present context we shall look at just two of the ideas he puts forward in his book *Der Leviathan in der Staatslehre des Thomas Hobbes. Sinn und Fehlschlag eines politischen Symbols* (1938), because they touch the nerve-centre of the Christian faith and hence of Christian theology too. The first of these ideas is the differentiation between spiritual and political power; the second is the liberty of private belief. In the first case, for Schmitt the distinction between religion and politics is 'Judaeo-Christian'. In the second, he claims that when Hobbes reserved the right to religious freedom in the private sphere, he paved the way for 'Jewish' undermining of the state and for the 'castration' of 'the vital Leviathan'. My concern here is not Schmitt's antisemitism, but the threat to the total state which he rightly perceived among Jews and Christians.

Appealing to Leo Strauss,[23] his Jewish discussion partner at the beginning of the 1930s, Schmitt maintained that in the question about the unity of the two powers Hobbes's position was 'contrary to typical Jewish-Christian doctrine, and that practically speaking he argued from a Gentile Christian viewpoint' (20). Strauss believed that Hobbes saw the Jews 'as the real authors of the rebellious distinction between religion and politics, which is destructive of the state'. Schmitt corrects this

to 'the Jewish-Christians'. For originally the differentiation of
the two powers was alien to the Gentiles, since 'for them
religion was part of politics'. Leo Strauss maintained that the
restoration of the original and natural pagan unity of politics
and religion was the real meaning of Hobbes's political theory.
'That is correct,' says Schmitt, and adds that the question is
'whether or not [the myth of the Leviathan] had proved its
worth as a political-mythical image in the struggle against
Jewish-Christian destruction of the natural unity, and whether
it was equal to the severity and malevolence of such a struggle'
(23). The context of what he says shows that by Judaeo-
Christians Schmitt means Jewish Christians in the *civitas
christiana* (not the early congregation in Jerusalem), and in
addition the influence of Jewish ideas in the Christian sphere.
The distinction between ecclesiastical and political power won
in the investiture struggle, the Lutheran distinction between the
two kingdoms, and not least, therefore, the freedom of the
church in the thus-differentiated constitutional state: for
Schmitt, these things count as Jewish corruptions of the
original, natural and thus vital unity of the all-ruling state.
Why this state should be 'original' and 'natural' and 'vital' is
admittedly something he never tells us.

In my view, however, this demonstrates the very converse:
that the freedom of the church from the state, and the self-
assertion of the church in the face of political religion or state
ideology, are the best securities against the totalitarian state,
because they do not allow the state, which is a human creation,
to turn into a monstrous Leviathan.

But it is not merely the 'Jewish' legacy in the Christian faith
which resists this transformation into religious politics or a
political religion – even if the state be a 'Christian' one. The bar
to any such transformation is remembrance of the Christ
crucified in the name of the Roman Leviathan. Christianity did
not come into being as a political religion. It was born out of the
free discipleship of the crucified Jesus. Christianity did not come
into being as a 'national' religion. It sprang up as a voluntary
community. Ultimately, it is always the cross of Christ which

stands between the church and the political unity of religion and politics, and tears that unity apart.[24] Erik Peterson rightly said of Schmitt's Leviathan: anyone who forswears the 'Jewish-Christian severance of political unity' ceases 'to be a Christian' and 'has decided for paganism'.[25]

To Schmitt's regret, Hobbes left a loophole in his unity of religion and politics, which was otherwise so self-contained and irresistible; and this later proved the Leviathan's undoing: it is the distinction between outward creed and inward belief, between loyalty to the state in public religion and freedom of thought and of faith in private life. In this distinction, or 'individualist proviso', Carl Schmitt sees the first approach to the free rights of the individual in the liberal constitutional systems that were to come. He maintains that from Spinoza to Moses Mendelssohn, and from Mendelssohn to Julius Friedrich Stahl, Jews have used this loophole in order to 'erode the life' of the Leviathan from within (87), for the inward life now determines the external one, and individual freedom of thought becomes the formative principle: 'One small, repositioning movement of thought, issuing from Jewish existence – and with the simplest logical consistence, the decisive turn in the destiny of the Leviathan was effected in the course of a few years' (89). The logical consequence of the Leviathan was really 'full, undivided state absolutism', over the inward sector as well: *cuius regio – eius religio*, a tenet which Schmitt viewed as 'the consummation of the Reformation'.

But Hobbes, knowingly or unknowingly, incorporated this Achilles heel into his *Leviathan*. Out of the faith forced to retreat to the individual heart the counteracting force slowly develops; for 'the moment the distinction between internal and external is acknowledged, the primacy of what is inward over what is outward, and hence of the private sector over the public one, is essentially speaking already a settled thing' (94). The power of the Leviathan will then be merely external, and thus hollow and empty, and a sub-human affair. Thus for 'the mortal god' the differentiation between the inward and the outward life becomes a sickness unto death. To demand of the state freedom of religion and conscience is to undermine and erode its sovereignty. In Moses Mendelssohn Schmitt detects just such a 'paralysis of the foreign (nation) for the purpose of emancipating his own Jewish people' (93). J. F. Stahl, he claimed, even 'ideologically confused and mentally paralysed' the very centre of the state, the monarchy, the nobility and the Protestant church (108). Carl Schmitt saw this correctly, but, as I see it, judged wrongly: the self-assertion of Christian and Jewish existence in the modern body politic has secularized it, neutralized it, and made of it a liberal constitutional state. Its re-mythologization by way of the Leviathan did not succeed. Hobbes wisely incorporated mortality into his political god, not because he himself failed to think consistently enough, but because of his 'Judaeo-Christian' beliefs. It was Spinoza, Mendelssohn, Stahl and the other emancipated Jews mentioned by Schmitt who, in Schmitt's own view, then saved the culture of liberal democracy from the Leviathan.

The socialist Leviathan too was apparently never able to dominate the inward sphere and private life, and because of that it foundered and died. But it is conceivable that through state control of the media even the private, inner life of the soul will be so much dominated by lies and fairy tales that there will no longer be either freedom of thought or freedom of belief. This was Noam Chomsky's analysis of the situation in the United States after the Gulf War.[26] The result will be the destruction of democracy. How can the 'individualist proviso' stand up to the economic marketing of everything? Perhaps here a new Leviathan is approaching us compared with which the Stasi octopus was a primitive monster.

(vi) The new political theology and democracy

A new political theology came into being in Germany after the war under the shock of Auschwitz, which only slowly made itself felt.[27] Those of us who came to theology after the war became painfully aware of having to live in the shadow of the Holocaust perpetrated against the Jews. For us 'after

Auschwitz' became the concrete location of theology. The long shadows of this historical guilt became our *locus theologicus*. We associated with the name Auschwitz not just a moral and political crisis of our own people, but a crisis of Christian faith too. Why was there so little resistance against the National Socialist Leviathan in the Christian churches? For personal courage was not lacking. But in the Protestant and Catholic traditions we discovered certain patterns of behaviour which apparently led to the failure of the churches at that time.

1. The opinion among the middle classes that 'religion is a private affair', and has nothing to do with politics, did not by any means rob the Leviathan of its life, erode it, and bring it to collapse, as Carl Schmitt believed. On the contrary, this 'inward immigration' allowed the external crimes to be perpetrated, and provided no point of departure for resistance. It was what he saw as the privatizing tendency of present-day theology which made Johann Baptist Metz demand and himself develop a politically critical and publicly responsible theology: 'The deprivatizing of theology is the primary self-critical task of political theology.'[28] It is not the person who holds his or her own private views who is enlightened. It is the person who is free enough to make public use of his or her reason. This saying of Kant's can be applied to the Christian faith too: freedom of belief does not mean being allowed to cultivate one's own personal faith; it means making public use of that faith, and practising it.

2. In the years of the German Leviathan, the separation between spiritual and worldly power, religion and politics, did in fact lead to resistance in the churches when they were supposed to fall into line. But it was resistance in the interests of the liberty of the churches themselves, not for the sake of the freedom of men and women. Through that separation, religion and conscience were restricted to the church, and life's other sectors were delivered over to unscrupulous power politics pursued without conscience. The new political theology pre-supposes the public testimony of faith, and freedom for the political discipleship of Christ, not just discipleship in private

life and in the church. It has no desire to 'politicize' the church, as its critics claim; its aim is to Christianize the political existence of the churches and of Christians, and to do so by applying the yardstick of the discipleship shown us in the Sermon on the Mount: the culture of non-violence. Politics is the widest context of every Christian theology. This must be critical towards political religion and religious politics, and affirmative towards the specific, practical commitment of Christians to 'justice, peace and the integrity of creation'. The distinctions between the inner and the outward life, private and political existence, or spiritual and wordly power, are not sufficient to restrain the Leviathan. The way – and this too Carl Schmitt saw rightly but judged falsely – must lead from within to without, and from faith to political praxis.

What distinguishes the new political theology from the old? It is its determining subject. For Carl Schmitt, political theology was limited to the doctrine of sovereignty. He saw as the determining subjects of political sovereignty only governments, revolutionary and counter-revolutionary movements. But the goal of his political theology was to fit religion into the confines of politics. The determining subject of the new political theology, however, is Christian existence in its difference from general civil existence, and the church in its difference from society and state. So the aim of the new political theology is to strip the magic from political and civil religion, and to subject to criticism the state ideologies which are supposed to create unity at the cost of liberty. In this way it places itself in the history of the impact of Christianity on politics, which means the desacralization of the state, the relativization of forms of political order, and the democratization of political decisions. Christianity has required political power to justify itself. It does not permit 'the innocence of power', which Nietzsche anachronistically invoked.

In closing, let us come back to the question raised at the beginning: how can we arrive at pluralism in freedom without chaos, and at unity in peace without dictatorship? Thomas Hobbes built the unity of the Leviathan on the notion of representation: 'Unity lies in the representer not the represented.' Carl Schmitt and Erik Peterson followed him. Duplessis Mornay and Johann Althusius saw the unity of society in the covenant. The crown sits on the constitution, said John Milton, not on the head of a man. Representative institutions ease the load of the people represented. My political representatives decide for me, and by so doing free me from the burden of my own responsibility. Representation of this kind is normal procedure in every form of social life. But this indispensable representation always involves the danger of estrangement.[29] Political estrangements result whenever the representatives get too much for the people they are supposed to represent, and the people capitulate before their own government. The consequences of this estrangement can be seen in spreading political apathy, in people's bored disinterest in politics, and in the separation of a 'political class' from the life of people as a whole. Because their representatives grow beyond their control, people revert to a passivity which in its turn permits the misuse of power. And that is not just a political estrangement. It is the beginning of every political idolatry. The early democrats and federalists saw the connection between estrangement from representatives and political idolatry quite clearly. John Quincy Adams, the sixth President of the United States, said that democracy has no monuments. It strikes no medals. Its coins do not bear the likeness of any person. Its true essence is iconoclasm. A merely representative democracy does not meet this claim. It is necessary, but it has to be supplemented by forms of direct democracy. Covenantal forms of social life, and the federalization of political life – a social contract, a generation contract and a contract with nature – can lead to a pluralism without chaos and to peace without dictatorship.

3

Political Theology and the Theology of Liberation

I am looking at this subject not as a neutral observer but as someone personally involved. What I am writing here is a contribution to a dialogue which has existed from the beginning of these theologies, and which today has to begin afresh, in view of the changed conditions in Europe. Now that 'the Second World' – the Communist bloc – has ceased to exist, the Third World and the First have to adapt to each other in a new way. My own context is Europe, and in Europe Germany, so I am talking about liberation theology from the viewpoint of European political theology. Many Latin American liberation theologians share Gustavo Gutiérrez's view that there is a 'breach' between the 'progressive' theology of the modern world, and liberation theology in the world of oppression engendered by that modern world. European political theology, it is said, is an academic theology, whereas Latin American liberation theology is a theology of the people. I shall try to examine this judgment, as someone whom it touches. I shall recount the history of political theology, in order to show that it is anything but a 'progressive' liberal theology of the established middle classes; it is a theology which is politically and socially critical, turned towards the victims of the First World, and can therefore be the natural confederate of the liberation theology of the Third World.

(i) Origins and beginnings

Liberation theology and political theology came into being round about the same time, between 1964 and 1968, but in very different circumstances – liberation theology among the poverty-stricken people of Latin America, political theology in the Cold War of divided Europe. The first was born out of the North–South conflict that divides humanity; the second evolved from the East–West conflict in the northern hemisphere.

At that time, Latin America was a continent that was just breaking free of its century-long colonial and economic dependence on Europe and North America. The successful socialist revolution in Cuba under Fidel Castro in 1959 was the bright and far-reaching signal for the rise of a 'popular movement' in many Latin American countries, with Christian participation. The theological interpretations of this awakening dynamic were at first tentative attempts to determine the future. The upwardly mobile and educated classes of the population took over the development programmes of the nations of the industrial West, and their theologians talked about a 'theology of development'. But the more it became clear that the development of the one was at the expense of the exploitation of the other, the more this model faded away, and was replaced by *the theology of revolution*. This was proclaimed in 1966 by Richard Shaull at the Church and Society Conference in Geneva, while in Colombia Camillo Torres lived it out, witnessing to it through the sacrifice of his own life.[1] For Torres, the revolution which brings justice to the oppressed people was a necessary part of Christian neighbourly love. But the goal of political revolution was socialism, as an alternative to the capitalism under which the people had suffered and were suffering. During the Allende era in Chile, the *Christians for Socialism* movement had its beginnings, holding its famous conference in 1972 in Santiago de Chile.

From 1972 onwards, with the publication of Gustavo Gutiérrez's epoch-making book, the *theology of liberation* took hold.[2] It is a formula which is unambiguous in its negative reference, but open in its positive one: liberation presupposes real, economic, political and cultural oppression, and is aligned towards a life in freedom and justice. It talks about a historical process, not a static condition. The process of liberation is sustained by 'the movement of the people'. Theology is reflection on this movement in the light of the gospel. Liberation theology is contextually localized and conditioned, deliberately so. Its *locus theologicus* – its *Sitz im Leben* – is the suffering of the poor. Participation in the movement of the people goes ahead of the theology: first orthopraxis, then orthodoxy! The church participates in the movement of the people by virtue of its 'preferential option for the poor'. Liberation theology uses sociological analyses in order to expose the causes of poverty (e.g., the dependence theory, which developed out of Lenin's imperialism concept). This theology no longer draws a dividing line between world history and salvation history; it testifies to the whole of salvation for the whole of this world. Liberation theologians formulated the better texts of the Latin American Bishops' Conferences in Medellin (1968) and Puebla (1979), and thus placed the church itself in the process of the transformation of Latin America.

In the 1960s Europe too had become a continent full of unrest. After the building of the Berlin Wall in 1961, the Cold War took on a new gravity. The Iron Curtain dividing East from West became impenetrable. West and East Germany were now the arena for the greatest concentrations of military power in the world: four foreign and two German armies confronted one another, with more than 12,000 nuclear warheads on both sides. Anti-communism in the one camp and anti-capitalism in the other dominated the political ideologies and made any inward opposition impossible. People lived in confrontation with each other, in two different blocks.

The first signs of hope came from West European social democracy – Willy Brandt's 'Risk more democracy!' – and from Czechoslovakia's reform Communism – Alexander Dubcek's 'Socialism with a human face'. Out of these two movements grew the first attempts to overcome the deadly schism in

Europe, to demilitarize the continent, and to build a 'shared house of Europe'. The *political theology* of Johann Baptist Metz, Helmut Gollwitzer, Dorothee Sölle, Jan Lochman and myself had its genesis in this historical situation. It was a theology that was ideologically and socially critical.[3] But why was it called 'political' theology?

The new political theology came into being in Germany after the war, under the shock of Auschwitz. Those of us who came to theology in those early postwar years were painfully aware of inescapably having to live in the shadows cast by the Holocaust perpetrated against the Jews. For us, 'after Auschwitz' became theology's specific, practical context.[4] The long shadows of this historical guilt became our *locus theologicus*. We associated with the name 'Auschwitz' not just the moral and political crisis of our people, but a theological crisis of the Christian faith as well. Why – with only a few exceptions – did Christians and church leaders remain silent? For personal courage was not lacking. But in our Protestant and Catholic traditions we found patterns of behaviour which led up to that failure. First, there was the opinion, general among the middle classes, that religion is a private affair, and has nothing to do with politics. This privatization of religion secularized politics. Christians who detested Hitler and deplored the fate of the Jews retreated into an 'inner emigration', thus preserving their personal innocence. Second, there was the separation between religion and politics that resulted from the (misinterpreted) Lutheran doctrine of the Two Kingdoms. Through this separation, religion and conscience were restricted to the church, and society was surrendered to unscrupulous power politics. 'No country can be governed by the Sermon on the Mount,' said Bismarck – and promised the Germans 'blood and iron' instead.

The new political theology presupposes the public testimony of faith and political discipleship of Christ. It has no desire to 'politicize' the churches, as it has often been accused of doing. What it does want to do is to 'Christianize' the political existence of churches and Christians in accord with the yardstick of Christian discipleship given us in the Sermon on the Mount.

Politics is the context of Christian theology – critical as it must be towards political ideologies and the civil religions of power, affirmative towards the practical commitment of Christians to justice, peace and the integrity of creation.

This political theology acquired its first profile in the Christian-Marxist dialogue organized during those years by the Catholic 'Paulus Gesellschaft': 1965 in Salzburg, 1966 in Herrenchiemsee, and 1967 in Marienbad, Czechoslovakia.[5] These conversations were unforgettable encounters between reform Marxists and reform theologians, between revolutionally inclined Christians and religiously enquiring Marxists. We came from Eastern and Western Europe, and moved 'from anathema to dialogue' and 'from dialogue to co-operation', as Roger Garaudy put it.[6] Political theology became the first post-Marxist theology – a theology, that is, which had addressed and absorbed the criticism of religion and idolatry put forward by Feuerbach and Marx, and which, challenged by Marxist social criticism, gave contemporary, actualizing force to Jesus's passion for the poor. An immense help in mediating to each side the best elements in Marxism and Christian theology was Ernst Bloch's *Principle of Hope* (1959).[7]

This was the state of things in which we found ourselves in the year 1968. For the liberation theologians it was a year of victory, since in that year they succeeded in exerting a decisive influence on the Medellin documents. For the political theologians it was a year of defeat, for in the autumn of 1968 Brezhnev sent the troops of the Warsaw Pact into Czechoslovakia, ending 'socialism with a human face' with brutal violence. In the outcome the Protestant theologian Joseph Hromadka died, as did the Marxist philosopher Viteslav Gardavski, a close friend of my own, after interrogations and torture. The names of the theologians who had been involved in the conversations were put on the 'state security' lists, my name among them. We were banned from the socialist countries as 'CIA agents, anarchists and convergence theorists'. Books, writings, quotations and the mention of certain names fell a victim to censorship. I am told that I said at that time: 'Now the lights are going out in Europe, and we shall not see them again for another twenty years.' It was just twenty-one years before the darkness lifted.

(ii) Developments in political theology in Europe

'Political theology' is not the description of a unified theological movement, any more than is the name liberation theology. Both are 'umbrella' terms, which gather together very different things, though with a shared alignment. So what I am about to describe as the different facets of political theology is simply my own view of things.

(a) Socialist theology

It was in 1968 that the student revolts in Paris and Berlin, Berkeley, Tokyo and Mexico City also reached a climax. These revolts were a young people's rebellion, a cultural revolution, a radically democratic and a socialist movement, and much more than that. In April 1968 the student leader Rudi Dutschke was gunned down in Berlin. And it was out of this student movement in Berlin that Helmut Gollwitzer's socialist theology emerged.[8]

Gollwitzer was one of Barth's friends, and he had been politically engaged ever since the time of the Confessing Church, during the Third Reich. Ten years imprisonment in Russia made him familiar with Marxism and the Soviet system. But it was the students who first convinced him of the reality of the capitalist 'crime against humanity', and the revolution of life that was required. In a multiplicity of writings after 1968 he presented capitalism as a 'revolution' which was going to end in the downfall of humanity, unless there was a conversion, a turn to life. In this conversion from destructive greed to the love for life he saw the dawn of the kingdom of God in this perverted world. At that time his 'Theses on Revolution as a Theological Problem' were passed from hand to hand. Gollwitzer saw capitalism as a contradiction to the kingdom of God that was hostile to life, while in socialism – following Barth – he discerned a true parable corresponding to, and anticipating, the coming kingdom. His 'Demands for Conversion' (*Forderungen der Umkehr*, 1976) are, in the words of its sub-title, 'Contributions to the Theology of Society'. His *Kapitalistische Revolution* (1974) brought the gospel and social revolution together, and tried to find an authentic location for the church in the class struggle. His main work during this period, *Krummes Holz – aufrechter Gang. Zur Frage nach dem Sinn des Lebens* (1970), set the individual aspects of this revolutionary process in the wider, life-embracing context of theology. Gollwitzer's socialist theology was close to 'the theology of revolution' affirmed by Camillo Torres, and it was to Torres that he also appealed. In those years Gollwitzer was not just the pioneering thinker of socialistically committed students; he was also a pastor to many people in the student movement.

(b) The theology of peace

The same year, 1968, also saw the beginning of the world-wide movement against the war in Vietnam. It was closely linked with the student revolts: 'Make love not war!' There were mass demonstrations in all the major Western and Asian cities, and in their wake, in 1973, the US abandoned the war.

Once the Vietnam war was over, the interest of the super-powers focussed once more on Europe, and rearmament was stepped up on both sides, particularly in the two parts of occupied Germany. This also led to growing resistance by the German peace movement. In the 1950s it had protested vigorously against the rearming of West Germany, and against the introduction of nuclear weapons: 'Fight atomic death!' At the end of the 1970s, the Americans stationed Pershing 2 and Cruise missiles in West Germany, and developed plans for a war in Europe against the Soviet Union. In East Germany the Russians set up their SS-20 missiles. The year 1983 saw the climax of the peace movement, as hundreds of thousands of people right across West Germany formed human chains in non-violent protest, and the German government acted against the will of the majority of the people at the behest of the United States.

At that time there were government discussions about 'security', and in the churches and among ordinary people discussions about peace. Opinion in the Christian churches was divided. Some people believed that nuclear weapons were necessary to keep the peace. Others were prepared to 'live without armaments'. In 1982 the Alliance of Reformed Churches declared the system of nuclear deterrent to be incompatible with Christian faith, and proclaimed the *status confessionis*.[9] In 1983 the Protestant churches in East Germany solemnly rejected 'the spirit, the logic and the practice of the system of nuclear deterrent'. In the German Democratic Republic a powerful peace movement developed which later, in 1989, led to the peaceful revolution. Its theologians included Heino Falcke, Dean of Erfurt, and Joachim Gastecki, later secretary of Pax Christi. Only the Catholic Bishops' Conference and the Union of Protestant Churches in Germany (the EKD) maintained that Christians could be either 'for' or 'against', and that the churches were there for people of both persuasions.

In West Germany, 1983 became the year of the Sermon on the Mount, to which the Christian peace movement appealed in its non-violent protests on behalf of peace. Politicians and political parties launched into attempts at biblical exegesis. The Sermon on the Mount made the front page of major newspapers. At this time political theology took on practical form in the theology of peace, and provided theological legitimation for the protest movements and civil disobedience campaigns. People as different in their way of thinking as Helmut Gollwitzer and Dorothee Sölle, Ernst Käsemann and Norbert Greinacher joined together in the peace movement.[10] In a situation of 'structural violence' such as exists in Latin America, the question of violence receives a different answer. But in Europe only non-violent campaigns enjoyed credibility. In the revolution in East Germany it was strict non-violence which alone led ultimately to the fall of the brutal socialist system.[11]

(c) Ecological theology

The beginnings of environmental awareness and the genesis of the 'green' movement cannot be precisely dated. After Rachel Carson's book *The Silent Spring* (published in 1962) had led to investigating committees in the USA, the Club of Rome's study *The Limits of Growth* (1972) made people all over the world aware of the problem. Environmental catastrophes were multiplying. Stranded oil tankers were poisoning the coasts. In Basel, the chemical industry destroyed all life in the Rhine. Acid rain is killing the trees in the Black Forest. CFC emissions from industry and transport, and methane from the rice fields, are destroying the ozone layer in the atmosphere. Finally, the Chernobyl disaster of 1986 has made large parts of White Russia uninhabitable for thousands of years, and up to now has cost 150,000 lives. Everywhere spontaneous groups sprang up to protect nature from destruction by human beings, the best known being Greenpeace and the 'green' parties in Europe.

In 1975 churches throughout the world were brought face to face with the problem through a lecture given by the Australian biologist John Birch at the General Assembly of the World Council of Churches in Nairobi. Most German regional churches appointed pastors with special responsibility for the environment, as a way of encouraging a lifestyle in the congregations that would be more caring and solicitous towards nature. Modern scientific and technological civilization began about 400 years ago with the subjugation of nature, justifying this with a biblical defence: that human beings were made to 'have dominion' over the earth – to be 'the lords of creation'. And for that reason Christianity in the West must share the guilt for the way our modern world has developed. Only a reformation of religious and moral values in the Western world can save nature, and ensure the survival of humanity.

The first ecologial theology was developed by the process theologian John Cobb in the USA, and in Germany by the Old Testament scholar Gerhard Liedke (see his book *Im Bauch des Fisches. Ökologische Theologie*, 1979). A series of church manifestos on 'reconciliation with nature' and a new creation spirituality followed. I added my own voice with an ecological doctrine of creation, *God in Creation* (1985; ET the same year).

Like socialist theology and the theology of peace, ecological theology aims to stir up Christians to participate in these initiatives, and in them to realize their own visions. On the other hand, like the other movements, ecological theology also brings the problems of society into the church, so that the church is present in the conflicts and sufferings of human beings and nature.[12]

(d) The theology of human rights

A less conspicuous but important dimension of political theology in Europe can be seen in theological reflections on human rights. In 1977, after seven years' study, the World Alliance of Reformed Churches passed a 'Theological Declaration on Human Rights'. A year later, the Lutheran World Federation published a similar study. The papal commission *Justitia et Pax* had already issued a declaration on 'The Church and Human Rights' in 1974.[13] All these declarations base the inalienable and indestructible dignity of human beings on their creation in the image of God; and by so doing they conjoin belief in God with respect for the beings he has created. All the declarations search for a balance between the individual human rights laid down in the Universal Declaration of Human Rights of 1948, and social and economic human rights, such as were resolved upon in the Human Rights pacts of 1966. As a practical consequence, all three declarations insist on the link between politics and human and civil rights – politics meaning both domestic and foreign affairs.

This insistence had considerable consequences in the 1970s. Human and civil rights groups were formed both in the military dictatorships of Latin America and in the party dictatorships of Eastern Europe. It is these groups above all to whom we are indebted for what we have experienced: the overthrow, without bloodshed, of those contemptuously cynical dictatorships. In

Europe these groups and movements put into practice the resolutions of the Conferences on Security and Co-operation in Europe, which began with Helsinki in 1975. And in this way human and civil rights became the foundation in constitutional law for the 'shared house of Europe'.

Today ecumenical groups of theologians and lawyers are working with the UN on an extension of human rights, which is to take the form of a declaration on the rights of future generations and the rights of nature, for an 'Earth Charter' which was resolved upon by the UN in Brazil in 1992.

(e) Feminist theology

No feminist theology emerged as an offshoot from political theology, but modern feminist theology nevertheless sees itself, too, as a political theology.[14]

The general feminist movement for the liberation of women from patriarchal oppression, and for full recognition of women's human rights, emerged first in the United States, although it really goes back to the impulses of the French Revolution. In 1974 the World Council of Churches organized a conference in Berlin on surmounting sexism in culture and church. In 1978 the first ecumenical conference on feminist theology was held in Brussels, and in 1981 the WCC Consultation on the Community of Women and Men in the Church took place in Sheffield. Since then, many church synods have addressed this subject, with greater or lesser success.

Feminist theology is political inasmuch as it presents theological vision and reflection for a comprehensive cultural revolution which will initially be sustained by women. It brings to light, critically and publicly, the everyday brutality and humiliation which takes place secretly in families and between men and women (the new women's refuges, or shelters, speak for themselves). It is also a movement for the human and civil rights of women in society and the churches. Finally, it also on the one hand motivates Christian women to participate in the general feminist movement, and on the other prepares the ground for these questions in the churches, which are even more patriarchally dominated than society – not to mention the rejection of women's ordination in the Roman Catholic and the Orthodox churches.

(iii) Where do we stand?

Let us take stock.

1. Political theology is not a purely academic theology. It is a theology which is related to the expectations and experiences of action groups and protest movements among ordinary people in the countries of Europe. In this sense it is related to Latin American liberation theology, although in quite different circumstances.

2. Political theology is not the same as 'progressive' theology, whether this be liberal Protestant theology or modernist Catholic theology. The differences and conflicts between the conservative Protestant Wolfhart Pannenberg and myself, or between the political theologian Johann Baptist Metz and the progressive post-modernist Hans Küng, are obvious. These others have never taken part in our initiatives and conflicts. On the contrary, they have often fought against us. Liberal theology was, and still is, the theology of the established middle classes. Political theology has its Protestant roots in Karl Barth's anti-bourgeois theology, and in the experiences of the Confessing Church in its resistance to National Socialism. In the early peace movement of the 1950s, we always looked in vain for Bultmann and his liberal followers. As I see it, political theology is the true dialectical theology: a theology of contradiction and hope, of negation of the negative, and the utopia of the positive.

3. Political theology in the countries of the industrial West has always critically challenged the self-justifications of the people in power. On the strength of Christian remembrance of Christ's suffering and death under the power of the Roman imperium and its agent Pontius Pilate, we have always tried to withdraw legitimation from tyranny in the name of its victims. We have grappled critically with political religion; with civil

religion; and with the ideologies of patriotism, 'the Christian West' and anti-communism. We have tried to 'demythologize' political and economic forces.

4. As I have shown, political theology has always tried to act as spokesman for the victims of violence, and to become the public voice of the voiceless: in socialist theology for the workers; in the theology of peace for the (potential) victims of a nuclear war in Europe, as well as for the (actual and present) victims of rearmament and arms exports in the Third World; in the theology of human rights for people robbed of their dignity and their rights under the East European dictatorships; in feminist theology for women who are imposed upon and mal-treated; and in ecological theology for the exploited creation. If it is true to say that liberation theology has a single theme – the liberation of the poor – then political theology must be said to have a whole number; but the point is always liberation of the victims and criticism of the perpetrators.

5. Political theology lives in the shared action groups, and brings into contemporary life the revolutionary traditions of the Bible and Christian history. That means Jesus's message about the kingdom of God, which comes to the poor of this world and the children – not at the spearheads of human 'progress' but among the victims of human violence. It was the Christian socialism of Leonhard Ragaz and Hermann Kutter, Christoph Blumhardt and Eduard Heimann which first grasped this. It also means the nearness of Jesus to the sick and the marginalized of his society, a nearness which today too draws people to Jesus and brings Christians to the victims of this society. And it means, finally, the Sermon on the Mount, as the basic law or constitution of God's kingdom in this world. For many of us this has become the guideline leading to peace in a world of violence.

If we sum it all up: the intention of our political theology is undoubtedly to make people who are the humiliated objects of the power and violence of others the free determining subjects of their own lives. In November 1989 we saw in East Germany a people which had been dominated and humiliated for forty years rebelling and bringing down not just the government but the whole system, with their self-confident cry 'We are the people'; for 'it is with the people that all power originates'. We should like to see the experience of this same freedom among the people who are suffering from the brutality of 'the free market economy' as well.

6. It is valuable for our theology to be related to its own context, so that it remains specific and practical. And this being so, some of us are in the nature of things Europeans in our thinking, and others Latin Americans. But it is wrong to use this fact to provincialize theology, saying that liberation theology is fine for Latin America, political theology is fine for Europe, black theology is fine for black people, feminist theology is fine for women, and so forth. Every theology is *contextually conditioned*, that is true. But every theology is *theology*, and therefore *universal*, and must be taken seriously everywhere. Moreover, every context is linked with every other context, whether it be by the one-sided tie of rule, or by the reciprocal bond of community. In the case of every theology, we have to say: think globally – act locally! In this sense liberation theology is just as global as political theology must be in its claim. But how are the two related?

(iv) The new situation: open questions

Ever since 1492, the modern world of North Atlantic society has been living at the expense of nature, and at the cost of the peoples of Latin America. What is suffered there is in actual fact the downside of the history whose upper side we ourselves experience. This can be said of the exploitation of natural resources just as truly as it can be said of the exploitation of cheap labour, and the burden of debt imposed on the Latin American nations. Approaches to a 'liberation of the oppressors' can be found in the political theology I have put forward (see my article in *Evangelische Theologie* 1978, 527ff.). It is part of the internal criticism of the contradictions of 'the modern world' – contradictions under which the Third World has to suffer most. Now that the so-called Second World of Eastern Europe has ceased to exist in its previous form, this internal criticism in the First World must make common cause with the protest of suffering people in the Third, so that at long last justice can be brought into the world-wide economic system. But where are the alternatives and the utopias?

1. The Cold War is a thing of the past. Centralistic socialism has disappeared from Eastern Europe. No one in Europe wants to talk about Marxism any more. Mikhail Gorbachev's offer to build 'a shared house of Europe' holds out tremendous new chances, both for good and evil. The European union will grow, and western and eastern European countries will join together in a democratic confederation. The problems lie in the steep decline of prosperity from west to east: how can equal living conditions be created in rich west Germany and poor east Germany? A truly united Germany and the European Union will have to be realized and make their way against the stream of men and women who are pushing from east to west. Without social justice there will be no peace in Europe. The free common market undoubtedly encourages personal initiative, but it also brings social inequalities in its wake. It is here that the future tasks facing the churches and political theology lie: the duty of maintaining, and maintaining publicly, criticism of capitalism, not in the name of any ideology, but in the name of the victims of the market-economy system; and the task of creating justice for human beings and nature through appropriate social and environmental policies. At the moment this is certainly not at all opportune; but ever since *Rerum Novarum* (1891) Catholic social doctrine has provided much critical potential for it. And the social movements in Protestantism are no less strong.

In our churches and congregations we have no base-community movement worth speaking of, but for the last 150 years the German churches have been strongly diaconal churches – strong, that is, in their service for others. In Germany, the greater part of social service on behalf of children, the disabled, the sick and the old is in the hands of the churches. This diaconal Christian ministry to the victims of the free market economy in our society would be misused if it were not bound up with prophetic criticism both of the people responsible and of the system that produces these victims. Now that the so-called Communist threat has ceased, I can see at this point inevitable internal conflicts between church and state, and between Christianity and society as a whole.

2. No less severe is the ecological conflict with nature in which industrial society finds itself. At this point environmental awareness, both private and public, has grown enormously during the past ten years, and has resulted in a cry for changes in production and consumption. Here ecological theology speaks for God's misused and despoiled creation, which we are sacrificing because we are living at its expense. This theology protests against the perpetrators and the system that produces these victims. Ecological theology too is Christian diaconal service, in this case on behalf of suffering nature; and at the same time it is prophetic criticism of the brutality which causes the suffering.

3. Political theology in Europe was ecumenical from the beginning, and developed in the framework of international relationships with Latin America, Korea and Africa. But with the new Europe, a new Eurocentricism has also developed among Europeans; and this the Christian churches have to resist by virtue of their world-wide catholicity. Christians in Europe must become the advocates of those who are outside. At the moment nationalism is on the increase in Europe. We need ecumenical solidarity which will be stronger than national and European loyalties. That is not just a moral duty. It is also the only reasonable commitment. Without social justice between the First World and the Third, there can be no peace. Without peace with the Third World the world of North Atlantic society will destroy itself. The ecological consequences of the Third World's impoverishment are already boomeranging back on to the world of Western industrial society. A human world cleft apart by violence and injustice will destroy the one earth on which we all live.

Political theology is the *internal* criticism of the modern world. Liberation theology is the *external* criticism of the modern world. Both speak in the name of the victims. Do we not have to develop an alliance between critical theology in the First World and liberation theology in the Third?

(v) The future of liberation theology

Up to now it has been only the Latinos who have spoken in the new Latin American theology.[15] When will the black descendants of the slaves in Brazil, and when will the Indigenos, raise their voices? And if the Indians find a voice, will they then still express themselves in forms of a Christian theology, or will they cut themselves off from their brutal Christianization and revert to their own ancient cultures and religions?[16] The black people in Brazil and in the Caribbean too could well find their ancient African Macumba cults more attractive than Christianity, even if that is represented by liberation theology.

If in the future Latin America also ceases to be a purely 'Christian continent', will Latin American liberation theology not then have to expand into interfaith dialogue? An interfaith dialogue within the perspective of liberation theology would be something new for these discussions, which up to now have served the peaceful co-existence of the religious communities – 'No world peace without peace between the religions', declares Hans Küng – rather than the common struggle against oppression, for the liberation of the people. The need for this expansion already became clear when an attempt was made to transplant Latin American liberation theology to Asia, and the people involved came to realize that the mass of Asia's poor are non-Christians, to whom a Christian theology has little to say. But if liberation theology is expanded in this respect, its own foundations must be expanded too. Hitherto this theology has been almost exclusively socio-economically orientated towards the antagonisms between poverty and wealth, oppression and liberation, and has expended too little attention on the cultural and religious dimensions in its own 'home countries' and among their peoples. When I cautiously intimated this in my 'Open Letter' to José Miguez-Bonino in 1976, the suggestion was indignantly repudiated. But today more and more people in Central and South America are turning to new religious movements, such as the Afro-Brazilian cults, while the Christian Pentecostal movement is drawing the mass of the poor; and this fact is surely connected with this defect in early liberation theology. The poor don't want just to be told what they don't have; they also want to be valued for what they are.

For a long time, ecological anxiety about the destruction of the rain forests in Latin America was thought to be a typically First World concern. For the poor landless farmers of Brazil, it is economic anxiety in the day-to-day struggle for survival which is in the forefront of their minds. It is only in recent years that the perception has begun to make its way in Latin American liberation theology too that economy and ecology belong indivisibly together, and that it is suicidal to despoil and consume the foundations on which one's own life is based. It was after the middle of the 1970s that an ecological-political theology developed in Europe (especially in over-industrialized Germany), following the North American model (represented by John Cobb, Harvey Cox and others); and now an ecological theology of liberation has also begun to grow (DEI in Costa Rica, Leonardo Boff, Reinerio Arce Valentin in Cuba). This has forged links with the first beginnings of an ecological policy in Brazil. Leonardo Boff's vison of a new planetary bio-ethic is theologically interesting; it fits very well into the new 'theology of life',[17] and introduces new viewpoints into our ecological discourse as well. From the viewpoint of liberation theology, concern is not merely with what the conciliar process calls 'the integrity of creation'. The aim is also to liberate nature from human oppression, and to reintegrate human culture into the living organism of the earth. This is the vision of Ernesto Cardenal's beautiful and powerful 'Cantico Cosmico'.[18]

In North America, the women's liberation movement developed parallel to the civil rights movement. Feminist theology began as a holistic theology, but soon took over its methods from liberation theology. In the United States and Europe, feminist theologians see themselves as liberation theologians (feminist/liberationist), and in the last ten years Latin America has developed a remarkable feminist liberation theology of its own. Mujerista theology corresponds to the black womanist theology of Dolores Williams and others, as distinct from white middle-class theology. The category 'poor' is egalitarian, but it can nevertheless be clearly differentiated: women as economically exploited, publicly and legally disenfranchised, and as culturally humiliated through 'machismo'. They are the victims of sexist violence as well as economic and political brutality. In addition to criticism of patriarchal images of God (which can be found in the USA and Europe too), Latin American women have taken over leading roles in the Christian base communities, and by so doing have called the male priestly caste in question. With Elsa Tamez, the Protestant Seminario Biblico Latinoamericano in San José, Costa Rica, now has its first woman rector.

But the most difficult and delicate point about the whole of liberation theology is not to be found in external conditions, but internally, in the church itself. Without a liberated church there can be no liberated society; without a reform of the churches there can be no social revolution. Ever since the famous Latin American Bishops' Conferences in Medellin (1968) and Puebla (1979), many people have hoped that the episcopate and theology together would implement the church's 'option for the poor', that the church in Latin America, as 'the church of the poor' and 'the church of the people', would begin to initiate a universal reformation of the Catholic Church, and that the theology of liberation would correspondingly play a leading part in the global class struggle (George Casalis). These hopes have foundered on Rome and the policies of the Vatican. Of course one can quote the pope's words, 'the theology of liberation is not merely opportune; it is useful and necessary'.[19] But we do better to look at what the pope actually does. Since Puebla, the bishops appointed have reduced supporters of liberation theology in the Latin American episcopate to a minority. Cardinal Arns and Cardinal Lorscheider were considerably restricted in what they were able to do. The see of the martyr bishop Oscar Arnulfo Romero is now occupied by an Opus Dei man. It is deeply depressing to have to mention that John Paul II sent a golden gift with personal greetings to General Augusto Pinochet, the murderer of so many Christians in Chile, on the occasion of his golden wedding. Of course one can mention the two letters from the Congregation for the Doctrine of the Faith in which Cardinal Ratzinger finally arrived at a balanced judgment of liberation theology; but we do better to look at what he does, and to listen to the long story of Leonardo Boff's sufferings. Forced to relinquish his priesthood and to leave the Franciscan order, he wrote bitterly in farewell: 'The doctrinaire power is cruel and merciless' (*Publik Forum*, 17 July 1992, 15f.).

Were Medellin and Puebla the church's dreams, in which the liberation theologians put too much faith? Have those theologians fought insufficiently for liberty in the church – Hans Küng's reproach? Certainly, the church of the base communities exists, and in many countries one has the impression that there are two parallel Catholic Churches: here the base communities – there the hierarchy. At all events, it is clear that it is impossible to build up a new, just and free society with an old, feudalistically authoritarian church. 'We are the people': that is true in politics *and* the church or it isn't true at all. As long as the feudalistically authoritarian, hierarchical structure of the colonial church of Latin America continues to exist, it will always serve as the model for a class society that matches it. To experience the church as 'the people of God' (which is what the Second Vatican Council declared it to be), and as the living community of Christ – men and women who long for this, and cling to hopes for a 'people's church' in the tradition of Medellin and Puebla – will in many cases join the congregations of the Protestant Pentecostal movement, which church leaders are still contemptuously terming 'sects'.

Here, it seems to me, comes the hardest but most important challenge to the theology of liberation: the liberation of the church from 'holy rule' so that it may become the community of the people.

(vi) The theology of our liberation

(a) The globalization of the Third World

The facts are obvious enough: the present globalization of the economy, the transfer of production to what are known as the low-wage countries, and the opening of the markets do not just bring our industries into the Third World. They also bring the Third World to us. We ourselves are becoming the Third World. And indeed the term was originally meant not just geographically but socially too, and meant the poor depressed classes in society. This is the way we are experiencing the Third World among ourselves today. The UNO report on human development (1996) points out the dangers that ensue when the many are impoverished through the enrichment of the few. The wealth of 358 multi-millionaires exceeds the total income of the poor countries, in which almost 45% of the world's population lives! Commenting on this, J.G. Speth, General Secretary of the UNO Development Programme, declared that if present trends continue, the economic drop between industrialized and developing countries will take on dimensions which are no longer merely unjust but are actually inhumane.[20]

But this injustice and inhumanity is also growing in the industrial countries themselves. This year, over 100 million people in North America, Europe, Japan and Australia are living below the official poverty line. Almost 30 million of them are homeless. In Germany too the figures are alarming: 7.5 million poor, 900,000 homeless. There are no signs of effective social policies designed to counter this development – rather political capitulation before 'the force of circumstances' in the economy, where businesses can increase their profits if they are globalized, and then avoid having to pay taxes in their home country. Among us, the impoverished are at least still surviving on the borders of the minimum for subsistence. But in the underdeveloped countries the UNO report tells us that 25,000 children are dying every day of hunger and of diseases which have long since been curable.[21]

The globalization of the economy is evidently leading in our societies to a shortfall of solidarity, as the never-ending lamentations about the excessive costs of the social services show. Health insurances are trying to get rid of the old and the chronically ill. In England, dialysis is no longer available for people over sixty unless they pay for it themselves. If people are judged only according to their market value, and are no longer respected in their human dignity, then a child with a high life expectancy may be worth eight million pounds while an old-age pensioner is not worth anything at all, because he or she can no longer produce anything. Consequently the fear that the disabled, the old and the 'useless' are running into serious danger in our society can no longer be dismissed out of hand. The countries of the so-called First World are also falling into a condition of apartheid: with the poverty of families and the lack of future for young people, crime is on the increase. Consequently the rich and the better off live in 'gated communities', in secure areas, and the other districts sink into slums, which is what we see happening in South Africa at the moment. The decline of a strong middle class means the end of political democracy, for the democratic idea of equality is incompatible with an economic system in which more and more inequalities are fabricated.

The more we in the countries of the industrialized West are clear about this development, and the more we discover the oppressed, impoverished and abandoned world in our own backyard, the more relevant we shall find the Latin American theology of liberation. It is better to heed its basic insights now, rather than to wait for the tragic end of capitalism, which has not foundered on its socialist alternative but is surely condemned to failure because it is increasingly at variance with human dignity, the life of this earth, and its own future.

(b) On the way to a common theology of life

If it is true that the globalization of production and markets is bringing the unjust and inhumane conditions of the Third World into what is still geographically (if not socially) 'the First World', then the relevance of the Third World's liberation theology also becomes universal. The Latin American theology of liberation is the first alternative theology to the capitalism which today goes under the name of 'the global marketing of everything'. It is contextual theology, not just for Latin America, but universally so, in the wake of the developments I have described. It speaks for the impoverished and marginalized in Los Angeles and Bangkok, England and Romania, East Germany and South Africa, to mention only a few places and countries. So it will be taken up by others, and translated into their conditions. In this process it will cease to be a specially Latin American theology and will become a theology whose social criticism has a universal scope. 'The Third World' is a class designation, not a geographical one. As the theology of liberation becomes universal, it will cross its Roman Catholic frontiers and become catholic in a wider ecumenical sense. It will reach out beyond the borders of the Christian community, in order to strengthen every impulse among the people which works for the liberation of humanity from injustice and oppression. Latin America may perhaps still count as a 'Christian continent'. This cannot be said of Asia and Africa. But the mission of liberation theology is as universal as the wretchedness of humanity.

In Europe, it seems to me important for the theology of the liberation of the poor to be embedded from the start in the wider context of the kingdom of God; for that gives a name to the positive goal which is to be reached through the liberation from oppression and poverty. But this positive goal is still tied up with the negative circumstances that have to be surmounted, for Jesus brought the kingdom of God to the poor, not to the rich. In history, however, ever since Constantine, kingdom-of-God theology has been linked with the Christian imperium or

Christian civilization. So we can only adopt it if it is indivisibly linked with the Beatitudes of the Sermon on the Mount, and with the call to the discipleship of Jesus. Otherwise kingdom-of-God theology has nothing to do with Christ. But what do we mean by the kingdom of God? Here Jon Sobrino says aptly: 'The kingdom of God is life, life in abundance and the fulfilment of life.' So in the context of liberation theology we can fill kingdom-of-God theology with 'life'. Structural and personal acts of violence against life characterize our world to a horrifying degree: violence against people, violence against nature, violence against the future of life. Love for life and reverence for life must be newly awakened, so that they may confront the growing cynicism that is widespread in the countries of the West. The protection of the life of the weak, the protection of the life of our fellow creatures, and the protection of the future of the life we share: these things must be reinforced, in order to counter the brutal structures of death.

Liberation from violence, brutality and poverty remains the theme of every practical theology and every theological praxis. But we have another theme as well as liberty, a theme which has almost been forgotten and edged out since the collapse of the socialist world. This theme is *equality*. Without equality there is no free world. It is in the spirit of early Christianity that we call the truth that all human beings are created *free* and *equal* 'self-evident'. Equality doesn't mean collectivism. It means equal conditions for living, and equal chances for living for everyone. As a social concept, equality means *justice*. As a humanitarian concept, equality means *solidarity*. As a Christian concept, equality means *love*. Either we shall create a world of social justice, human solidarity and Christian love, or this world will perish through the oppression of people by people, through a-social egotism, and through the destruction of the future in the interests of short-term, present-day profits. The alternatives are either social justice or increasing crime and continually more expensive security; either international justice or revolts by the hungry in the poor countries; either long-term investments today for the future of our common life, or short-term profits today and the calculated bankruptcy of humanity in the near future.

In Europe, the Latin American theology of liberation can awaken a new social kingdom-of-God theology which will reach back to the left wing of Catholic social doctrine, and to the 'religious-social' movement of Leonhard Ragaz, Eduard Heimann, Paul Tillich and the young Karl Barth. It will pick up the thinking of Walter Rauschenbusch in the United States (*A Theology for the Social Gospel*, 1918) and the concerns of the earlier English group round F. D. Maurice, pursued later in his own way by William Temple. This new social kingdom-of-God theology would gather together the different approaches of political theology, ecological theology, feminist theology, and the new social-critical theology. Not least, Pope John Paul II could fall in with it also; for it would fulfil his dream of a 'culture of life'.

II

Theology
in the Changing Values
of the Modern World

Christian Faith in the Changing Values of the Modern World

In this section I am not about to uphold the 'values' of the Western world in the dreaded 'clash of civilizations',[1] defending them against the representatives of the Islamic theocracies (such as Iran) and the Confucian 'educative dictatorships' (such as Singapore). Nor do I propose to prop up Western self-esteem, and weigh up what the West is 'worth'. The modern and Western worlds must cope with the present crises of their values by themselves. Every defence against attacks from outside merely stands in the way of the 'revaluation of values' which is required in the West today if humanity and the earth are to survive.

But as a Christian theologian I have to ask: what does the Western world and the modern era owe to the biblical traditions, which have come down to them through the medium of Christianity especially, and in what way do Christianity and the biblical traditions act on them as a burden? In the phrase 'biblical traditions' I am including Judaism, to which the modern Western world owes more than it is aware of. Above all I mean the particular impress put on the Western world by the 'Old Testament' – by Abraham's Exodus, by Israel's God, by the Ten Commandments of Moses, and by the visions of the prophets. The Western world has let itself be profoundly inspired by the biblical traditions, which have penetrated right down to the fundamental ideas and values of modern times. In the biblical story of God, it found again its own history of freedom, and it has continued to identify itself with that history, even in its now secular forms. But since we have discovered 'the dialectic of enlightenment',[2] and suffer from the inward contrarieties and contradictions of modernity, it may well be that a postmodern world will take leave of the driving force of the biblical traditions at the same time as it departs from modernity, because it identifies the one with the other.

We therefore have to ask ourselves whether in the light of our traditions and hopes we can co-operate in overcoming the inward conflicts and contradictions of the modern world which we, or our predecessors, have evidently provoked, and if so, how? Society's values and their re-evaluation are primary tasks for public theology. And by virtue of its origin and its goal, Christian theology *is* public theology, for it is theology of the kingdom of God.[3] Its historical traditions tell 'the history of the future', and its prophetic traditions shape the visions of that future. So what do these traditions have to say to us in our present crises of values?

(i) The God of the Bible and the experience of history

The values we acknowledge and our experience of reality correspond; so we shall begin with the biblical experience of history,[4] and then ask about the values of the human person and the human community.

The God about whom the biblical traditions talk is not always already revealed in the laws and cycles of nature. He reveals himself through men and women and in contingent events of human history. Consequently God is named after the people he called, and the events through which he revealed himself to men and women. This is unique in the history of religion. There is 'the God of Abraham, Isaac and Jacob' and 'the Father of Jesus Christ'. There is 'the Lord' who liberated his people Israel from the historical power, Egypt, and there is 'the Father' who liberated Christ from the power of history, death. The God of historical callings and liberating experiences is rightly called 'the God of history', in distinction from the gods of nature.

Judaism, Christianity and Islam, which are at one in their appeal to the God of Abraham and to Abraham's experience of God, understand themselves, each in its own way, as 'historical religions'. For them, historical remembrance is just as constitutive as expectation of the future. Abraham's experience of God is the experience of liberty and of exile: 'Go out from your country and your kindred and your father's house to the land that I will show you . . . and in you all the families of the earth shall be blessed' (Gen. 12.1–3).[5] Abraham's experience of time as he 'goes out' is the experience of a past which he leaves behind him, never to return, and a future which he has to seek in the hope that he will one day find it.

What experience of time has the meditating Buddha, compared with Abraham? The Buddha, lost within himself, experiences timelessness in the eternal moment. For him, past and future have vanished. Every comparison with the great Asian cosmic religions shows the unique character of the Abrahamic religions: the future is something new; it is not the return of the past. The world is not held in the great equilibrium of the cosmos and its harmony. As God's creation, it is aligned towards the future of his eternal kingdom and hence is temporal. The 'time pointer' dominates all systems of matter and life which are caught up in the movement of evolution. In the process of tradition and innovation, time is not reversible; it is irreversible. It is experienced in the unbridgeable difference between past and future. The past is the reality which can never be brought back, the future is the potentiality which can never be caught up with, and the present is the interface at which the possibilities of the future are realized or neglected – the point, that is, where future and past are mediated to one another. The Abrahamic religions discovered and sanctified not space but time. Elsewhere the divine was worshipped in the ever-returning orders of the cosmos. But here it meets us in the contingent events of history – events, that is, which are undeducible and unhoped for – and in 'the new thing' which the future brings. And with this human beings lost their home in the natural environment.

The view of reality which I have described here – if only briefly – as the time of history has a special affinity with the modern view of reality, for the modern world emerged out of the detachment of human civilization from its dependencies on and its concurrences with nature. The agrarian world gave way to the world of industry, the village to the megalopolis.[6] Industrialization and urbanization engender a human world which is constructed according to human wishes and criteria, and it is through these alone that human values are given effect. In the modern megacities – Mexico City, Calcutta, Lagos, Shanghai and the rest – in which, in a few years, more than half the human race will have to exist, the sun is darkened through smog, and nature has been replaced by transportation systems. These cities need neither plants nor animals, but live from their own creations. The real world which can be perceived by the senses is simulated and replaced by the 'virtual world' of computers and information highways. The course of every individual life is no longer determined by the cycles of the earth and the rhythms of the body, but only by the pace of the modern world. The sensory perception of reality is reduced to the senses that convey remote impressions – hearing and seeing. What were originally the more immediate senses – feeling, tasting and smelling – wither and atrophy. We shall look at this more closely in the light of time as it is experienced by inhabitants of the modern world.

The detachment of the world of human civilization from nature generated the ecological crisis which can condemn the whole project of the modern world to failure. The devastations inflicted on nature are growing in proportion to the urbanization of human beings and the centralization of industry, as well as the growing demand for energy and the increasing industrial emissions in the mega-cities.

The ecological crises of the natural environment in the external world in which human beings live are matched by the psychosomatic crises of modern men and women in their inner world, and in their mental and emotional life.[7] Alienation from nature without is matched by the alienation from nature within, by growing spiritual and emotional paralysis, and by estrangement from the senses. 'The desert is growing – woe to the one in whom the deserts hide,' prophesied Friedrich Nietzsche; and we all hide within us the deserts of alienation which we outwardly deplore.

If it is the interpretation of reality as history which has edged out nature within us and round about us, then the task of modern cultural therapy is to develop values which will reconcile human beings with nature outside themselves and with nature within, in their own bodiliness and sentient life, and to work for a new harmony between human civilization and nature. 'Progress' is the *Leitmotif* of the modern age. Equilibrium was the *Leitmotif* of pre-modern civilizations. If humanity wants to survive, we need to find a balance between the values of 'progress' and the values of 'equilibrium', so that we can arrive at a sustainable development and an ecological culture.[8]

For this, do we have to leave behind us the Abrahamic religions, which have brought us, together with 'the God of history', the estrangements from natural life as well? Have the values that are bound up with human *freedom* from nature been transmuted into demons of *estrangement* from nature, and nature's devastation? Is it only if our souls take wing to India that we overdriven denizens of the West can be healed? I believe that we can 'drink from our own wells' too. Only we must discover them once more. And by our own wells I mean the mystical traditions in Christianity and the sabbath traditions of Judaism.

The God of the Bible is by no means simply the unresting 'God of history'. He is also in the same measure the God of the sabbath rest, which interrupts time and history. According to the creation story, God 'rested' on the seventh day, and by coming to rest consummated and blessed his creation.[9] In creating, God goes out of himself; resting, God returns to himself again, and takes leave of his works like an artist who only completes his work when he can draw back from it and let it go. The active, labouring human being is meant to correspond to the active creative God – but only on six days. On the seventh day he is intended to be in accord with the resting God, who rejoices over his work and himself. This sabbath rest is meant for men and women, rulers and ruled, human beings and animals alike. In the sabbath year even the land and the vineyards are to remain unplanted, so that 'God's earth may celebrate its sabbath', and can restore itself as it lies fallow. The sabbath laws set a clear limit to the history of human works, for the sake of nature's well-being, and for the healing of body and soul.

In Christian mysticism we again find the biblical wisdom of the sabbath in time, but now it is turned inwards. Out of the alienations and wildernesses of their world, men and women find themselves through meditation and self-examination. When they arrive at themselves, they also come to rest in God; and the converse is also true: once they find rest in the eternal God they also find themselves in the darknesses and abysses of their souls. Just as the sabbath falls on the seventh day, so in mysticism there are always seven steps that lead to healing in 'the interior castle', as Teresa of Avila called it, or on 'the seven-storey mountain' (Thomas Merton's phrase). *Contemplation in a World of Action* is the title which Thomas Merton gave to one of his books.[10]

We find contemplative rest not just by turning inwards and analysing our souls. We find it too if we deal wisely with our time, which we must interrupt on the sabbath if time is not to devour us entirely. God does not merely inhabit the depths of our being. He dwells in time too.

(ii) Does being human mean being part of nature or being a person?

In all the Asian and African religions men and women see themselves as part of nature. It was the biblical traditions that led to the understanding of the individual human being as person.

People see themselves as part of nature if they believe that the earth is their 'mother' and the moon their 'grandmother', and that their life in the great family of all the living oscillates in the cycles and rhythms of sun, moon and earth. People see themselves as part of nature if they believe in reincarnation, since every individual living thing emerges out of life's great warp and weft, and turns back to that, so as to return once more in other forms of life. Finally, individuals understand themselves as part of nature if they see themselves as only one link in a long succession of generations. The members of the family who went before them are the ancestors who must be revered; the members of the family who come after them are the children for whom they work. The tiny individual consciousness knows itself to be embedded in and sustained by the great collective consciousness. The death of the individual has no great importance, for the sequence of the generations remains, as the generation registers in the Old Testament and in Korea, for example, show. The UN's Earth Charter of 28 October 1982 therefore calls human beings 'part of nature'.

Over against this, however, every declaration of human rights begins with a foundational article on the 'human dignity' which is inviolable. But what constitutes this unique human dignity? It is the dignity of every individual human person, each for himself or herself, and its premise is the individuality of each and every human being. This individual human dignity is the source of all individual human rights, such as those laid down in the Universal Declaration of Human Rights of 1948 – a declaration signed by all the nations belonging to the UN. The right to be a person, the equal rights of men and women, as well as freedom of belief, conscience, opinion and assembly all follow from individual human dignity. How is this individual human dignity protected? By treating no one as an object, but by respecting everyone always and everywhere as a determining subject. So to reduce human beings to their market value as slaves, pure work force, or an object of commerce (as in prostitution) is forbidden. It is with this principle – the principle that all human beings are created free and equal – that the modern democratization of politics begins. It is with this principle that all liberation movements and liberation theologies work. No one must be disadvantaged because of some disability. The principle of all humane medicine is that 'the patient is a person'. We do not need to go into the consequences any further, because we all know what they are.

But what is a person? A person is not an individual. As the derivation of the word tells us, an individual is like an atom, something ultimately indivisible. But something ultimately indivisible has no relationships and cannot communicate itself either. So Goethe was right with his dictum that '*individuum est ineffabile*' – the individual transcends expression. If an individual has no relationships, it has no characteristics and no name either. It is unknowable and does not know itself. In German and Spanish it used to be a term of abuse to call a particular human being an 'individuum', because that meant an anonymity. A person, on the other hand, is the individual human being in the field of resonances constituted by his or her relationships: I – you – we, I – myself, I – it. In the network of relationships the person becomes the active subject of taking and giving, hearing and doing, experiencing and touching, perceiving and responding.

In the theological sense, the 'person' comes into being through God's summons, which calls human beings out of their relationships 'in their fatherland and among their kindred' (Gen. 12.1).[11] Abraham and Sarah, who follow God's call and 'go out', are the prototypes of biblical persons. In the same way God calls Moses too by name, and Moses comes forward and says: 'Here am I' (Ex. 3.4). It is on the model of Moses that the prophets are called, and according to Isa. 43.1 the model is valid for everyone: 'Fear not, for I have redeemed you; I have called you by your name, you are mine.' The God who is not part of nature but stands over against it independently as its Creator makes human beings, as his image, correspond to him in standing over against both the visible creation and themselves (Psalm 8). People become responsible persons before God on earth. That makes their life unique and unrepeatable. That raises them above other created beings, with relative freedom for the special task given them in the name of that transcendent God. And it also burdens them with special responsibility for other living things. According to the biblical traditions, the dignity of human beings is constituted by the fact that they are created in the image of God. In his famous oration *De dignitate hominis* (1486), Pico della Mirandola introduced this idea into the Renaissance culture of the Western world, and by doing so prepared the way both for the recognition of human rights and for Western anthropocentrism.[12] The consequences, both positive and negative, were momentous. Let me try to put together a list of the merits and demerits.

1. *The children of Abraham, Sarah and Hagar.* If human beings are persons called out of the world by the transcendent God, then they lead an Abrahamic existence. They leave their familiar environment – family, home and country – and become strangers in what is for them an alien world. They do not feel at home anywhere. Everywhere they are responsible for themselves until their hope in God's promise is fulfilled. That is a freedom which is above the world, but it is the freedom of the desert. The mark of Abraham's children is openness to the world, and homelessness. No present gives them rest and entices them to linger. As long as the divine promise is not fulfilled, their hearts remain restless. For good or ill, they become *bestia rerum novarum cupidissima*, animals voracious for new things, content with no environment but breaking through all limitations. Their desires are measureless, as Freud complained, because those desires are wakened by the infinite God. Abraham becomes 'the father in faith' of Jews, Christians and Muslims, and Sarah and Hagar are his constant companions; they are not stay-at-homes, like Penelope, who lets Odysseus go off on his adventures alone. But this being so, what results in the corresponding civilizations is not just domination over nature; it is alienation from nature too. Anyone who follows the God of promise like Abraham and Sarah cannot have nature as 'mother'. But then what *is* nature for the children of Abraham and Sarah?

Nature then becomes in the positive sense the 'sister' and companion on the way of hoping and seeking human beings:[13]

that is the way Paul describes it in Romans 8. It is not only human beings who live from hope, and long for the redemption of the body from the bondage of death. All other earthly creatures and the earth itself sigh under the power of transience, and long for the glory of eternal life which 'the children of God' in their freedom already experience. It is God's Spirit itself which in believers and in all transitory creatures sighs for the new world of eternal life, and reveals the sufferings of this present time as being the birth pangs of that eternal home of all things. This means that the restless heart of the children of Abraham finds its correspondence in the restless world – *natura sperans*, in hoping nature. Together with Abraham's children, all transitory creatures are on the way to that future in which the restless God will come to rest and find a home in the house of consummated creation. There Abraham's children also find the home of their identity. All creatures are companions on the way trodden by the children of Abraham and Sarah, and the children of Abraham and Sarah are in profound harmony with all other created being. They do not view the world as divided into cosmos and chaos, but see it bound into a unified move- ment that draws towards their redemption, a movement in which cosmos and chaos are merely two complementary characteristics.

2. *Augustine's solitary soul.* The inhabitants of the Western world are blessed and burdened by Augustine's 'soul', for no one has moulded Western psychology more fundamentally than this Latin Father of the church, or justified Western indi- vidualism more profoundly.[14] Augustine desired to know 'God and the soul'. 'Nothing else? No, nothing else.' Why the soul particularly? Because the human being's soul carries within it the image of God as if in a mirror. So those who want to know God must forget the world, close the door on all their senses, and withdraw into themselves through meditation. Then they will simultaneously come to know both themselves and God. 'Withdraw into thyself: in the inner man dwells truth.' For Aristotle, the soul was an organ, part of the human being like other organs too. He could describe the powers of the soul

objectively. However, for Augustine the soul became the human being's inner self, mysterious and unfathomable, like God. Through the reflexive inwardness by way of which he sought God in himself and himself in God, Augustine became the discoverer of the human being's subjectivity. Descartes, with his philosophy of subjectivity, merely followed him.[15] He took over Augustine's argument: I can doubt all sense impressions, but not that it is I who doubts; I can be deceived in all things, but not that it is I who is deceived. The inward certainty of the self is stronger than the outward certainty of any object, for it is immediate, whereas certainty of the object is only mediated through the senses. In simple terms this means that we are all closest to ourselves, for we know ourselves best. Consequently neighbourly love has self-love as its precondition, and only self-love leads to the love of God. If the soul is the subjectivity of the self, then it dominates the body and the senses, and is not ruled by them. In this respect too the soul corresponds to God: as God is the ruler of the world, so the soul, which corresponds to God, rules the body. It is in self-mastery and self-control that the human being's nature as the image of God finds expression: this was the teaching of puritanism and pietism.

But Augustine was wrong when he saw the image of God only in the soul of the individual person: 'God created man in his own image, male and female he created them' (Gen. 1.27). So God's image is to be found in the mutual relationship of man and wife, and this is always mediated through the senses and the body.[16] We find no suggestion in the Bible that the self-regarding individual soul enjoys pre-eminence. It is not when we withdraw into the self that we find God; it is when we go out of ourselves. It is not in the I that God is hidden; it is in the Thou. The whole human person is made in the image of God, in the unity of soul and body, of inward and outward, of spirit and the five senses. The whole human community of women and men, parents and children, is intended to correspond to God, and to become his reflected radiance on earth. The differentiated unity of person and nature tallies with God's thought in creation: the person represents nature, and nature sustains the person.

Today, weighed down by 'Augustine's soul', we are seeking the return of the body and the rediscovery of the senses and the world we can perceive through the senses – and men are listening to feminist theology.

The separation of the person from nature is life-threatening and leads to moral irresponsibility. Radical humanism of the kind advocated by Peter Singer defines the human person as the subject of understanding and will.[17] People who are not yet in control of their understanding and will – or are no longer in control of them – or are never in control of them – are not considered to be human persons; they are viewed merely as human material. To this category belong embryos and foetuses, the severely handicapped, and people suffering from geriatric diseases. In actual fact, indeed, it is only the healthy male between thirty and fifty who is a person in the full sense. Before that he is in training for personhood, and afterwards his personhood has been pensioned off. The logical consequence is that only the person in the full sense of the word has any claim to human rights. Human material, on the other hand, can be treated like objects of nature. This radical humanism therefore leads to perfect inhumanity, for it withdraws human dignity from what is allegedly 'worthless life', life that is unfit to live.

Theologically, the human being's likeness to God is not based on the *qualities* of human beings. It is grounded in their relationship to God. That relationship is a double one. It means God's relation to human beings, and the relation of human beings to God. Human beings' objective likeness to God subsists in God's relation to them. This is indestructible and can never be lost. Only God can end it. The dignity of each and every person is based on this objective likeness to God. God has a relationship to every embryo, every severely handicapped person, and every person suffering from one of the diseases of old age, and he is honoured and glorified in them when their dignity is respected. Without the fear of God, God's image will not be respected in every human being, and the reverence for life will be lost, pushed out by utilitarian criteria. But in the fear of God there is no life that is worthless and unfit to live.

(iii) The person between personal liberty and social faithfulness

In traditional societies, the whole life of the individual was pre-determined and regulated from the cradle to the grave. Membership of families, castes, social classes and peoples determined the course of life. There was little scope for personal decisions and developments. The person's own name counted for very little. Among some peoples, daughters were simply given numbers, because on their (arranged) marriage, they took their husband's surname. The family name, in contrast – the surname as we call it – meant everything. To belong to 'a good family' secured one's social position. One simply had to come from 'a good house', as the phrase went in Germany. In traditional societies stability was everything, and individuality counted for very little.

In modern societies, the values of personal liberty are paramount, placed higher than the values of sociality, of belonging to a certain group. Life is no longer moulded by tradition. We live in free-choice societies, because we believe that a society can only be creative in the individual persons that constitute it. Consequently with us nothing must be accepted as predetermined and decreed. Everyone must be able to decide everthing for himself or herself: free choice of school, free choice of job or profession, free choice of a partner, free choice of where to live, free political choice, free choice of religion, and so on. We are even working on the possibility of being able to decide our genetic make-up for ourselves. Nothing must be 'just fate', not even a person's gender. We must be able to determine everything ourselves. In semi-traditional European societies, one is still addressed by one's surname, one's 'family' name. In very modern societies and among young people, first names are the only ones that count.

The modern mega-cities individualize and isolate people. It is only in villages or small towns that people can live in 'family clans'. Modern apartments and modern cars are designed for four people at most: father, mother and two children. A free choice of jobs and the moving of homes tears the old extended families apart. Since our children live in Berlin, Hamburg and New York, we seldom see our grandchildren. In the major German cities of Berlin, Hamburg, Frankfurt and Munich, more than 50% of all households are 'single' households. Earlier, people were members of a family; now they are increasingly becoming single persons. This doesn't necessarily mean isolation, although isolation also exists to an alarming degree, for instance among the elderly. But freely chosen friendship is increasingly taking the place of the predetermined family. House-sharing is becoming the new way of life, and new patchwork families are developing in which no one knows or cares any more who father or mother is, or who is related to whom. All that matters is who is living with whom, or who is living in whose house. The person one relates to replaces family ties: a relationship, yes – a bond, no; or a bond, yes – but without commitment.

Public life is brought into every living room by way of television. It is true that there each individual sits in front of the screen alone, but they all participate in everything that happens in town, nation and world – or at least they think they do, although in actual fact they participate only in the 'virtual' world of pre-selected information and entertainment. Of course they can switch the television on and off – but that is not media control. It is true that we can participate in everything if we watch the news; but we cannot help to determine things, because we receive without being able to transmit anything. This distinguishes the public life brought to us by television from any kind of discussion. Individualization is always the way in which people can be dominated: 'divide and rule.'

Finally, there are signs that a new culture of death is growing up. In traditional societies people were in religious terms 'gathered to their fathers', and were buried in the earth in the family grave. In the ancestor cult, at the Korean Chosuk festival, on All Souls Day among Catholics or – in the Lutheran Church – on 'the Sunday of the Dead', people visit the graves of their ancestors and dress them with flowers. In modern societies it is becoming more and more difficult for people to look after their family graves personally, because they no longer live near the burial place. The religious interest in family tradition is vanishing. So in the secular lives of modern men and women there are more and more anonymous burials: the body is cremated and the ashes are scattered in a field, or at sea, and 'no one knoweth the place thereof . . .' The isolated persons who determine themselves by themselves disappear into nothingness. This is really quite logical, because the surname – the family name – had already ceased to mean anything even in life. So why should it bind the children to the graves of the dead?

The liberty of persons cannot be maintained through progressive individualism of this kind.[18] Nor can it be relinquished again in favour of membership of the traditional society. In my view, it can be preserved only through reliability and faithfulness. The free human being is the being who can promise, said Nietzsche – and who must keep that promise. Through the promises I give, I make myself in all my ambiguity unambiguous for others and for myself. In promising, we commit ourselves and become dependable. We acquire a firm configuration or Gestalt, and make ourselves people who can be addressed. In faithfulness to our promise we acquire identity in time, because in being reminded of our promise we are reminded of ourselves. It is only in promising and fulfilling the promise that the free person who is not predetermined by tradition acquires continuity in time, and with it his or her identity. Those who forget their promises forget themselves; and those who remain true to their promises remain true to themselves. If we keep our promises, we come to be trusted; if we break our promises, people mistrust us. We lose our identity and no longer know ourselves. The identity of a person's whole life history is indicated by his or her name. Through my name I identify myself with the person I was in the past, and anticipate myself as the person I will be in the future. With my name I can be addressed. With my name I sign my contracts and stand by my promises. The shared social life of free persons is a densely woven fabric of promises and promise-keeping, agreements and dependabilities, and it cannot exist without trust. The paradigm of a free society is not predetermined membership. The paradigm is the covenant. A free society rests on social consensus.

(iv) Our modern lack of time and 'the discovery of slowness'

Modern men and women are 'always on the go', so wherever they are, they are always pressed for time.[19] Is it the Christian understanding of time as irreversible, and as an unstoppable 'ever-rolling stream', flowing out of the future into the past, that has plunged us into this shortage of time? How can we be rescued from it? Never before did human beings have as much *free* time as they have today, and never did they have so little *time*. Time has become 'precious' too, because 'time is money'. The world offers us endless possibilities, but our life-span is brief. Consequently many people fall into a panic in case they should miss out on something, and they try to step up their pace of living. The utopia of overcoming space and time by way of high-speed trains, faxes and E-mail, Internet and videos, is a modern utopia. Everywhere we want to 'keep up' with things – the phrase is significant in itself. We want to be omnipresent in space and simultaneous in time. That is our new God-complex.

The difference between our life-span and the possibilities offered by the world tempts us into 'a race against time'. We want to save time, so as to get more out of life, and miss out on life in the very attempt. Only the person who lives faster gets most out of his brief life, we think. What we so proudly call 'our modern world' gets its name because we are compelled to modernize faster and faster. We move more and more rapidly from place to place, and collect so many 'experiences' in the adventure park or the adventure holiday that sociologists like Gerhard Schulze (see n. 19) talk about this 'experience' society of ours. We have more and more 'contacts' and 'know' a great many people. Fast food has become the symbol of our fast life.

The modern revved-up human is fed by McDonald's, poor

devil. He has plenty of experiences, but actually experiences none of them because he wants to have seen everything and to hold on to it on slides or videos; but he doesn't take it in or assimilate any of it. He has contacts in plenty but no relationships, because he 'can't stay', but is always in a hurry. He gulps down his fast food, standing up if possible, because he is incapable of enjoying anything any more; for to enjoy something takes time, and time is what one doesn't have. Modern men and women have no time, because they are always out to 'save' time. Because we can't prolong our lives to any appreciable degree, we have to hurry in order to 'get as much as possible out of life'. Modern men and women 'take their own lives' in the double sense of the phrase: by snatching at life, they kill it. The brevity of time is not diminished one single second by accelerated life. On the contrary, it is by being afraid of not getting one's share and missing out on something that one falls short, and misses out on everything.

We tourists have been everywhere but have got nowhere. There is always only enough time for a flying visit. The more we travel, and the more rapidly we chase after time, the more meagre the spoils. Everywhere we are just in transit. The person who lives more and more rapidly so as to miss nothing lives more and more superficially, and misses the depths of experience life offers. In that person's world, everything is possible, but very little is *real*.

The clock is the modern world's key machine, for it regulates everything. An Indian sage said to a friend of mine last year: 'You have the clock – we have time.' The mechanical time of our omnipresent clocks dominates our lives.[20] For the clock, it is a matter of indifference whether the time it ticks off was empty or filled, whether we were sickened by boredom or whether 'time flew'. Sixty minutes, and the hour is past. Mechanical time takes no account of time as we experience it, and makes all times equal. But experienced time is the quality of our life – measured time is simply its quantity. Happiness is timeless, we say. So whenever we experience life most intensively, it is important to put our watch away, or at least to stop looking at it. Life only becomes living when we break the dictatorship of the time that is measured by the clock.

It is probably our suppressed fear of death which makes us so greedy for life. Our individualized awareness tells us: 'Death is the finish. You can't hold on to anything, and you can't take it with you.' The unconscious fear of death shows itself in the stepped-up haste for living. In traditional societies, individuals felt themselves to be members of a larger whole: the family, life simply as such, or the cosmos. When the individual dies, the wider context in which he or she participated lives on. But modern individualized consciousness knows only itself, relates everything to itself, and therefore believes that death is the end of everything.

Perhaps we can no longer go back to the old sense of belonging to a greater whole which endures when we disappear.[21] But we can surrender our finite and limited life to the eternal divine life and receive our life from that. This is what happens when we experience communion with God in faith. To experience the presence of the eternal God brings our temporal life as if into an ocean which surrounds us and buoys us up when we swim in it. In this way the divine presence surrounds us from every side, as Psalm 139 says, like a wide space for living which even finite death cannot restrict. In this divine presence we can affirm our limited life and accept its limits. We will then become serene and relaxed, and will begin to live slowly and with delight.

It is only the person who lives slowly who gets more out of life. It is only the person who eats and drinks slowly who eats and drinks with enjoyment. Slow food – slow life! Sten Nadolny's book *The Discovery of Slowness* (ET 1981) rightly became a bestseller, and a comfort for harrassed modern minds and hearts. Only the very rich can squander time. Those who are assured of eternal life have time in plenty. Then we linger in the moment, and lay ourselves open to the intensive experience of life. In the moment which is fully and wholly lived we experience eternity. Isn't the living intensity of a single lived moment more than all the hastening through the times of life in their extensiveness?

It is only the suppressed fear of death that makes us so hurried. The *experienced* nearness of death, by contrast, teaches us to live every moment with full intensity as an eternal moment. Our senses are sharpened in an undreamed-of way. We see colours, hear sounds, taste and feel as never before. The experience of death which we permit ourselves makes us wise for life and wise in our dealings with time. The hope of resurrection to which we hold fast opens up a wide horizon beyond death, so that we can leave ourselves time to live.

Finally, the modern world emerged out of the Western world, even if this is no longer realized, for example in Asia. The Western world emerged out of Christianity, and especially out of Protestantism. Human rights and personal liberties, freedom of religion, freedom of belief and of conscience, democratic forms of government and liberal views of life: all these things grew up together with Protestantism. The crisis in the values of the modern and Western world are also crises in Protestantism. So we are called to a special degree to work together for the revaluation of values which is required so that the world may live and not perish.[22]

The Destruction and Liberation
of the Earth: Ecological Theology

*(i) The destruction of the earth by the First World and the
Third World*

The destruction of the environment which we are causing
through our present global economic system will undoubtedly
seriously jeopardize the survival of humanity in the twenty-first
century.[1] Modern industrial society has thrown out of balance
the equilibrium of the earth's organism, and is on the way to
universal ecological death, unless we can change the way things
are developing. Scientists have shown that carbon dioxide
and methane emissions are destroying the ozone layer in the
atmosphere, while the use of chemical fertilizers and a multitude
of pesticides is making the soil infertile. They have proved that
the global climate is already changing now, at the present day,
so that we are experiencing an increasing number of 'natural'
catastrophes, such as droughts and floods – catastrophes which
are actually not natural at all, but man-made. The ice in the
Arctic and Antarctic is melting, and in the coming century, the
scientists tell us, coastal cities such as Hamburg, and coastal
regions such as Bangladesh and many South Sea islands, are
going to be flooded. All in all life on this earth itself is under
threat. The human race can become extinct, like the dinosaurs
millions of years ago. What makes this thought so disquieting is
the fact that we can no longer retrieve the poisons which are
rising into the earth's ozone layer and those that are seeping into
the ground. Consequently we don't know whether the die has

not already been cast, as far as the fate of humanity is concerned. The ecological crisis of our century has already become an ecological catastrophe, at least for the weaker living things, which are the first to perish in this struggle. Year by year, hundreds of plant and animal species are becoming extinct, and we cannot call them back to life. 'First of all the forests die and then the children.'

This ecological crisis is in the first place a crisis brought about by Western scientific and technological civilization. That is true. If everyone were to drive as many cars as the Americans and the Germans, and were to pollute the atmosphere through as many toxic emissions, humanity would already have suffocated. The Western standard of living cannot be universalized. It can only be sustained at the expense of others: at the expense of people in the Third World, at the expense of coming generations, and at the expense of the earth. Only a universal 'equalization of burdens'* can lead to a common standard of living and a sustainable development.

At the same time, it is mistaken to think that environmental problems are problems for the industrial countries of the West alone.[2] On the contrary, the ecological catastrophes are intensifying still more the already existing economic and social problems of countries in the Third World. The Western industrialized countries can try by means of technology and statutory provisions to preserve a clean environment in their own territories; the poorer countries are unable to do so. The Western industrial countries can try to foist environmentally harmful industrial plants on the countries of the Third World, and to sell these countries dangerous toxic waste; and the poor countries of the Third World have no defence.[3] But even apart from that, Indira Gandhi was right when she said that 'poverty is the worst pollution'. I would add that the worst environmental pollution

---

* An 'equalization of burdens' of this kind (a so-called *Lastenausgleich*) was attempted in West Germany at the end of the Second World War for the benefit of refugees and displaced persons from the eastern parts of Germany which had now passed to the USSR, Poland and Czechoslovakia.

is not the poverty as such; it is the corruption that causes poverty. It is a vicious circle leading to death: impoverishment leads everywhere to over-population, because children are the only security life has to offer. Over-population leads to the consumption not only of all the foodstuffs, but of the very foundations from which people live. That is why it is in the poor countries that the deserts are growing most rapidly. In addition, the global market is compelling the poor countries to give up their own subsistence economy and to plant monocultures for the world market; to cut down the rain forests and overgraze the pastureland. They have to sell not just the apples but the apple trees as well – and that means that they can survive only at the cost of their children. In this way these countries are being inexorably forced towards self-destruction. In countries with massive social injustice, ruthlessness is part of 'the culture of violence'. Violence against weaker people justifies violence against weaker creatures. Social lawlessness reproduces itself in lawless dealings with nature.

The first ecological law is that for every intervention in nature there must be a compensation. If you cut down a tree you must plant a new one. If you sell a piece of land you must buy another piece, for you must pass your land on to your children just as you received it from your parents. If your city builds a power station, it must plant a forest which produces just as much oxygen as the power plant uses up.

Where the destruction of nature is concerned, both worlds, the First and the Third, are imprisoned in a vicious circle. The interdependencies of the depredations can easily be seen. The Western world destroys nature in the Third World and forces the Third World countries to destroy their own natural environment. Conversely, the destruction of nature in the Third World – the cutting down of the rain forests, for instance, and the pollution of the seas – strikes back at the First World by way of climatic changes. The Third World dies first, and then the First World: first the poor die and then the rich; first of all the children and then the adults. Isn't it cheaper in the long run, as well as more humane, to combat the poverty in the Third World now, and to dispense with our own growth, rather than to combat natural catastrophes all over the world in the next few decades? Is it not more sensible to restrict driving now rather than to run round in gas masks in the future? Without social justice between the First and the Third Worlds, there will be no peace; and without peace in the world of human beings there will be no liberation of nature. In the long run this one, single earth of ours cannot sustain a divided humanity. And this one, living earth will no longer endure a hostile humanity. It will free itself from men and women, either through counter-evolution, or through the slow suicide of the human race.

In the light of these sombre vistas of the future we have to set new priorities, politically and economically. Up to now 'national security', safeguarded through armaments, has been in the forefront. In the future *environmental* security, safeguarded through the common protection of the common foundations of life, will take first place. Instead of more and more weapons turned against each other, we need joint efforts turned against the threatening destruction of the living space we share on this earth. We need a sustainable development in the Third World, and a policy of environmental security in the First. We need what Ernst von Weizsäcker calls a joint 'earth policy', and a global market that is ecologically orientated, an 'earth market'.[4]

I believe that the ecological crisis of the earth is a crisis of modern scientific and technological civilization itself. The great project of the modern world is threatened with failure. So this is not just a 'moral crisis' either, as Pope John Paul II maintained; it is a profounder crisis still – a religious crisis of the things in which people in the Western world put their trust. In the next section of this chapter, I shall try to show how this is so. I shall then go on to show three perspectives, drawn from the religious traditions of the Western world, which can lead us from the destruction of the earth to harmony and consensus with it.

(ii) The religious crisis of the modern world

The living relationship of a human society to its natural environment is determined by the human techniques by means of which human beings acquire their foodstuffs from nature and give it back their waste. This 'metabolism' with nature is really as natural as breathing in the air and breathing it out again. But ever since the beginning of the Industrial Revolution it has been increasingly determined and governed solely by human beings, and not also by nature. In our throwaway society, we think that what we throw away 'has gone'. But a something never becomes a nothing, so nothing we throw away has ever 'gone'. That is the error of nihilism. It is still somewhere or other in nature. Where? Everything returns in the cycles of the earth.

Human technologies are the modalities in which the sciences are invested. Technology is applied science, and all scientific knowledge will, some time or other, be technologically applied and utilized, since – as Francis Bacon declared – 'knowledge is power'. Natural science is knowledge about the power of disposing over things and dominating them. Philosophy and theology, in contrast, have to do with orientation, and are disciplines which address the meaning of reality.

Technologies and sciences are always developed under the pressure of particular human interests.[5] We never have them value-free. Interests precede them, direct them, and put them to work. These human interests, for their part, are guided by the fundamental values and convictions of a given society. And these fundamental values and convictions are quite simply what everyone in a particular society takes for granted, because within the system of that society they are self-evident and plausible.

Now if a crisis arises in a life-system of this kind, which links a human society with the nature surrounding it, because nature is dying, the logical result will be a crisis of the whole system, its attitude to life, its life-style, and not least its fundamental values and convictions. The dying of the forests outside us is matched by the spread of neuroses in the mind and spirit within. The pollution of the waters finds its parallel in the nihilistic feeling about life which prevails among many people in the mega-cities. So the crisis which we experience is not just an 'ecological' crisis; nor can it be solved merely by technology. A conversion of convictions and fundamental values is just as necessary as a conversion in attitudes to life and in life-style.

What interests and concerns, and what values, rule our scientific and technological civilization? To put it simply: it is the boundless *will towards domination* which has driven modern men and women to seize power over nature, and is driving them still. In the competitive struggle for existence, scientific discoveries and technological inventions are used by the political will to acquire, secure and extend power. Among us, growth and progress is still gauged by increase of power, economic, financial and military. When economic growth stops, we talk of zero growth; for growth simply has to be.

If we compare our civilization with pre-modern cultures, the difference leaps to the eye. It is the difference between *growth* and *equilibrium*. Those pre-modern civilizations were anything but 'primitive' or 'underdeveloped'. On the contrary, they were highly complicated systems of equilibrium which ordered the relation of people to nature and to the gods. It is only modern Western civilizations which for the first time are one-sided, being programmed solely towards development, growth, expansion and conquest. The acquisition of power and the securing of power, to which may be added the American 'pursuit of happiness': these are the fundamental values which really count and regulate everything in our society. Why did this come about?

The deepest reason can probably be found in the religion of modern men and women. The Judaeo-Christian religion is often made responsible for the human seizure of power over nature, and for the unbridled thrust of the human will for power.[6] Even if ordinary modern men and women do not see themselves as particuarly religious, they have at least done everything they could to obey the divine commandment of their own destiny: 'Be fruitful and multiply, and fill the earth and subdue it.' One might say that they have done more than enough to meet the target! But this commandment and this image of the human being are more than 3,000 years old, whereas the modern culture of conquest and expansion grew up in Europe with the conquest of America, no more than 400 years ago. So we have to look elsewhere for the reasons. And in my view they can be found in the picture of God which modern men and women have adopted.

Ever since the Renaissance, the understanding of God in Western Europe has been increasingly one-sided: God is 'the Almighty'. *Omnipotence* has been considered the pre-eminent attribute of his divinity. God is the Lord, the world is his property, and God can do with it what he likes. He is the absolute determining subject, and the world is the passive object of his sovereignty. In the Western tradition, God moved more and more into the transcendent sphere, while the world was understood in a purely immanent and this-worldly sense. God was thought of without a world, and so the world could be understood without a God. It lost the divine mystery of its creation, the 'world soul', the *anima mundi*, and could be stripped of its magic by science, to adopt Max Weber's apt description of this process.[7] The strict monotheism of modern Western Christianity is an essential reason for the secularization of the world and nature, as Arnold Gehlen already acutely pointed out in 1956.

> At the end of a long history of culture and intellect, the view of the world as an *'entente secrète'* has been destroyed – the metaphysics of the concurring and conflicting powers of life. It has been destroyed by monotheism on the one hand, and on the other by the scientific and technological mechanism for which monotheism, for its part, first cleared the way, by de-demonizing and de-divinizing nature.[8]

God and the machine have survived the archaic world and now confront one another, just by themselves. A terrifying picture, because not only has nature disappeared from this final confrontation between God and the machine; the human being has vanished too.

As God's image on earth, human beings were bound to see themselves, in complete correspondence with him, as rulers – that is, as the determining subjects of knowledge and will, standing over against their world, which was their passive object, and subduing it. For it is only through lordship over this earth that the human being can correspond to God, who is the Lord of the world. God is the Lord and owner of the whole world, and human beings must therefore strive to become the lords and owners of the earth, in order to prove themselves God's image. Human beings come to resemble their God, not through goodness and truth, not through patience and love, but through power and sovereignty. It was in this sense that at the beginning of modern times Francis Bacon lauded the sciences of his time: 'Knowledge is power'; and it was through their power over nature that human beings were to be restored in their character as the image of God. In his *Treatise on Scientific Method*, René Descartes declared that science and technology make human beings 'maîtres et possesseurs de la nature'.[9]

If we compare with this the famous indictment made by the Indian chief Seattle in 1855, the point we have reached is immediately evident:

> Every part of this earth is sacred to my people, every glittering pine-needle, every sandy beach, all the mists in the dark forests . . . The rocky hills, the gentle meadows, the bodily warmth of ponies – and of people – they all belong to the same family.[10]

Today this brings us face to face with the decisive question: is nature our *property*, so that we can do what we like with it? Or are we human beings *one part* of the wider family of nature, which we have to respect? Do the rain forests belong to us human beings, so that we can cut and burn them down – or are the rain forests the home for a multiplicity of animals, plants and trees, so that they belong to the earth, to which we also belong? Is this earth '*our* environment' and '*our* planetary home' – or are we human beings merely guests: guests who have arrived very late on this earth, which up to now has put up with us so patiently and graciously?

If nature is nothing more than our property – unclaimed property, which belongs, it is said, to whoever takes possession of it – then we shall counter the ecological crisis of nature solely by technological methods. We shall try through new products of genetic engineering to make plants resistant to climate and animals of increased utility. By means of genetic engineering we shall breed a new human race which does not need a natural environment at all – merely a technological one. We could in fact be in a position to create a world capable of sustaining our numbers and our practices; but it would be an artificial world – a global laboratory.[11] Alternatively we could change our practices and our numbers, restore nature, and let her live again. But how can we change the way we go about things? Isn't the destruction of nature the result of our disrupted relationship to nature and to ourselves and to God?

At the Global Forum Conference in Moscow in January 1990, we heard the moving message of the North American Indians. These 'indigenous children of the earth' talked about their thousand-year-old great goddess: 'The earth is our mother, the moon is our grandmother, and we all participate in the sacred cycles of life.'[12] The Indian ambassador V. T. Singh and the Mongolian high priest, the African rain-maker and the Californian New Age adherent, all implored us to return to 'the womb' of the earth, from which all life comes. It all sounded splendid. But can the religious symbols of pre-modern times, when human beings were still hunters and gatherers, help the urbanized masses of the post-modern world to solve the eco-logical problems of industrial society – the people in New York, Mexico City or Sao Paulo, where the sun often cannot be seen for smog? Isn't that just poetry? All the politicians and scientists present assumed that human beings have caused the ecological problems of industrial society, so human beings have to solve them. The message of the earth's indigenous peoples and the modern 'depth ecologists' aims to free human beings from the burden of this responsibility, so as to make them once more happy and infantile 'children of the earth'. But can we again give up the liberty we have acquired, once it becomes dangerous? Will nature take over responsibility from us again, if it becomes too heavy for us? I do not believe it. But we can translate pre-industrial ideas of harmony with the earth into post-industrial conceptions of an ecological culture.

(iii) The liberation of the earth: three Christian perspectives

(a) Cosmic spirituality

The first conversion begins with the picture of God, for the way we think about God is the way we think about ourselves and nature too. 'Tell me what you believe in, and I will tell you who you are.' Belief in God, the Almighty Lord in heaven, led to the secularization of the world, and robbed nature of its divine mystery. What we need theologically is to rediscover the triune God. I know that sounds dogmatic, orthodox and old-fashioned, but it could still be true for all that. Even when we simply hear the name of 'the Father, the Son and the Holy Spirit', we sense that the divine mystery is a marvellous community. The triune God isn't a solitary, unloved ruler in heaven who subjugates everything as earthly despots do. He is a God in community, rich in relationships. 'God is love.'[13]

Father, Son and Holy Spirit live with one another, for one another, and in one another in the most supreme and most perfect community of love we can conceive: 'I am in the Father and the Father is in me,' says the Johannine Jesus. If that is true, then we correspond to God not through domination and sub-jugation but through community and relationships which further life. It is not the solitary human subject who is God's image on earth; it is the true human community.[14] It is not separate, individual parts of creation that reflect God's wisdom and his triune livingness; it is the community of creation as a whole.

In the high-priestly prayer in John 17.21, the Johannine Jesus prays 'that they may all be one, even as thou, Father, art in me and I in thee, that they also may be in us'. As we know, this is the foundational saying for the ecumenical movement. And it can become the foundational saying for theological ecology too. Mutual indwelling is the innermost mystery of the triune God. Mutual indwelling is also the secret of the divine love: 'He who abides in love abides in God and God abides in him' (I John 4.16). And mutual indwelling is also the secret of the community of creation which corresponds to God. The term for this in the patristic church was *perichoresis* or *circuminsessio*.[15]

According to Christian understanding, creation is a trinitarian process: God the Father creates through the Son in the power of the Holy Spirit. Seen from the other side, this means that all things are created by God, formed 'through God', and exist in God.

'See in the creation of these beings the Father as the preceding cause, the Son as the creative cause, and the Spirit as the perfecting cause, so that the ministering spirits have their beginning in the will of the Father, are brought into being through the efficacy of the Son, and are perfected through the assistance of the Spirit.' That was already Basil's explanation.[16] For a long time the church's Western tradition stressed only the first aspect, so as to distinguish God, the almighty Creator, from his creation, and to stress his transcendence. By so doing it stripped nature of her divine mystery and surrendered her to de-sacralization through secularization.

The important thing today is therefore to rediscover *the Creator's immanence* in his creation, so as to include the whole of creation in our reverence for the Creator. Through whom, or through what, did God create the world? According to Prov. 8.22–31, he created the world through his daughter, Wisdom:

The Lord already had me at the beginning of his ways, before he created anything I was there. From eternity I was set up, from the beginning, before the earth . . . Then I was beside him as his master workman and was daily his delight, playing before him always, playing upon his earth, and delighting in the children of men.

This divine daughter Wisdom (*hokmah*) was translated by Philo as *Logos*, the Word. Whenever 'the Logos', 'the Word', is used in the New Testament, as it is in the prologue to the Gospel of John, we should think of Wisdom.[17] According to Wisdom literature, this creative Wisdom can also be called God's Word or God's Spirit. But it is the presence of God in all things which is invariably meant, *a presence immanent in the world*. If all things are created by God, then their protean variety is preceded by *an immanent unity*. It is through Wisdom that God forms the community of created beings, who exist with one another and for one another.

Christian theology has recognized in Christ not just personal salvation but also the cosmic Wisdom through which all things *are*, as the Epistle to the Colossians shows. Christ is the divine mystery of the world. The person who reverences Christ also reverences all created things in him, and him in everything created. Where was Jesus after the devilish temptations in the desert? 'He was among the beasts, and the angels ministered to him' (Mark 1.13).

In the apocryphal Gospel of Thomas, Logion 77, Jesus says:

I am the light that is over all,
I am the universe: the universe has gone out of me,
and the universe has returned to me again.
Cleave the wood and I am there.
Lift up the stone and there thou shalt find me.[18]

This means that what we do to the earth, we do to Christ.

Where God's *Word* is, there God's *Spirit* is too. According to Gen. 1.2, creation through the Word is preceded by the vibrating energy of God's Spirit. God creates everything though his naming, differentiating and judging words. That is why all things are individually different, 'each according to its kind'. But God always speaks in the breath of his Spirit, which gives life. Where the community of creation is concerned, Word and Spirit complement one another. The Word specifies and differentiates. The Spirit joins and forms the harmony. The words are different, just as they are when human beings speak; but they are communicated in the same breath. So in a transferred sense we can say that God speaks through the individual things he has created, and – in the words of an English hymn – 'God breathes through all creation'.[19] The totality of creation which I have here called 'the community of creation' is sustained by the breath of God's Spirit: in the words of Ps. 104.30: 'Thou sendest forth thy breath and renewest the face of the ground.'

Through Word and Spirit the Creator communicates himself to his creation, and enters into it, as the Book of Wisdom says (12.1):

Lord, thou art the lover of life,
thy immortal Spirit is in all things.

That is the way Calvin saw it too: 'For it is the Spirit who, everywhere diffused, sustains all things, causes them to grow, and quickens them in heaven and on earth . . . In transfusing into all things his energy, and breathing into them essence, life, and movement, he is indeed plainly divine' (*Institutions*, I, 13–14). So creation must not just be called, in detached objectivity, a 'work of his hands'. It is the indirect, mediating *presence of God* as well. All things are created so that as 'the shared home' of all creation they may be 'the house of God' in which God can live beside those he has created, and where those he has created can eternally live beside him. This is expressed biblically through the image of God's cosmic temple: 'The Most High does not dwell in houses made with hands; as the prophet says, "Heaven is my throne, and earth my footstool. What house will you build for me, says the Lord, or what is the place of my rest?"' (Acts 7.48f., following Isa. 66.1f.).

That place is the cosmos!

This viewpoint – the Spirit of God *in* all things and the preparing of all things to become God's dwelling – leads to a cosmic adoration of God and an adoration of God in all things. What believers do in the churches is representative, and related to, and on behalf of, the whole cosmos. Solomon's temple was built according to the dimensions of the cosmos as the cosmos was then understood to be, so that it might be a microcosm to represent and correspond to the macrocosm.[20] The presence of God's Word and Spirit in Christ's church is the advance radiance and beginning of the presence of God's Word and Spirit in the new creation of all things. The church is orientated towards the cosmos, by reason of its foundation and its essential nature.[21] It was a dangerous modern contraction that restricted the church to the human world alone. But if the church is orientated towards the cosmos, then the ecological crisis of earthly creation is the church's own crisis too, for through the destruction of the earth, which is 'bone of its bones and flesh of its flesh', it too will be destroyed. When the weaker creatures die, the whole community of creation suffers. If the church sees itself as representing creation, then it will feel this suffering of creation's weaker creatures as conscious pain, and it will have to cry out this pain in public protest.[22] It is not just 'our human environment' that is suffering; it is the creation which is destined to be '*God's* environment'. Every intervention in nature which can never be made good again is a sacrilege. Its outcome is the self-excommunication of the perpetrators. The nihilistic destruction of nature is practised atheism.

Astonishingly enough, it was Christian mysticism which taught us to be alive to the language of God in nature. Let us listen to a modern mystic, the Nicaraguan poet and revolutionary Ernesto Cardenal. In his book *Love* he writes:

> The bird chorus in the early morning sings to God. Volcanoes, clouds and trees shout about God. All creation cries out with a loud voice that God is, is beautiful and loves. Music sings in our ears and beautiful countryside tells our eyes . . . God's signature is on the whole of nature. All creatures are love letters from God to us. The whole of nature is bursting with love, set in it by God, who is love, to kindle the fire of love in us.
> . . . Nature is like God's shadow, reflecting his beauty and

splendour. The quiet blue lake has the splendour of God . . .
The image of the Trinity is in every atom, the figure of God
the three in one. . .

And my body was also made for the love of God. Every cell
in my body is a hymn to my creator and a declaration of
love.[23]

In case anyone thinks that this is a typically Catholic eulogy in
celebration of 'natural theology', we may listen to the Reformer
John Calvin too, for Calvin saw the presence of God in nature
in just the same way. In his *Institutions* he writes:

'The final goal of the blessed life . . . rests in the knowledge
of God. Lest anyone, then, be excluded from access to happiness, he not only sowed in men's minds that seed of religion
of which we have spoken, but revealed himself and daily dis-
closes himself in the whole workmanship of the universe. As
a consequence, men cannot open their eyes without being
compelled to see him. Indeed, his essence is incomprehensible;
hence his divineness far escapes all human perception. But
upon his individual works he has engraved unmistakable
marks of his glory, so clear and so prominent that even un-
lettered and stupid folk cannot plead the excuse of ignorance
. . . Wherever you cast your eyes, there is no spot in the universe wherein you cannot discern at least some sparks of his
glory.' 'But,' laments Calvin, 'it is in vain that so many burn-
ing lamps shine for us in the workmanship of the universe to
show forth the glory of its Author. Although they bathe us
wholly in their radiance . . . we have not the eyes to see . . .'[24]

(b) The new earth science: 'the Gaia hypothesis'

For us 'the earth' means two things. On the one hand it means
the ground *on which* we stand; on the other, it is the planet
earth, with its biosphere and atmosphere, *in which* we live.
Photographs of the earth taken from satellites or the moon
show our planet with its very thin atmospheric covering within

which all life goes on. In this second meaning of the word, we live *in* the earth, not on it.

How are we to understand in its totality this earth 'in' which we live? Modern astro-scientists have shown the repicrocal influence of the lived and the unlived sectors of the planet. This suggested the idea that the earth's biosphere, together with the atmosphere, the oceans and the expanses of land, form a single complex system. Since this has the capacity to preserve our planet as a place suited to life, it can also be seen as a unique 'organism'.[25] Through the constant absorption of solar energy, life is developed and sustained. That is the generally accepted theory of the English scientist, James E. Lovelock, which he put forward in his book *Gaia – a New Look at Life on Earth* (1979). Lovelock actually proposed calling this earth system 'a universal bio-cybernetic system with a trend towards homeo-stasis'. But his neighbour, the novelist William Golding, offered him the old Greek name for the earth goddess, Gaia. And so this theory became known as 'the Gaia hypothesis'.[26] This thesis does not imply a remystification of the earth. It means understanding the total system of our planet as a system of interactions and feed-backs, which strives to create the best possible environmental conditions for life on earth. We call the preservation of relatively constant conditions by way of active controls, homeostasis. Lovelock has shown that our earth system has this tendency, and also makes use of living things in the process, especially the micro-organisms in the seas.

As Lovelock himself says, the Gaia hypothesis offers an alter-native to the modern viewpoint which sees nature only as the embodiment of a primitive power which has to be subjugated and dominated. It also offers an alternative to the depressing notion that our planet earth is a mindless spaceship which circles the sun without meaning or purpose, and will do so until the day when it burns out or grows cold. But in fact the Gaia hypothesis also offers an alternative, which can also be scientifically tested, to the anthropocentrism which is funda-mental to modern civilization. For this hypothesis compels us to think biocentrically or, better, to orientate our thinking towards the earth.[27]

The earth system 'in' which the human race has spread and developed its civilizations works like a super-organism. With its own kind of subjectivity, it fashions life-forms out of macro-molecules, micro-organisms and cells, and is in a position to keep these forms alive. The Gaia language of all living things is *the genetic code*, a universal language which is used by all cells. There is also an inbuilt ingenious and elaborate security system which resists genetic combinations hostile to life. And since this organism 'earth' has finally produced intelligent living things such as human beings, then inherent in the organism itself must be a higher intelligence, and a memory which bears the imprint of millions of years – as Cicero already argued. It can therefore be said that the earth itself is 'alive'. According to Gen. 1.24, God created it to 'bring forth' living things. This is said of nothing else in creation. According to a rabbinic tradition, God creates human beings *together with* the earth (Gen. 1.26).[28]

The inward link between human beings and the earth's whole biosphere is the genetic code. Through this code the cells and organisms communicate. The human genetic code is only one variant of the codes of all living things, from the micro-organisms to the whales, from the first protozoa to the dinosaurs. By way of the genetic code, all living things are related and in communication. What we call consciousness, understanding and will is only a small part of the organism which is steered by our genetic code. Is it possible to be conscious of the genetic code? Our total constitution shows it, as we see in people suffering from Down's syndrome, and among others too. But does it say anything to our conscious-ness? About that we know very little. Some people have supposed that the genetic code speaks to us through bodily Gestalts and body rhythms – through 'body wisdom' – in the way that dreams also speak to us. Peoples which have cultivated a particular closeness to nature have always had a dream culture of their own. Through scientific knowledge of the genetic code, it ought actually to be possible today to establish conscious concurrences between the *genetic* and the *cultural* code.

The importance of the Gaia hypothesis can hardly be over-estimated:

1. It makes it possible to recognize the global functions of local and regional ecosystems, and prevents them from being isolated.

2. It reverses classical scientific methods. Knowledge is no longer split up into more and more detailed specialist fields. Instead, scientific disciplines co-operate, and are integrated into 'earth sciences' for the investigation of wider connections and cohesions in the system of the earth.

3. Integrated knowledge is no less scientific than isolated knowledge. But it no longer serves the interests of domination, according to the method 'divide and rule'. Instead it is guided by the concern for shared life and survival, by way of co-operation and symbiosis.

4. The Gaia hypothesis forces us to put an end to the anthropocentric self-understanding and behaviour of men and women, and constrains them to fit democratically into the life of the earth as a whole.

5. Politically, the threatening nuclear catastrophe has com-pelled us to to re-think national foreign policies, and to see them as part of a shared 'global domestic policy', as C. Graf von Krockow and C. F. von Weizsäcker put it. The threatening ecological catastrophe forces us to understand this shared global domestic policy as 'earth politics', to use E. von Weiz-säcker's phrase. Without democracy, biocracy is not viable. It is only when, as the species 'human being', we understand our-selves in our relation to the earth as 'creatures of the earth', and no longer as conflicting peoples, nations or races, that we can enter into relationship with other species of the living, and see ourselves as one form of life among, and together with, other forms of life on earth.

This has nothing to do with the return of the earth goddess; nor does the Gaia hypothesis ascribe any divine power to the earth, as some conservative Christians fear. But it has everything to do with the survival of the human race. This survival will only be possible in symbiosis, co-ordination and concurrence with the total organism of the earth.

(c) Human beings and nature in covenant with God

We believe that God loves his creation and wants to bring its life to its full development and flowering. In God's eyes nothing created is a matter of indifference. Every creature has its own dignity and its own rights, for they are all included in his covenant. That is what is said in the story about Noah: 'Behold,' says God, 'I establish my covenant *with you* and *your descendants after you,* and *with every living creature*' (Gen. 9. 9–10). It is this covenant 'with us' which provides the basis for fundamental *human rights.*[29]

Out of this covenant 'with us and our descendants after us' follow *the rights of future generations.*

Out of this covenant 'with us and our descendants after us and with every living creature' follow *the rights of nature.*[30]

Before God the Creator, we *and* our descendants and all living things are partners in his covenant, and enjoy equal rights. Nature is not our property. But we are not just part of nature either. All living things are partners in God's covenant, each in its own way. All living things must be respected by human beings as partners and confederates in God's covenant: the earth brings forth; human beings are God's image on earth. Anyone who injures the earth injures God. Anyone who hurts the dignity of animals hurts God.

Today, now that the Universal Declaration of Human Rights of 1948 has become generally accepted, it is time to draw up a Universal Declaration of the Rights of Nature which will be generally accepted too. In so far as nature – air, water and land, plants and animals – is at the mercy of acts of violence committed by human beings, it must be protected by human law. A first attempt to free nature from human despotism and caprice was the World Charter for Nature, proclaimed by the General Assembly of the United Nations on 28 October 1982.

It is true that this charter does not yet go so far as to concede to nature rights of its own, and to recognize it as the subject of its own rights. But there are approaches in what is said which indicate that it is reaching out for ways to get beyond the anthropocentric and egotistical viewpoint of the modern world, according to which nature is only there for human beings as 'unclaimed property'. 'Mankind is a part of nature,' says the preamble, and, 'Every form of life is unique, warranting respect regardless of its worth to man.'[31]

But this moral appeal, right though it is in itself, must also be given a legal basis, so that nature is not dependent on the goodwill of human beings, but is recognized as an independent subject, with its own rights. It was not the goodwill of the masters that finally brought about the abolition of slavery; it was the fight of the slaves for their freedom and human rights, together with the efforts of the abolitionists and the gradual public recognition that slavery is inadmissible. It is only through the recognition of its rights that nature will be liberated from its oppression, and recognized as a partner for human beings, and a confederate in God's covenant.

But how? The protection of nature from destruction by human beings is thought by some politicians to be part of the minimum guarantee of individual human rights. Just as every human being has a right to freedom from bodily harm – which means freedom from torture – so every human being should have a right to an intact, unscathed environment: clean air, pure water and unspoiled earth. But according to this viewpoint, nature is aligned solely towards human beings. It is required only as 'human environment', but is not recognized for its own sake.

Yet if this earth, together with all living things, is *God's creation*, then its dignity must be respected for *God's* sake, and its continued existence must be protected for its *own* sake. Because nature is being destroyed by the economic forces of the free market, it must be put under the special protection of the state. By virtue of its constitution, the state has to respect human rights as the rights of all its citizens; and in the same way it must also, by virtue of its constitution, protect *the rights of stricken nature*.

I would therefore propose that the following sentences should be included in our constitution: 'The natural world is under the special protection of the government. Through the way in which it acts, the state shows respect for the natural environment and protects it from exploitation and destruction by human beings *for its own sake*.' Every democratic government has two responsibilities: 1. to protect the people; 2. to protect the land.

The German Animal Protection Act of 1986 is the first German law which no longer views animals merely as human property, but sees them as 'fellow creatures' of human beings, and protects them in their dignity as such. 'The purpose of this law is to protect the life and wellbeing of the animal out of human responsibility for it as a fellow creature. No one may inflict pain, suffering or harm on an animal without reasonable grounds.'[32]

To call animals 'fellow creatures' is to recognize the Creator, the creature and the community of creation. The theological word 'creation' is more appropriate than the philosophical term 'nature', because it shows respect for God's rights to his creation, and therefore restricts the rights of human beings: God has the right of ownership – human beings only have the right of use.

The rights of nature. Here is a proposal by a group of theologians and lawyers belonging to the universities of Berne and Tübingen, laid before the World Alliance of Reformed Churches in 1989, the Ecumenical Assembly in Seoul in 1990, and the UN Conference in Rio in 1992:

1. Nature – animate or inanimate – has a right to existence, that is, to preservation and development.
2. Nature has a right to the protection of its eco-systems, species, and populations in their interconnectedness.
3. Animate nature has a right to the preservation and development of its genetic inheritance.

4. Organisms have a right to a life fit for their species, including procreation within their appropriate ecosystems.
5. Disturbances of nature require a justification. They are only permissible
   – when the presuppositions of the disturbance are determined in a democratically legitimate process and with respect for the rights of nature
   – when the interests of the disturbance outweigh the interests of a complete protection of the rights of nature, and
   – when the disturbance is not inordinate.
   Damaged nature is to be restored whenever and wherever possible.
6. Rare eco-systems, and above all those with an abundance of species, are to be placed under absolute protection. The driving of species to extinction is forbidden.

We appeal to the United Nations to expand its Universal Declaration of Human Rights and to formulate explicitly the rights mentioned above.

Simultaneously, we appeal to the individual nations to incorporate these rights into their constitutions and legislation.[33]

This proposal was put before the major United Nations Conference in Rio de Janeiro in 1992 and was incorporated in the 'Earth Charter'.

(iv) The sabbath of the earth: the divine ecology

For a long time men and women viewed nature and their own bodies only under the dominating interest of *work*. This meant that they perceived only the utilitarian side of nature, and only the instrumental side of their bodies. But there is an ancient Jewish wisdom which teaches us to understand nature and ourselves once more as God's creation. We find this wisdom in the celebration of the sabbath, the day of rest, on which human beings and animals find peace and leave nature in peace.[34]

According to the first of the creation stories, the Creator 'finished' the creation of the world by celebrating the world's sabbath: 'And God rested from all his work.' And through his resting presence God blessed his creation. God was no longer active, but he was wholly present as God himself.

The seventh day is rightly called the feast of creation. It is the crown of creation. Everything that exists was created for this feast. So as not to celebrate the feast alone, God created heaven and earth, the dancing stars and the surging seas, the meadows and the woods, the animals, the plants, and last of all human beings. They are all invited to this sabbath feast. All of them are God's fellow celebrants, each in its own way. That is why God had 'pleasure' in all his works, as the psalms say. That is why the heavens declare the glory of the Eternal One. Everything that is, is created for God to rejoice over, for everything that is, comes from God's love.

This divine sabbath is 'the crown of creation' – not the human being. On the contrary, human beings, together with all other created beings, are crowned by the divine 'Queen Sabbath'.[35] Through his sabbath rest, the creative God arrives at his goal, and people who celebrate the sabbath recognize nature as God's creation, and *let it be* God's beloved creation. The sabbath is wise environmental policy and an excellent therapy for our own restless souls and tense bodies.

But the sabbath has another significance too: the significance of the sabbath year for the land and for the people who live from the land. Leviticus 25.4 says: 'In the seventh year the land shall keep its great sabbath to the Lord.'

According to Exodus 23.11, every seventh year Israel is not to plant or till the ground, but is to let it rest, so that 'the poor of your people may eat'. According to Leviticus 25.1ff., every seventh year Israel is not to plant or till the ground, so that 'the land may come to rest'. The social reason is complemented by the ecological one.

For the book of Leviticus (26) this sabbath rest for the land is of paramount importance. All God's blessings are experienced by the obedient, but the disobedient will be punished. How?

Leviticus 26.33ff.: 'And I will scatter you among the nations
. . . and your land shall be a desolation, and your cities shall be
a waste.'

Why? 'Then the land shall enjoy its sabbaths as long as it lies
desolate, while you are in your enemies' land; then the land
shall celebrate and enjoy its sabbaths.'

This is a remarkable interpretation of Israel's Babylonian
exile – we might even call it an ecological interpretation. God
wanted to save his land. That is the reason why God permits his
people to be defeated and to be carried off into captivity. God's
land is to remain unworked *for seventy years!* By the time the
seventy years are over, it will have recovered, and God's people
can return to the land promised to them. We might call the
sabbath year for the land God's environmental policy for those
he has created, and for his earth.

All ancient agrarian cultures were familiar with *the wisdom
of fallowing*, as a way of preserving the soil's fertility. When I
was young, every fifth year the arable land in North Germany
was left unplanted, so that plants and animals could return,
and we children could play there. It was only the great empires
which exploited the fertile regions non-stop, in order to feed
their armies and their capital cities, until the soil was exhausted
and became a desert. That is what happened in Persia, Rome,
Babylon, and perhaps also to the Mayas on the Yucatan
peninsula.

Today the fallowing principle has almost entirely disappeared
from agriculture. Its industrialization means the introduction of
more and more chemical fertilizers into the soil. Monocultures
have replaced the old rotation of crops. And the result is that
artificial fertilizing has to be intensified, and the soil and the
crops are increasingly polluted.

The end will resemble the end that Israel of old experienced.
The uninterrupted exploitation of the land will lead to the exile
of the country population, and in the end to the disappearance
of the human race from the earth. After the death of the human
race, God's earth will then celebrate the great sabbath which
modern humanity has hitherto denied it. If we want our

civilization and nature as we known it to survive, we should let ourselves be warned, and permit the land 'to celebrate its great sabbath'. The celebration of the sabbath, and reverence for 'the sabbath of the earth', can become our own salvation and the salvation of earth from which we live. Simply to restrict ourselves on the sabbath, and to refrain from intervening in creation – this extolling 'let it be' helps both the land and ourselves.[36]

During the first oil crisis in 1972, one Sunday was declared to be a 'car-free' day in West Germany. It was one of the loveliest days I can remember. Children played football on the motorways, grown-ups sat around at the crossroads, dogs jumped about on the streets. It is possible. 50% of our traffic is superfluous.

How would it be if we were to include in the festivals of the church year an 'earth day', to celebrate the creation tormented by us human beings? An 'earth day' of this kind is unofficially celebrated by many congregations and churches in America on 22 April. How would it be if in Europe we were to declare 27 April, the day of the Chernobyl disaster, such a day?

On 'earth day' we should bow before the earth and beg for forgiveness for the injustice we have inflicted on it, so that we may once more be accepted into community with it. On 'earth day' we should renew the covenant which God made with Noah and the earth.

According to the Bible, the sabbath laws are God's ecological strategy, designed to preserve the life which he has created. In its rest and its rhythmical interruption of time, the sabbath is also the strategy which can lead us out of the ecological crisis and, after the one-sided forms of progress made at the expense of nature, can show us the values of sustainable development and harmony with nature.

3

Human Rights – Rights of Humanity – Rights of the Earth

(i) Human rights as we have them

Insight into fundamental human rights and obligations developed in many civilizations at the same time as recognition of the 'humanity' of human beings. Wherever there came to be a concept of 'the human being', the rights of human beings as such were formulated too. These are not exclusively Christian or European ideas, although it was at the time of the Western Enlightenment that human rights, explicitly formulated as such, made their way into the North American and European constitutions, and it is just because they were admitted into these fundamental constitutional codifications that they acquired the world-wide validity they enjoy today. Like other universal ideas too – mathematics, for instance – human rights have cut adrift from their specifically European origins and development and make a directly convincing appeal to all people who accept that they are not just Americans or Russians, black or white, men or women, Christians or Jews, but that they are first and foremost human beings. So there are no copyright claims to human rights. They are neither exclusively Jewish-Christian, nor do they derive solely from Enlightenment humanism.

Today the peoples of the earth are entering a shared global history, because they are all mortally endangered, on the one hand by the nuclear threat they pose to one another, and on the other by the ecological crises they share. And the more this global history develops, the more important human rights will become, if we are to build a world-wide human society capable of warding off these perils. Human rights will therefore increasingly become the universally valid framework, capable of winning general acceptance, by which humane policies are judged and legitimated. The recognition and realization of human rights for all human beings is going to be *the* factor which decides whether a global human community, in harmony with the cosmic living conditions of the earth, develops out of this divided and perilous world, or whether human beings destroy themselves and this earth. Because of the extreme danger of the present situation, the authority of human rights must be placed above all the particularist interests of nations, groups, religions and cultures. Today, the religious claims to particularist absoluteness and the ruthless implementation of particularist political interests are a threat to the continued existence of humanity itself.

The existing formulations of human rights are in themselves inadequate. We have to work to expand them if human rights are not themselves to be a factor in the destruction of our world. As I see it, human rights must be expanded in two directions: 1. in the formulation of the fundamental *rights of humanity*; and 2. in the incorporation of human rights into *the rights of the earth and other living things*.[1]

The declarations of human rights which apply today in the United Nations are, first, the Universal Declaration of Human Rights of 1948 and, second, the International Covenants on Human Rights concluded in 1966 (on Economic, Social and Cultural Rights, on Civil and Political Rights, The Optional Protocol). They have very little force under international law, for the preamble to the 1948 Declaration says simply that human rights are intended to be 'a common standard of achievement for all peoples and all nations'. Nevertheless these declarations have proved to have astonishing force in the civil rights movements in many countries and, in the Conferences on Security and Co-operation in Europe (CSCE) which followed Helsinki in 1975, have increasingly come to exert an influence on international law in both Western and Eastern Europe.[2]

Right down to the end of the Second World War, it was internationally accepted that the way a country treats its own people is a matter solely for its own sovereign decision. Today this is no longer the case. Even though many countries still complain about 'interference in their internal affairs', the way a government treats its own nationals is legally considered a matter for other countries and their peoples too; for today every person is also subject to international law in so far as this protects human rights.

The divisions and categories of human rights already emerge from their history. In the wake of the crimes of the Fascist dictators, and after the Second World War, the North Atlantic states formulated *individual human rights*, over against the powers of state and society. In the struggle against capitalism and class rule, the socialist states emphasized *economic and social* human rights. And the wretched and impoverished people of the Third World are demanding the *right to existence*, the right to live and survive. We can also distinguish the categories in the following way. There are 1. *protective rights*: the right to life, liberty and security; 2. *rights to freedom*: freedom of religion, opinion and assembly; 3. *social rights*: the right to work, to food, home, and so forth; and 4. *rights of participation*: the right to co-determination in politics and economic life.

The root of the different human rights and the bond uniting them is termed *human dignity*. Human rights exist in the plural, but human dignity is simply and solely singular. Human dignity is one and indivisible. There is never a greater or a lesser degree of human dignity. It exists only entire or not at all. Human dignity is the term that describes the quality of being human, however the different religions and philosophies may specifically interpret that. Human dignity, at all events, means that human beings may never be exposed to treatment which in principle calls in question their 'quality as subject' (to use Kant's term). Because the dignity of human beings is one and indivisible, human rights are also a single whole, and cannot be expanded or restricted at will.

But to base human rights on human dignity also shows the

limits and the dangers of their inherent anthropocentricism.[3] Human rights must be brought into conformity with the rights of nature – the earth from which, with which and in which human beings live. Human dignity is not something that elevates men and women above all other living things. It is merely a special instance of the dignity of all natural life – in Christian terms, the dignity of each of God's creatures. Human dignity cannot be upheld through human rights at the expense of nature and other living things, but only in harmony with them, and for their benefit. Unless human rights come to be integrated in the fundamental rights of nature, these human rights will be unable to claim universality. Instead, they themselves will become factors in the destruction of nature, and will thereby ultimately lead to the self-destruction of humanity.

In the economic discussions after the end of the war, interesting shifts of emphases emerged. From 1948 onwards (the year when the General Assembly of the World Council of Churches met in Amsterdam) until about 1960, the question of *religious liberty* was at the centre of concern, until people realized that freedom of religion can be attained only in association with other individual human rights. The CSCE conferences, as well as conditions in Turkey, show that it is still important, even today, to promote both. Freedom of religion is being recognized step by step, together with individual human rights, even in countries with state ideologies and state religions.

Since about 1960, questions about *social and economic* human rights have come to the forefront of attention. Racism, colonialism, dictatorship and class rule are under attack as severe violations of human rights. Personal rights to liberty cannot be protected in a world of gross political injustice and economic inequality. It is only economic and social rights which put people in a position to implement their liberties for themselves. The ecumenical consultation in St Polten, Austria, in 1974 was a milestone in the history of discussions in the Christian churches about human rights, because there representatives of people in the Third World spoke, and were listened to, for the first time. Today the *ecological* discussion is at the centre of interest in the industrialized countries. It sets human rights irrefutably in the context of living conditions on earth, and in the framework of the life-sustaining cosmos.

At the end of the 1970s we saw the declarations on human rights made by the major churches. In 1976 'The Theological Basis of Human Rights' came from the World Alliance of Reformed Churches, and in 1977 the declaration of the Lutheran World Federation, 'Theological Perspectives on Human Rights'; while a working paper prepared by the papal commission *Justitia et Pax* on 'The Church and Human Rights' has been in existence ever since 1974. Unfortunately human rights have not as yet been made the subject of any joint Christian declaration.

If I see the matter rightly, only the declaration of the World Alliance of Reformed Churches has addressed today's problems about the rights of humanity and the rights of nature – though even so without expanding the framework in which human rights have to be set if they are really to be universal and life-sustaining.

Let us now try to arrive at a systematic survey, in the form of a spiral of human rights in which the one points to the other, and the whole thrusts towards universality.

1. No individual human rights without social human rights.

2. No human rights without the right of humanity to protection from mass annihilation and genetic change, and to survival in the sequence of the generations.

3. No economic human rights without ecological obligations towards the rights of nature.

4. No human rights without the right of the earth.

(ii) Individual and social human rights

'We hold these truths to be self-evident,' says the American Declaration of Independence, 'that all men are created equal . . .' If this means all human beings, irrespective of their sex, race, religion, state of health, and so forth, then it also means every individual. Every human being is a person, and as person is endowed with inalienable human rights. With the maxim about the liberty and equality of all human beings, the American Declaration of Independence and the constitutions of the French Revolution admittedly also raised the essential problems of modern constitutional states: how to mediate between a person's rights to individual liberty, and the protective rights of society, which have to ensure social security and economic provision – the conflict, in short, between liberal democracy and socialism.

In the 'prophetic' religions, Judaism, Christianity and Islam, the liberty and equality of all human beings is derived from belief in creation – which the American Declaration of Independence also talks about ('. . . endowed by their Creator . . .'). The fact that all human beings are made in the image of God is the foundation of human dignity. Human beings are intended to live in this relation to God. That gives their existence its inalienable, transcendent depth dimension. In their relationship to the transcendent God, human beings become persons whose dignity must not be infringed. The institutions of law, government and economy must respect this personal dignity, which is the endowment of all human beings, if they claim to be 'humane institutions'. They would destroy themselves if they were to treat human beings as objects, things, commodities, or merely as underlings or members of the work force. They would lose their legitimation.

In the myths about power and sovereignty which we find among many peoples, it is only the ruler who is worshipped as 'God's image on earth', as 'the Son of Heaven' and 'Son of God'. 'The ruler is the shadow of God, and men are the shadow of the ruler,' says a Babylonian code for princes. But according to the Jewish, Christian and Islamic belief in creation, it is not any ruler who has been created to be the image of God on earth. It is 'the human being' – which means each and every human being. It follows from this that all human beings are kings or queens, and no one may dominate the others. The mediaeval 'Saxon Code' already commented (Land Law, Book 3, Article 42): 'God has created and formed men after his own image, and has redeemed them through his Martyr, one like another . . . As I see the matter, I am unable to understand that anyone should be [the property] of the other.'

In Europe's political history, the belief that everyone is created in the image of God, and respect for the liberty and equality of all human beings, led to the democratization in principle of all rule by human beings over other human beings. Any exercise of rule must legitimate itself before other human beings. Rulers and ruled must at all times be recognizably 'human', in the same degree and together. That means that all the citizens of a country must be equal before the law, to which rulers too are subject. The democratization of the way in which political objectives are formed; the time limit set to the commission to rule; the control of rule through the separation of powers and through popular representation; the binding of rule to the charge given under the constitution; and, not least, the extensive power of self-determination given to the people and the self-administration of local communities – all these have become the political means through which the image of God in each human being, and the human dignity of all, are paid due respect.

But when liberty was developed in Europe and North America, it was one-sided to stress only the rights of individuals over against the structures of political rule, and to neglect their social equality and economic security. It was the fault of Western liberalism to overlook the social dimension of freedom, which is to be found in the solidarity of people together, one with another. Here the religious history of the West also went astray, from Augustine onwards. For it is not the disembodied individual soul that is the image of God; it is the human being together with other human beings, since the biblical creation story tells us that 'male and female he created them'.

Although they spring from different intellectual roots, and although they have still never been gathered together in a single document, individual and social human rights logically belong together and call for one another in their realization. Human sociality has in principle the same dignity as human personhood. The person does not 'take precedence' over the community, nor does the community 'take precedence' over the person. Persons and community are mutually related entities, in the same way as the individuation of human beings and their socialization. Consequently individual human rights cannot in principle take precedence over social human rights, although this is always the assumption in the Western world. The rights of persons can be implemented only in a just society, and a just society can be attained only on the foundation of personal rights. The liberty of persons can develop only in a free society, and a free society grows up only out of the liberty of persons. The free choice of work cannot be attained without the right to work. And the right to work presupposes the free choice of work, if people are to live in freedom.

(iii) Human rights and the rights of the human race

Up to now, human rights have been formulated only in the perspective of persons and society, not yet for the human race itself, although the term 'human' logically implies the collective term 'humanity'. Has humanity as a whole rights and obligations too? Little thought has been give to this, because the life and continuing existence of humanity has been presupposed as self-evident, divinely willed, and 'natural'.

   1. But ever since Hiroshima in 1945, nuclear weapons and the production of chemical and biological methods of mass destruction have made one thing increasingly clear: the human race is mortal, and has a time-limit. The continued existence of humanity is under deadly threat through the crime against humanity which is possible at any time – the crime of starting a war waged with nuclear, biological or chemical weapons. Yet humanity is meant to survive, and wants to survive. This fundamental affirmation of human life is the presupposition underlying every declaration on human rights. It is now time to formulate and acknowledge publicly the existence and right to survive of humanity as well, because this is something which people can negate. There are even specific situations in which

the rights of humanity take absolute precedence before the particularist rights of special classes, races and religions, and when all particularist interests, legitimate though they may very well be, must be subordinated to humanity's own right to exist. Even 'the class struggle', said Gorbachev, can fruitfully lead to the liberation of the oppressed only within the framework which makes possible the survival of humanity. Even the absolute claim of certain human religions must be subordinated to the right of humanity to exist and to survive, because otherwise the claim could lead to the suicide of the human race.

Because the threat to humanity can proceed from the power of the nation that possesses nuclear, biological and chemical weapons, the limitations of that power must be more closely defined, with a view to humanity as a whole. To threaten potential enemies with instruments of mass annihilation which can lead to the extinction of the human race goes beyond the right of any country which claims to be humane. Individual governments have an obligation, not just towards their own people but also towards humanity as a whole. They have to respect not just the human rights of their own citizens but the human rights of people in other countries too; for the rights of humanity are indivisible. National foreign policies based on rivalry with other countries and systems must give way to a 'global domestic policy' which is in duty bound to promote the survival of humanity, a policy which serves the reciprocal advancement of life and the shared security of all. Human solidarity in overcoming mutual threats therefore takes precedence over loyalty to one's own nation, race, class or religious group. Individual states and communities of states have human obligations towards the rights of the human race to live and survive.

2. If human dignity forbids the violation of the quality of human beings as determining subjects or their extinction, this is true not only for individual persons but for coming generations too, and for the human race as a whole. Modern genetic engineering and new reproductive medicine could make it possible not only to heal hereditary illnesses, but also to breed changed generations through 'eugenics'. Prenatal diagnostics

make the evolution of new generations through inter-uterine selection possible. Manipulations of the germ-line can essentially change the genome of the human race. Of course therapeutic interventions are permissible if their aim is to heal. But manipulations designed to breed living things lacking in the human quality of 'subjecthood', and manipulations the purpose of which is to breed so-called supermen, destroy the essential nature of human beings, and hence the dignity of humanity too. If, together with the protection of human dignity, the state has also taken over the duty of protecting every human life, then it is also in duty bound to safeguard the truly human character of human life in this and coming generations. Otherwise it would lose its legitimation. Genetic intervention in the human species – 'optimizing', 'advantageous', or whatever it may be called – belongs to a new category of crimes against humanity, just as much as the annihilation of life that is allegedly 'unfit', and of races which are declared to be 'inferior'. There is a new racist application of evolutionary theory and eugenics to the future of the human race which destroys its dignity and humanity. Not only the nuclear threat but also the genetic self-destruction of humanity is a new and growing danger.

3. 'Humanity' does not just mean all human beings in the cross-section of a particular time. It also means people down the ages – in the sequence of human generations. At a particular time and in a particular place, different generations always live together and look after each other. Parents care for their children, the young for the old. Because the human race consists of the temporal sequence of the generations, up to now there has been a generation contract which has always been taken for granted because it is natural; and this has guaranteed the survival of the human race. Laws of inheritance ensured a degree of justice between the generations, so that there was a certain balance between the chances in life enjoyed by those born earlier and later.

Today this unwritten generation contract is threatening to break down, and this can be deadly for the human race. In the industrial nations we are in the process of exhausting most of the non-renewable sources of energy (oil, coal, gas, and so forth) in our present generations; and in our national budgets we are leaving generations to come appalling mountains of debt which they will sometime or other have to pay off. We are using up the benefits of industrial production in our own time, and are foisting their costs on to the times ahead. We are producing giant rubbish dumps which coming generations will have to 'dispose of', although we know that nuclear waste cannot just be 'disposed of' but has to be guarded until the year 3000 or 10000, depending on the half-life of the material.

But the human race can survive only if the generation contract creates justice between the generations, which are the form humanity takes in time. Since today this contract can be irreparably broken, it must be formulated and publicly codified. In our situation, particular regard must be paid to the rights of children, and the right of coming generations to live, because children are the weakest link in the generation chain, while coming generations do not as yet have any voice, and are therefore the first victims of the collective egoism of the present generation.

(iv) Economic human rights and ecological obligations

Part of human dignity is the right to lead a life of dignity. This involves certain minimum social and economic preconditions, such as protection from hunger and illness, and the right to work and to personal property. Recently, protection of the natural environment has also come to be numbered among the minimum guarantees of personal human dignity. We can develop economic human rights analogously to the right to political liberty. Just as in the political sphere it is at variance with people's dignity if they are made the mere object of state authority, in the same way it is at variance with their dignity if they are reduced economically to the status of mere members of the work force and to pure purchasing power. In order to be able to live out their 'quality as subjects' in the economic sphere too, human beings must be able to acquire a just share of work, property, food, protection and social security. The concentration of the means of production and of foodstuffs in the hands of a few, and the oppression and exploitation of the many, is a severe violation of human dignity. A world-wide economic situation which allows millions of people to starve is unworthy of humanity, and in Christian terms it is a violation of God's honour and glory, which is present in all human beings, since they are the image of God.

If all human beings are created with the dignity of being made in the image of God, and hence 'free and equal' – not particular races or classes – the economy must be democratized in correspondence to the democratization of politics. The trade union movements and worker participation in factories and businesses are steps in this direction. But the democratization of the global economy is proving to be particularly difficult, because there the interests of capital have combined with the interests of the nations in the industrial West. Yet it can be shown that without more justice through a democratization of the global economy, humanity is going to be faced with an economic and ecological catastrophe; for the increasing exploitation and indebtedness of countries in the Third World are compelling the people there to cut down their rain forests, and to over-exploit their arable land and pastures to the point where they become dustbowls and deserts. And in this way they are destroying large parts of the foundations from which the whole of humanity lives.

The fundamental economic rights of each and every human being are intrinsically linked with certain fundamental ecological obligations. The stock of fundamental economic rights cannot be multiplied indefinitely in the wake of a rapidly growing world population and the increased claims of certain nations because, as everyone knows, on this earth ecological limits are set to economic growth. The human struggle for survival cannot be waged at the cost of nature, because the ecological collapse of nature on this earth would be the beginning of the end for all human life. Economic rights must therefore be brought into harmony with the cosmic conditions of nature on the earth in which humanity is living and spreading. Economic justice among people in a society, between human societies, and between the generations of the human race must therefore be matched by ecological justice between human culture and nature. But up to now economic injustice has been matched only by ecological injustice: the exploitation of the human work force finds its precise correspondence in the exploitation of natural resources. The exploitative relationship of human beings to nature will only find an end when the exploitative relationship of human beings among themselves stops; and the converse is equally true. Since today the technical means of exploitation have been stepped up to the point when the natural foundations from which people live are being totally destroyed, this is not just a moral judgment. It is a counsel of wisdom too. It is stupid to destroy the foundations of our own life for the sake of short-term profits, because it is suicidal.

(v) The rights of the earth and the dignity of its community of the living

If we look at the world only from the aspects of private or civil law, there are apparently only 'persons' and 'things', just as according to the modern world-view there are only subjects and objects. But are animals really only 'things' in relation to the human persons who can possess and make use of them? Do they not have rights of their own, and a kind of subjectivity which human beings have to respect?

Ever since the beginning of modern Western civilization, we have got accustomed to looking at nature merely as our own environment, related to us ourselves, viewing all other living things in nature only from the angle of their utility for human beings. Only human beings are there 'for their own sake'. Eveything else is supposed to be there for the sake of human beings. This modern anthropocentricity has robbed nature of its soul and made human beings determining, bodiless subjects. The pre-modern view of the world – the view held in antiquity – saw the whole world as 'ensouled'. Aristotle still talked about the souls of plants, the souls of animals, and the souls of human beings, as well as about the world soul, which differentiates them all and at the same time holds them all together. Post-modern world-views, on the other hand, assume that human beings are a unity of body and mind or soul, so that out of their bodily needs and their relationships to all other natural living things it is possible to develop the concept of a cosmic community in which human beings are integrated.

Both ways of thinking – the ancient and the post-modern alike – point to the fact that the modern fissure between person and thing, subject and object, does justice neither to the natural community of life in which and from which human beings live on this earth, nor to the bodily existence of human beings. Rigorously carried through with modern methods, it destroys the natural community of the living, and deadens human bodiliness. Modern anthropocentricity is ultimately lethal for human beings themselves. Of course we can hardly revert to the old cosmocentricity in our view of the world and life (even if some modern thinkers see that as a way out of the impasses of the modern world); for modern anthropocentricity is the basis of modern industrial society, whereas cosmo-centricity was the foundation for the agricultural societies of pre-modern times. But modern anthropocentricity can be fitted into the living conditions of the earth and into the community of all the living in a way which does not turn its back on indus-trial society, nostalgically and in pursuit of an alternative culture, but reforms that society until it becomes ecologically compatible with the earth, and integrated into the earth's community of life.

Yet a community of life shared with all other living things on earth remains no more than an illusion and a dream unless it is realized in the form of a community of all the living which has *a legal basis*. A community under law embracing the whole earth would have to open the human community under law for the rights of other living things and the rights of the earth, or would have to incorporate these in the earth's universal laws of life. That presupposes that earth, plants and animals are respected as having a value for their own sake, before there is any estimate of their utility value for human beings. Just as human dignity is the source of human rights, so the dignity of creation is the source of the natural rights of other living things and the earth. A Universal Declaration of Animal Rights should be part of the constitutions of modern states and international agreements. This would correspond to the Universal Declaration of Human Rights of 1948, would be in conformity with it, and in certain circumstances would correct it. A draft of just such a declaration has already existed since 1977.

'No one may without justification inflict pain, suffering or harm on an animal, or terrify it . . .' 'Pain, suffering or harm may be inflicted on an animal only to the extent to which this is unavoidable for the purpose in hand.' Experiments on animals must be reduced, replaced by other experiments, and as far as possible be avoided altogether. They must at all events be subject to authorization.

An animal is not a human 'person', but it is not a 'thing' or a 'product' either. It is a living being, with its own rights, and it requires the protection of public law. To respect this fact means putting an end to industrial, hormone-controlled 'meat production' and to go over to ways of keeping livestock which will meet the requirements of their species. It also follows from this that the use of millions of animals in industrial experiments (animal experimentation) must be reduced as far as possible, and be replaced by other techniques, for example simulators. In the United States, at least seventeen million animals are 'used' or 'expended' in laboratory experiments every year, 85% of them rats and mice. More and more people are asking, rightly: 'Do the practical benefits of animal experimentation outweigh the moral costs?' (*Newsweek*, 16 January 1989). The moral loss is undoubtedly to be found in the growing indifference towards other life, whether it be the life of animals, embryos or other people, an indifference which has a backlash effect on our own lives. Faced as we are with the impasses of industrial societies, hostile to nature as they are, we must define afresh the place and the role of human beings within the total fabric of life on earth;

and as the logical consequence of that we must also fit human rights into the comprehensive rights of nature, if we want to survive.

This requirement seems to me self-evident. But it poses a serious question about the religious foundations of modern Western civilization. Hasn't the Jewish-Christian tradition, ever since the biblical creation accounts, conceded godlike privileges to men and women, over against all other living things? Aren't human beings alone God's image on earth, destined to rule over the earth and earth's other living beings? Wasn't it this anthropology which provided the basis for the development of special human rights in the West? This is the way we are in fact bound to see things, because right down the centuries this is what the churches and the theologians maintained. And yet it is not the whole truth, for the special destiny of human beings enjoys its validity only *within* the community of all creation, a community that is to be respected by human beings, as Psalm 104 quite clearly states. We can talk about special human dignity if the premise is our recognition of *the creation dignity* of all other creatures – not otherwise. As the image of the Creator, human beings will love all their fellow creatures with the Creator's love. Otherwise, far from being the image of the Creator and lover of all the living, they will be his caricature. Consequently special human rights to life and existence are valid only as long as these human beings respect the rights of the earth and of other living things.

According to the biblical traditions, there is a community under law shared by the earth and human beings which reaches out beyond the human community, with its laws, and which is rooted in the special divine law, the right of the Creator to his creation.

We find this wider community in the laws about the sabbath. The weekly sabbaths and the regular sabbath years are meant for human beings and the animals which they have domesticated and which live with them. But *the sabbath of the earth* (Leviticus 25 and 26) is emphasized as being of special importance. In the seventh year the earth is to lie fallow, so that it may renew itself. That is *the earth's right*. People who observe 'the sabbath of the earth' will live in peace, but those who disregard it will be visited by drought and famine, because they destroy the earth's fertility. Today the right of the earth and its biosphere to renewal is largely ignored. Chemical fertilizers and pesticides force the earth into a permanent state of fertility which is contrary to nature. The result is erosion which can never again be made good, and unavoidable catastrophic famines. Anyone who disregards the right of the earth threatens coming generations and the survival of humanity.

(vi) *The world religions in the forum of human rights*

Because our present life and the future survival of the human race are dependent on the observance of human rights, the rights of humanity and the rights of nature, the world religions too must subordinate themselves to the preservation of this world. In all the different religions there is nothing higher than truth. Today the religions will really only become 'world' religions when they begin to integrate themselves into the living conditions and the developing *community under law* of this *one world*, and are prepared to surrender their particularist claims to truth in favour of the universalism of truth. The religions must learn to respect individual religious liberty as a human right, and in this framework to act tolerantly towards one another, and to be prepared for dialogue. That also means subordinating their legal codes – the Torah and the Sermon on the Mount, canon law and the Sharia, Hindu and Confucian ethics, and so forth – to the minimum demands of human rights, the rights of humanity and the rights of nature. To cling to the divergencies and contradictions between the religious groups would make them enemies of the human race.[4]

On the other hand, the further development of human rights and the rights of humanity depends on the creative contributions of the different religious ideas about the world. Up to now, formulations of human rights have been based on the tradition of modern Western humanism. This, for its part, developed in the context of the Judaeo-Christian religion – a culture with a strongly anthropocentric stamp. Judaism, Christianity and Islam have therefore been termed 'religions of history', over against the Asian and African 'nature religions'. And it is true that they are concerned with human hope and historical progress, whereas the nature religions cultivate the wisdom of equilibrium and equivalence. These religions of history have therefore also been called 'prophetic religions', or 'book religions', in distinction from the directly sensory spirituality of the Indian and Chinese religions, which are closely bonded with nature. However we may define the differences in these general terms, as far as the ecological problem of modern society is concerned, the balance between progress and equilibrium, the harmony between human history and nature, and the concurrence between person and nature are of vital concern. Today interfaith dialogue will be directed towards these questions, which are of such vital concern for the human race, if that dialogue is to be meaningful and useful for the Western and Eastern religions, and for humanity as a whole.

4

The Knowing of the Other and the Community of the Different

(i) The problem of like and unlike

Knowledge and community are mutually related. In order to arrive at community with one another we have to know one another, and in order to know one another we have to come closer to one another, make contact with one another, and form relationships. In both personal and political life, community depends quite essentially on whether we are able to perceive 'the others' and to know and acknowledge them; or whether in 'the others' we see only the reflection of our own selves, and embrace them in our own image, so as to subject them to our own ideas. On the other hand, our perceptions and our ideas of 'the others' are always shaped by our social relationships to them, and by the public form our community with them takes. So we might say: without knowledge there is no community, and without community no knowledge.

If this rather general disposition is correct, it follows that epistemology and sociology are so closely related that the laws of the one sector recur in the other, and changes in the one sphere bring in their wake changes in the other. I should like to analyse this correlation, and to put it up for discussion. I am proceeding from a conjecture which I made earlier and have expressed more than once since.[1]

Ever since Aristotle, the principle of *knowledge* has been: '*Like is only known by like.*'[2]

Ever since Aristotle, the principle of *community* has been: '*Like draws to like.*'[3]

The principle of correspondence in epistemology and the principle of homogeneity in sociology correspond precisely.

But are they true? Do they contribute to the knowing of 'the others'? Do they lead to living fellowship with others? Are we not ourselves 'the others' for other people?

It is already clear at first glance that in themselves these principles effect nothing, or merely the opposite of what they purport to say. If like is only known by like, why should it be known at all? Surely what is no different is, for the one who is no different, a matter of complete indifference?[4] If I know only what is like me, or what already corresponds to me, then, after all, I know only what I know already. The fascination of knowing is missing. The interest in knowing is paralysed. When two people say the same thing, says a Russian proverb, one of them is superfluous.

If, in social life, like draws only to like, is the result in a society not total stultification? The rich for themselves, and the poor for themselves, the whites for themselves and the blacks for themselves, the men for themselves and the women for themselves, the healthy for themselves and the disabled for themselves – we all remain with the people who are like us, and no one knows 'the others', for as Sartre said: 'Hell – that is the others.' This would be the total segregation-society of unrelated ghettos, and in every ghetto death through boredom would hold sway.

If this is so, must we not try to start from the opposite principles, in order to arrive at knowledge of others and community with others?

In epistemology, must we not start from the principle *'Other is only known by other'*, and in sociology from the principle *'The acceptance of others creates community in diversity'*?

I shall call the tenet cited above the principle of analogy and homogeneity, and this second tenet the principle of difference and diversity of kind, or: analogous and dialectical thinking. Having looked at the first principle in more detail, I shall go on to the second. And in each case I shall test the principle against knowledge of other people, knowledge of nature (as other than

ourselves), and knowledge of the Wholly Other God, asking
what forms of community they lead to. Finally I shall enquire
about *the foundation* of knowing – the knowing of human
beings, nature and God – in the elemental wonder over existence.

(ii) Correspondence in knowing leads to community between the same and those who have been made the same

'Like is only known by like.' Strictly understood, this principle
of likeness in epistemology means that the unlike – that is to say,
what is 'other' – cannot be known at all. All cognition is then
merely a re-cognition of what is already known, and knowledge
is nothing other than 'the eternal return of the same thing'. Early
Greek philosophy therefore at once expanded this principle to
cover 'the similar'. 'Similar is known only by the similar.' We
know by analogy when we ask about the *tertium comparationis*,
the factor linking the two elements we are comparing. In the
spheres of those that are different, the knower always perceives
only what is similar – that which corresponds to him. Why?
Because he perceives only that which finds a correspondence in
his own inner life. The macrocosm without corresponds to the
microcosm within. Every perception of things in the world outside evokes a resonance in the world within, and that is how
knowledge comes into being. Today we should say: the receiver
can hear the transmitter only by being tuned into the same
wavelength. That is why Empedocles (from whom this epistemological principle derives) said: 'Thus sweet reached out for
sweet, bitter rushed to bitter, sour to sour, the warm poured
itself into the warm. Thus fire pressed upwards, striving towards
what was like it.' For 'with the earth (i.e., in us) we see the earth;
with the water, water; with the air, the divine air; but with fire
the destroying fire; with love, love; and strife with sorry strife.'[5]
  Here the concern that prompts knowing (Habermas's 'knowledge-constitutive interest') is the *union* of like in human beings
with like in the cosmos. Like strives to like in order to be
united with it. It is the force of Eros which leads to the know-

ing of like by like, Eros being the power which creates the universe and holds it together. Likeness of essence between the macrocosm and the microcosm makes it possible for human beings to know the world, and this knowing in its turn leads them to community with the world through the correspondence of within and without. 'All that is separated finds itself again,' said Hölderlin. This goal of community is the concern and purpose of knowing. Its foundation is the cosmic fact that, in Eichendorff's phrase, 'Everything is eternally related within.' This ontological principle makes union through knowing possible. Because in the ancient Greek world – indeed in the world of the Old Testament too – knowing always confers community, knowing is always erotic through and through. 'Then Adam knew Eve . . .' (Gen. 4.1) – and the outcome was their son Cain. But what constitutes the power of Eros? It is the *attractive power* exerted by the lovable (*eidos*) on love (*eros*), by the desirable on desire, and by excellence on appreciation of its value. The power of Eros is the power to know and to be united, and must hence be viewed as the foundation of both this epistemology and this sociology.

Let us now apply this principle to the knowing of *other people, other things,* and *the Wholly Other God.*

1. If only like and like know one another, then I recognize in other people only that which corresponds to me myself in my own nature. I do not perceive what is different in kind and alien in other people. I filter it out. I perceive only the things in which we are alike, and only this can become the foundation of community between us. 'True friendship,' says Aristotle, 'rests on the foundation of likeness.'[6] The friendship of those who are alike was the quintessence of Greek social doctrine. Its correspondence is the spirit of equalizing, 'even-handed' justice which requites like by like – good by good, evil by evil. Some heroes, indeed, were called 'friends of the gods', but it is not really possible to talk about friendship between human beings and Zeus, the father of the gods. The same may be said of friendship between men and women, freemen and slaves. If friendship is based on likeness, it has an exclusive effect. Only

closed societies issue from people who are all the same. In these societies people who are alike mutually endorse each other's identity through the exclusion of others and the repeated assurance of not being like the others. Even in what Karl Popper designates as our 'open society',[7] like consorts with like in exclusive circles. Quite apart from the fact that behaviour of this kind is hurtful for 'the others' who are excluded, the result for 'the insiders' is deadly boredom, because they have already heard the stories and jokes with which closed societies are accustomed to amuse themselves a hundred times over.

The principle of correspondence does not lead to any increase in knowledge, but only to the continually reiterated self-endorsement of what is already known. The principle of like-ness leads to caste and class societies, and destroys interest in the livingness of life, which consists of polarities and contrasts.

2. If we apply this epistemological principle to *nature*, the effect is ambivalent. In the ancient world, knowledge meant participation: I perceive nature outside myself through the nature within myself, so that with my own nature I may partici-pate in nature as a whole, and may unite myself with her. Reason was then essentially an observing reason (*theorein*), a thinking with the eyes which see what is there.

But in modern times the human being came to be understood as a person and determining subject over against nature, which was made the object of human knowledge. Ever since Francis Bacon and René Descartes, to know has meant to dominate. I want to perceive nature outside myself in order to dominate it. I want to dominate it in order to acquire it for myself. I want to acquire it for myself in order to do what I like with my posses-sion. That is a thinking with the rapacious hand: I grasp that – I've mastered it – I've got it – I've seized the meaning – I have it. In the modern civilization to which we give the name 'scientific and technological', reason is no longer understood as an organ of perception; it is now an instrument of power.[8] Moulded by science, the reason of the modern world sees with Kant (who rationalized Newton's world picture philosophically) 'only that which it produces after a plan of its own . . . (it) must itself show the way with principles of judgment based upon fixed laws, constraining nature to give answer to questions of reason's own determining'.[9] Human reason behaves to nature like a barrister-at-law (Kant, from his German background, says 'like a judge') who subjects the witnesses to cross-examination. According to Francis Bacon, experiment is the torture to which nature is exposed so that she may give an answer to the questions human beings put to her, and yield up her secrets.[10]

Yet if this aggressive reason understands in nature only that which it itself 'produces' according to its own design, then what is other and alien in nature remains for ever hidden from it. 'The thing in itself' – *Das Ding an sich* – can never be known, as Kant made clear when he related the modes of appearance to the active subject. But if this is true, then humanity lives in the nature which has been made manifest by the sciences as if in a hall of mirrors. Wherever we look, we see only the projections, the reflections and the traces of human beings. Productive reason can recognize only its own products. It knows nothing of the inner being of things, and of nature's own individual life. If 'like is only known by like', then this human reason knows only the nature which it has adapted to itself, made the same as itself, subjugated to itself. But that destroys nature's own life, isolates human beings and makes them lonely. All that is left is technopolis and the desert. We have made the earth the exhausted quarry of our civilization, and our own rubbish dump.[11]

3. Applied to *God*, the 'likeness' principle leads either to the divinization of human beings or to the humanization of God. In the ancient world, people saw in every true knowledge of God a deification of the human being (*theosis*). For knowledge is participation, and creates community. But we can know the divine *above* us only by means of the divine *within* us, for 'God is only known by God'. It was in this sense that Goethe wrote:

Were the eye not like the sun, how could then the sun be seen?
Were not God's own power within us, how could the divine delight us?

Knowing confers community, and only the community of like beings makes this knowing possible. Here again we see that according to the view held in antiquity, perception changes the perceiver, so that the perceiver corresponds to what he perceives. But is God then knowable at all by beings who are not themselves divine?

Goethe gave the theological principle of likeness a particularly distinctive turn. If God is only known by God, then the reversal is also true: *Nemo contra Deum nisi Deus ipse* – no one is against God unless it be God himself. It is not clear from whom Goethe took this tremendous statement, or whether he or F. W. Riemer invented it, passing it off as old. Goethe takes the saying as the motto for the fourth book of his autobiography *Dichtung und Wahrheit* ('Poetry and Truth'), which he wrote in 1830. There he talks about 'daemonic personalities' who seem to be beyond good and evil, and concludes: 'Seldom or never do such men simultaneously find their like, and they can be defeated by nothing, unless it be the universe itself, with which they have begun their struggle; and it is from such observations that that strange but tremendous saying may well derive: *Nemo contra Deum nisi Deus ipse.*' Eduard Spranger followed this up,[12] and in Riemer's *Mitteilungen über Goethe* found Goethe's own interpretation: 'A glorious dictum, of endless application. God encounters always himself; God in man encounters himself again in man . . .' In the sense of Goethe's revered Spinoza, this then means: God is all and in all. If there is anything counter-divine, this contradiction of God too is within God himself. For outside God there is no one who could contend with God. Even the harshest *contra Deum*, the counter-divine, still conceals the *deus ipse*, God himself.

Taken by itself, however, this statement makes God himself the only conceivable atheist. If no one except God himself can be 'against God', then human atheism is impossible – either that, or the statement divinizes every serious atheist who is 'against God' into God himself. Tremendous though the declaration is, and fascinating though the possibilities are which it opens up to the speculative mind, it can also be used for the pupose of theological self-immunization: God is known only by God; no one can be against God except God himself. But this then eludes the grasp of theology to such an extent that we cannot even be against it. It really has nothing more to do with us at all.

The reason of the modern world understands the process of cognition in precisely the opposite way from antiquity: through the knowing, the known is subjected and adapted to the knower; for to know means to dominate. Applied to the divine above us, the 'likeness' principle therefore means that all knowledge of God must be viewed as a projection of the human fantasy. All imaginations and concepts of the divine are nothing more than human products, and tell us nothing about the divine itself. 'You are like the spirit you understand, not me,' cries the Earth Spirit to Dr Faust in Goethe's drama, after Faust has conjured it up. So human beings create their gods in their own image: the male gods, the white gods, the black gods, the female gods. The other and the alien, and the Wholly Other of the divine (Karl Barth's phrase,[13] following Rudolf Otto[14]) – all this is so unknowable that it cannot even be thought. The 'likeness' principle makes the reason of the modern world in principle agnostic. As Feuerbach's modern criticism of religion shows, it even makes it narcissistic. Like the beautiful youth Narcissus, modern human beings, wherever they may turn – whether it be to other people, to other 'nature', or to the Wholly Other of the divine – always see everywhere only their own reflection. But we have meanwhile lost the entranced self-love of the Narcissus of old, and in many people this self-love has already turned into the self-hate which befalls people when they have shut themselves in and never get out again. A kind of claustrophobic self-pity has developed, and it is only occasionally that out of it springs what Max Horkheimer calls 'a longing for the wholly Other'.[15]

Let us take as example the great event which stands at the beginning of modern times, because it has changed the world: the so-called discovery of America by Columbus, Cortes, and the Conquistadores, from 1492 onwards. As Todorov has shown,[16] the Europeans never really 'discovered' America at all in its unique character and difference. The Conquistadores saw nothing, and 'discovered' only what they were looking for – gold and silver. The Indian kingdoms were never known. They have never been understood, right down to the present day. They were subjugated, destroyed and exploited, and were missionized and colonized according to European blueprints. The 'other' people were accommodated to the rulers, as their subjects. The Christian missionaries too, as their diaries show, understood only what they could make the same as themselves through conversion. Spaniards, Portuguese and the Protestant Pilgrim Fathers failed to perceive the difference in kind and unique character of the Indians. Because they could only recognize what was like themselves, and because it was only that which they had the will to understand, they were bound to destroy the alien culture, and level down 'the others' to be like themselves. The sorry result was the uniform colonial culture, the uniform imperial religion, and the uniform, all-levelling language.

(iii) Knowledge of the other leads to community in diversity

'Other is only known by other.' This epistemological principle too has its roots in ancient Greek philosophy, though in a tradition which had little influence on our own culture.

Aristotle quotes Euripides as saying:

'The parched earth yearns for rain,
and the high heavens, great with rain, desire to fall to earth.'[17]

'Everything living springs out of strife,' the mysterious Heraclitus had said. But it was Anaxagoras who first formulated the epistemological principles which are the exact opposite of the principles maintained by Empedocles:

'Anaxagoras holds that sense perception comes to pass by

means of opposites, for the like is unaffected by the like . . .
We come to know the cold by the hot . . . the sweet by the
sour, the light by the dark . . . All sense perception, he holds,
is fraught with pain, for the unlike when brought into contact
[with our organs] always brings distress.'[18]

This last comment about the connection between perception
and pain is important. If our organs of perception encounter
something like, something familiar, or something that already
corresponds to ourselves, we feel endorsed, and that is pleasing
to our senses. If our organs of perception encounter something
different, strange or new, then the initial effect is pain.[19] We feel
the resistance of the alien. We feel the contradiction of the
other. We sense the claim of the new. The pain shows us that
we must open ourselves, in order to take in the other, the alien
and the new.

But how do we perceive this other? Not through its
correspondence but through its contradiction. We might say, in
general terms, that we perceive things first through their
contrast to the thing they are not. We perceive the other with
what is opposite in us ourselves. It is through dissonance, not
consonance, that we become alive to the new. To take up
Anaxagoras's imagery: the darker it is in us, the more we sense
the holiness of light. The colder we are, the more intensely we
feel a fire's warmth. When we are among people who are black,
we notice that we are white. Among people who are white, we
see that we are black. In a transferred sense, and in the dialectical formulation of the young Schelling: 'Every being can
become manifest only in its opposite – love only in hate, unity
only in strife.'[20] To put it somewhat less dramatically: it is only
in the foreign land that we understand what home is. It is
only in the face of death that we sense the uniqueness of life. It
is only in strife that we know how to appreciate peace. It is in
our encounter with others that we experience our own selves. In
the like, we do not notice what is like in ourselves at all. For us,
it is a matter of course. It is so close to us that we cannot perceive it. It is first in the distance, even more in the difference,

and then lastly in the contradiction that we perceive the other, and learn to value it.

Here too the concern that guides perception – the 'knowledge-constitutive interest' – is union. But the goal is not a unity in uniformity; it is a unity in diversity. Those who are different can complement each other, and long for reciprocal complementation as the earth longs for rain, and the rain for the earth. Those that are different can clash too, and out of the contention new life can be born. Antagonisms do not always have to be deadly. They can be life-giving as well, and can promote life. In spite of Heraclitus, what the Greeks meant by strife (*agon*) was competition and play as 'the father of all things'.[21] In the Chinese concept, these are the polarities Yin and Yang, which rhythmically and fluidly divide and unite, divide so as to unite, unite so as to divide, and thus advance the process of life.[22] Here too, the power in those who are united is Eros, but in a more profound interpretation than the one cited above. It is Hegel's dynamic dialectic of love which creates unity in division and division in unity, because it itself is the union of division and unity.[23]

Let us now apply these dialectical principles to the knowing of other people, other things, and the Wholly Other God.

1. If the unlike know themselves, then interest in the difference of the other must be greater than interest in its likeness. In the others I do not look at what is like myself, but at what is different in them, and try to understand it. I can only understand it by changing myself, and adjusting myself to the other. In my perception of others I subject myself to the pains and joys of my own alteration, not in order to adapt myself to the other, but in order to enter into it. There is no true understanding of the other without this empathy. Together with the other I enter into a process of reciprocal change. These pains of alteration and the joys of new insights are inherent in every learning process. In Greek, *mathein* (to learn) and *pathein* (to suffer) go together, as we see from many proverbs and sayings. Understanding empathy then engenders a connecting sympathy, once the empathy leads to mutual understanding. It forms the

community in the diversity and the diversity in the community. The basic law of a society like this is 'recognition of the other' in his or her difference. Societies which develop according to this principle are not closed societies. Nor are they uniform societies, where people are brought into line. They are 'open societies'. They can live not only with different and dissimilar people, but also, as Karl Popper required, with 'their enemies' too; for they can even make the enmity of their enemies fruitful for the things that are of concern to them.

How is this possible? Must a society's enemies not be told: either adapt or emigrate? I do not believe so. While the foundation of a society consisting of people who are like each other is normally *the love of friends,* the foundation of the society made up of the different is, if the worst comes to the worst, *the love of enemies*. To love our enemies means taking responsibility not just for ourselves and those who belong to us, but for our enemies too. We then no longer ask merely: how can we defend ourselves against our possible enemies? Our question now is: how can we take away their enmity, so that we can all survive together? In this sense, love of our enemies is the foundation for a shared life in conflicts.[24]

2. If we apply this dialectical epistemological principle to *nature*, then we replace analytical thinking, with its objectification of nature, by the systematic and *communicative* thinking which respects nature in its unique character and lets it be what it is, in its contradistinction to the human being. That means on the one hand perceiving natural beings in their totality and in their own biospheres, no longer isolating them and splitting them up for the purposes of acquisition. It means on the other hand recognizing them in their relative subjectivity, and no longer debasing them to the status of passive objects. The heuristic interest is no longer domination and control; it is communication. 'Holistic thinking'[25] brings people once more into the warp and weft of life shared in the greater organism of this earth, from which they have isolated themselves ever since the time when – on the strength of science and technology – they set themselves up to be nature's rulers and possessors. To put an

end to this self-isolation does not mean a romantic return to a paradisal 'state of nature' and to 'Mother Earth'. What it does mean is a new integration of human culture into nature through a balance and harmonization of their different interests in life. On the human side, this would involve a reintegration of the rationality that differentiates and dominates into the reason that receives and participates. But it goes further than that.

The new participatory reason is always at the same time an *involved* reason. It observes, and does not dominate things and other beings in the reality they have become. It understands their reality, together with their potentialities, in order to avert the potentialities that would be destructive, and to encourage the possibilities that are conducive to life. 'Involved' thinking does not just ask how things *are*. It also asks what they can become.[26] It perceives the present condition of things, but their future too. It understands everything in its time, and living things in their processes.

This, in its turn, presupposes understanding the 'objects' of nature as *systems open to the future,* systems whose past is fixed, whose future is partially undetermined, and whose present lies in the anticipation of their possibilities.[27] If all beings are open systems, from the atom to other people, as Prigogine and others rightly say, then in nature there are no objects in the true sense. There are only subjects with varying degrees of complexity.[28] Human knowing of things in nature is thus nothing other than communication between open systems with different gradations of complexity. It is therefore a cognitive process between subject and subject. But between these different subjects there is community in recognition of the diversity. Domination and control by one side would merely destroy the protean character of the living and the relationships in which they live.

3. Applied to *God*, dialectical thinking leads to the recognition of diversity in community. 'God is only known by God,' says the 'likeness' principle. Dialectical thinking says that God appears as God only in the sphere of what is other than God,

that is to say, in the realm of the finite and in the sphere of human beings who are in contradiction to him; dialectical thinking says that for human beings God is the Wholly Other.[29] It is only when human beings see themselves simply as human beings, no longer as gods, that they are in a position to perceive the wholly other nature of God. It is only when we cease to be unhappy supermen and pathetic mini-gods and permit ourselves to become human beings through and through again that we let God be God, as Luther said. We can even go a step further and say: it is only when we men and women become wholly godless, in the sense that we dispense with every self-deification or presumptuous pretence of resembling God, that we can perceive the wholly other reality of the true God; and conversely, where we experience the wholly other God, we can dispense with our anxious and aggressive 'God complex', and become true human beings.

'To know God means to suffer God,' says a wise old Greek saying, drawn from experience. The experiences of the God of Abraham, Isaac and Jacob, Moses and Jesus, endorse the truth of this saying. It is with pain that people first perceive the wholly other reality of God. According to Christian experience, these are the pains of dying from God and the joys of being born again out of God. Only through the total change of our selves do we perceive the wholly other reality of God. This kind of knowledge of God has received its concentrated theological form in the theology of the cross, which says that God is hidden beneath cross and suffering, so that the true misery of men and women, which seems to be so God-forsaken, is the place where God encounters us. 'In the moments of God's profoundest revelation there was always suffering of some kind: the cry of the oppressed in Egypt, the cry of Jesus on the cross, the birth pangs of the whole creation as it waits for its redemption.'[30] 'In so far as God is revealed in his opposite, he can be known by the godless and those who are abandoned by God, and it is this knowledge which brings them into correspondence with God and, as I John 3.2 says, enables them even to have the hope of being like God.'[31]

Is this dialectical knowing out of diversity, out of difference and out of contradiction, identical with that mediaeval principle of analogical knowing, according to which between the creature and the Creator, in spite of all similarity, there is always a still greater dissimilarity? '*Quia inter creatorem et creaturam non potest tanta similitudo notari, quin inter eos major sit dissimilitudo notanda*' ('Because between the Creator and the creature so great a likness cannot be noted without the necessity of noting a greater dissimilarity between them').[32]

This dissimilarity in all the similarity distinguishes the Creator from those he has created in an ideal sense. But in our reality what we are faced with is the sinner's contradiction of God, and God's revelation to the godless through his compassion with them. The knowledge of God in the truly godless can only be found in the event of their acceptance by God, and that means in the crucified Christ: 'Emmanuel – God with us – with us godless men and women.'[33] It is only on the basis of this knowledge of God in the event of justification that it is possible to talk again about the correspondence of human creatures to their Creator, and to speak of the analogies of the human being who corresponds to God. Only God's contradiction of our contradiction creates correspondences and similarities even in still greater ontological dissimilarity.

(iv) The origin of knowing in wonder

In the practical process of knowing, we always link the elements that correspond and the elements that contradict. If there were no likeness there would be no common ground and therefore no possibility of knowing. And if there were nothing 'other', then there would be no need to know. In knowing in the specific sense, we need both the endorsement of the correspondence and the pain of the contradiction. Knowing is remembrance and expectation, remembrance of what is familiar and expectation of what is new. It is therefore both re-cognition and a fresh cognition.

But where do we find the root of knowing? Of course knowledge is guided by as many interests as there are human desires. But that is merely to name the subjective factors which empower the capacity for the knowing which is already existent and must be presupposed. The root of knowing itself is not just subjective; it is objective at the same time. It lies in the elemental form of encounter between the awakening human senses and the impressions made on them by the world. The Greek philosophers therefore called the deepest ground of knowing *wonder*. In wonder the senses are opened for the immediate impression of the world. In wonder the things perceived penetrate the senses fresh and unfiltered. They impose themselves on us. They make an impression on us, and we are impressed.

In wonder, things are perceived for what they are *for the first time*. The wondering child still has no ideas with which to grasp its impressions, and as yet no concepts with which it can circumscribe them. It is only the second or third time that it remembers, and exercises a repeatable approach to the impressions that crowd in upon it. By the twentieth time, this perception is then already familiar, and we react in understanding and will, as we have learnt. It no longer astonishes us. We are no longer surprised. We are prepared for it, as we say. That is why we grown-ups attribute wonder to the childlike eyes which perceive and experience the world for the first time.

And yet, even at the depths of the perceptions of adult people there is still a little element of wonder. In the reality of life in time, nothing ever repeats itself in the strict sense; every moment is unique and once for all. Consequently it is only the wonder in us that is capable of grasping the non-recurring moment. People who can no longer be astonished, people who have got used to everything, people who perceive only as a matter of routine and react accordingly: people who live like this let reality pass them by. Every chance is singular and unique. That is its nature. The same chance never comes twice. There is never a 'second' chance, for time is irreversible. 'No one enters the same river twice,' said Heraclitus. The people who have kept their original capacity for wonder sense the uniqueness of the moment. They perceive that uniqueness with the openness with which they grasped the firstness of things.

In wonder we do not yet grasp *what* things look like, but we grasp that they are *there*. We perceive with astonishment that they are there. We understand in an elemental way the wonder of existence – of *Dasein*, the being-there itself. We are often astonished that we ourselves are *there*, although we do not know why we are there or what for. Those who are cast into astonishment by this 'there-ness' also experience that they themselves are really there, and are not an illusion. That means that through wonder we grasp the 'being there' of the world and our own thereness. It is only later that we grasp the what and how. But simple 'thereness' we never understand. It remains astonishing.

Is it not important to trace back again and again our knowing, our interest in knowing, the ideas which we form out of experience, and the concepts with which we order our ideas to the elemental wonder over existence itself? Otherwise we could come to perceive only our perceptions, and see nothing more of the phenomena. Otherwise we could come to see only what we want to see, and go almost blindly through life. Otherwise we could cease to know other people because we have tethered ourselves fast to our pre-judgments about them, and simply want to have these confirmed. Otherwise we could come to think that the products of our religious fantasy are God, and notice nothing of the living God. Reality is always more surprising than we are capable of imagining.

'Concepts create idols, only wonder understands,' said the wise Gregory of Nyssa.[34] People whose unique character we respect continue to astonish us, and our wonder opens up the freedom for new future possibilities in our community with them. The wonders of nature too still astonish us, if in our busyness we can pause and sink into the contemplation of a flower or a tree or a sunset. But the most astonishing thing of all seems to me to be the ground of the 'being-there' of all things, the ground whom we have to thank for there being anything there at all. The One we call God eludes our ideas, which nail him down, and our concepts, which try to bring him within our grasp; and yet he is closer to us than we ourselves – *interior intimo meo*, as Augustine knew.[35] For 'in him we live and move and have our being'. In 'the darkness of the lived moment'[36] we become aware of God's presence. Wonder is the inexhaustible foundation of our community with each other, with nature, with God. Wonder is the beginning of every new experience and the ground of our creative expectation of the new day.

5

Freedom in Community between Globalization and Individualism: Market Value and Human Dignity

(i) The double danger

Like all other life, human life is shared life, communicated and communicating life, communion in communication. Today the necessary communities which make up human life are threatened from two sides: on the one hand by the stepped-up *individualism* of modern men and women, and on the other by the *global marketing* of everything, including relationships. So what is true freedom: individual freedom of choice, or the principle of the free market economy?

The global marketing of everything and every service is much more than pure economics. It has become the all-embracing law of life.[1] We have become customers and consumers, whatever else we may be. The market has become the philosophy of life, the world religion, and for some people even 'the end of history'.[2] The marketing of everything destroys community at all levels, because people are weighed up only according to their market value. They are judged by what they can perform or by what they can afford.

The traditional *family* community is being weakened by the overwork of some and the long-term unemployment of others. Its capacity for social integration is diminishing. After the reunification of Germany, many women in the east had themselves sterilized, so that they would be in a position to compete in the job market. The birth rate sank drastically. In the cities, the number of single parents, mostly women, is about 40%. Men are turning into workaholics, with the three typical male Cs: career, competition, collapse.[3]

The *civil* community is becoming increasingly polarized: a rich upper class on the one hand, and impoverished masses on the other. The rich live in gated communities – in a gilded prison; the poor vegetate in the slums and ghettos and in prisons of iron. Is there a social contract between rich and poor? That was already Rousseau's ironical question. Every modern democracy is based on the principles of liberty and equality. The American Declaration of Independence maintained that 'all men are created equal, and are endowed . . . with the right to liberty'. Is liberal democracy possible in the unbridled market economy – in pure, deregulated capitalism? The disagreeable answer is: probably not, for liberal democracy presupposes a certain degree of economic equality – which in sociological terms means a strong middle class – and this is eliminated by the neo-liberal laws of the market.

Not least, the internationalization of production has weakened the *national* community, and with it the national welfare state. Article 14.2 of the German constitution or Basic Law (the *Grundgesetz*) states that 'Property involves obligation. It must be used for the benefit of all.' But how can transnational corporations be sued for their neglect of this social obligation which property involves? Their only goal is the dividends of the shareholders. On a national level they can no longer be either controlled or obligated. What American or German can compete with Indians or Chinese who work for less than a dollar an hour? The internationalization of the flow of capital makes it impossible for national governments to exercise any control over it. On the contrary, they are dependent on it themselves. Has the nation state become obsolete? What communities in which people can identify themselves still exist in the global and total marketing of everything?

Are there any alternatives? Unlike Francis Fukuyama, I do not believe that the end of history will have been reached once there are no more alternatives – only when no *challenging contradictions* thrust forward to a new solution. But the global marketing of everything produces enormous discrepancies, personal and social, economic and ecological, which can mean the end of humanity unless new solutions can be found.

(ii) Three Dimensions of Human Freedom

Let us turn first to the personal side of the danger, and ask whether progressive individualism can sustain personal human dignity and personal freedom.

(*a*) The first definition of freedom, familiar to us from political history, is *freedom as domination*. Because all history up to now can be viewed as a permanent struggle for power and the increase of one's own power, the only person who is called free in this struggle is the one who acquires the power, and rules. The losers and the subjugated are called 'unfree'. One linguistic root of the word freedom comes from the slave-owning society: only the masters are free – not their slaves, women and children. But people who understand freedom as domination can be free only at the expense of other people. Their freedom means oppression for others; their wealth makes other people poor; their power makes the weaker powerless. That is why the liberty of those who are 'free' always brings in its wake those tiresome security problems.

People who understand freedom as domination really know only themselves as determining subjects, and everything else as their property, their object. Freedom is a function of property. They do not know other people as persons. Even if we say today that people are free if they can do and leave undone whatever they like, we are still understanding freedom as rule – as the human being's autonomy over himself or herself. C. B. Macpherson has shown[4] how the liberation of the bourgeois world led from feudalism to 'possessive individualism': no one may be any master's slave or serf, everyone is his own master, everyone belongs to himself. The very words 'lordship' and 'mastery' themselves show the degree to which the understanding of freedom as rule and self-rule derives from the male world.

The middle-class liberalism which succeeded princely absolutism in Western Europe held on to the model of the feudal autocrat, and democratized it. Everyone has the same right to liberty. This individual liberty is limited only by the liberty of all the rest. So anyone who lays claim to liberty must respect the same liberty in other people. Everyone is the boundary of other people's liberty. No one determines over anyone else; everyone determines over himself. Everyone is free and on his own, and no one takes any interest in the others. Notionally, or in the abstract, this is the society of solitary individuals who do not meddle with each other – a society of social frigidity.[5] In this way freedom becomes general. But is it true freedom?

No: for a *person* is not an *individual*. The distinction is simple, but is seldom made. According to its Latin meaning, an *individuum* is something ultimately indivisible, like 'atom' in Greek.[6] A person, in comparison, is – as Martin Buber showed (following Feuerbach, Hegel and Hölderlin)[7] – the individual human being in the resonant field of his or her relationships, the relationships of I, Thou and We, I-Myself and I-It. In the network of relationships, the person becomes the human subject of taking and giving, listening and doing, experiencing and touching, hearing and responding. We approach humanism only when we pass from individualism to personalism.

That is why I would maintain that the freedom of human persons cannot be safeguarded by increasing individualism. On the contrary, the increasing individualism of people in modern society contributes to their fresh enslavement. 'Divide and rule' was the proven Roman method of domination. If we want to rule over other people, we must separate them from each other as far as possible, isolate them, drive them apart and individualize them. When in this division we arrive at the final and indivisible entity, that is the subjugated person *per se*. The modern individual is therefore the end-product of the divide-and-rule method. What we have are individuals in an atomized world.

How can human persons protect their dignity and freedom in spite of the pressure of individualization? By becoming capable of community, and prepared for community. That is the truth of the communitarian network.[8] But we cannot revert to the predetermined affiliations of traditional societies. We should then have to give up the personal liberties we have won, and let traditions or hierarchies rule over us again, and decide for us. But we can keep our personal dignity and freedom if we take a step forward.

The person who is free is 'the being who can promise', said Nietzsche, with penetrating insight; and I would add: 'and the being who must keep his promise.' Through the promise I make, I make myself – equivocal though I am – unequivocal for others and for myself. In promising we commit ourselves and become reliable and calculable for other people.[9] People who forget their promises, forget themselves as well. People who remain true to their promises remain true to themselves too. If we keep our promises, we win the trust of others. If we break them, other people distrust us – and rightly so, for then we lose or deny our identity, and in the end no longer know ourselves.

Yet 'trust is good, control is better', said Lenin, the Communist, who mistrusted his own people. And with this principle he laid the foundation stone for the self-destruction of the socialist world. Control is so costly and so endlessly extravagant because the controllers always have to be controlled too, so the state security services eat up the national budgets, and a profound mistrust of each against all spreads among the people: 'Your neighbour could be an informer. Be on your guard!'

Promising and keeping promises, giving and receiving trust, are not restraints on personal freedom. They are the concrete form freedom takes. Where do I feel personally free? In a supermarket, where I can buy what I want (as far as my money goes), but where no one knows me, and not even the girl at the checkout looks me in the eye? Or in a community where others affirm me just as I am?

The first is the reality of modern, individual freedom to

choose. The second is the reality of communicative freedom. The first freedom is related to things, the second to persons.

(*b*) The other definition, familiar from social history, defines *freedom as free community*. Here freedom is not an attribute of the determining subject. It is a qualification of the intersubjective relationships in which and from which the human subjects live. That is the concept of communicative freedom.[10]

Not every community is a liberating community. There are communities which are highly exclusive and repressive, which we have to break out of if we want to experience freedom. German linguistic history shows that friendliness or kindness (*Freundlichkeit*) is the other root of freedom (*Freiheit*). The person who is free is friendly, affectionate, open, pleasant and loving, says Kluge's *Etymologisches Wörterbuch*. People who are what German calls *gastfrei* – hospitable – have many guests and 'give freely'. They let other people participate in their lives and are interested in the welfare of others. Intersubjective relationships are called free if they are marked by mutual respect and by friendliness on both sides. If I know that I am respected and loved, then I feel free, because I can come out of my shell and can behave as I really am. If I open myself for others, I recognize them for what they are, and love them. I open a free space for them socially, so that they can blossom.

In a community of mutual respect, of liking, friendship and love, the other person is no longer a restriction of my personal freedom. That person is the social complement of my own limited freedom. The result is reciprocal participation in the life of other people. People become free beyond the frontiers of their own lives, and the outcome of this mutual participation is shared life, 'the good life'.

We call this 'a free society'. It is the social side of freedom, which is often so neglected. In the Christian community we call it love, and in sociology solidarity. A free society is therefore not a collection of private, free individuals. It is a community in solidarity, where people intervene on one another's behalf, and especially for the weak, the sick, the young and the old. In this society we experience a coming together of the individuals who

are otherwise isolated and solitary. The community in solidarity is a resistance movement against domination through the
'divide and rule' method.

If a human subject is related to objects, then freedom takes
the form of rule. If human subjects are related to each other,
then freedom takes on the form of community. There is no other
way in which the dignity of human beings can be respected, for
human dignity means that human beings are determining
subjects always and everywhere, and must never, ever, be
degraded into objects – into slaves, work force or 'human
material'. The freedom to rule and the freedom of a community
must be strictly distinguished if freedom is to be preserved.

(*c*) The third definition of freedom takes us beyond both these
others. *Freedom is the creative passion for the possible.* Freedom is not just turned towards things as they are, as it is in
domination. Nor is it directed only to the community of people
as they are, as it is in solidarity. It reaches out to future, for
future is the unknown realm of possibilities, whereas present
and past represent the familiar sphere of realities.

The Greeks understood freedom as a harmonious assimilation of individuals into the human *polis*, and of the human
polis into the divine cosmos. 'To live according to nature' was
accounted to be the true life in freedom. Marx and Engels too
still made use of this idea when they taught that freedom was
'insight' into the 'necessity' of world history, through which
capitalism was to be replaced by socialism, and socialism by
communism.

When we align freedom towards future and understand it as
creative expectation, we are drawing on the biblical – the Jewish
and Christian – 'principle of hope' (Ernst Bloch). Creative
passion is always fascinated by a project for the future, which is
anticipated in creative imagination. We want to realize new
possibilities. That is why we expect from the future the new day.
Our rational understanding becomes productive fantasy, no
longer aligned towards the present condition of things but looking towards ways of improving them. Like Martin Luther King,
we have visions and dreams of another life, a life healed, just

and good. We explore the possibilities of the future in order to realize these dreams, visions and projects. All cultural and social innovations belong to this sphere of freedom for the future. Christian possibility-thinking has lent powerful impulses to this understanding of freedom: 'With God all things are possible' and 'All things are possible to him who believes.'[11]

Up to now we have understood freedom either as rule – the relation of a subject to objects – or as community, in the relation of subject to subject. But in relation to *projects*, freedom is a creative *movement*. Anyone who in thought, word and act transcends the present in the direction of the future is truly free. Future is the free space for creative freedom.

'*Denken heisst überschreiten*' – thinking means going beyond: that is the epitaph written on Ernst Bloch's tombstone in Tübingen. It is true that for this we need hope. But a community must permit this creative freedom too, and must not hinder it. Many communities, however, have conservative tendencies; they want to preserve what is actually there, and to curb the possible. They are focussed on stability, not innovation. In the former German Democratic Republic, students were trained to work together. All the members of a seminar were given the same mark at the end. In my seminars in a West German university, the groups were creative in 'brainstorming', but not when they wrote their seminar papers. Those had to be conceived and written by individuals. Will the 'communitarian movement' promote the spirit of hope and innovation? If it hinders that spirit it will soon be superseded.

One final thought in this connection: freedom as rule by a subject over objects is *a function of property*. Freedom as unhindered, life-furthering community is *a social function*. Freedom as a transcending into the possibilities of the future is *a creative function*. The first has to do with having, the second with being, and the third with becoming.

In this last respect, freedom is not a possession, nor is it a quality. It is *a happening*. We have our creative liberty only in the process of liberation. We are never free once and for all, but we can continually *become* free. And only the people who make use of their freedom remain free. If it is not used, freedom is an empty slogan. In history, freedom is experienced in liberating events, processes and movements. We are not yet in 'the realm of freedom' itself, but only on liberating paths which lead out of the old conditions of the past into the new possibilities of the future. In history, and if we follow the remembrances of the Bible, we find freedom in the continual exodus from enslavement and lethargy, and on the long march through the desert; but not yet in the promised land, which is 'the end of history'. Freedom is like the manna in the wilderness. It cannot be stored up. We can only trust that tomorrow it will be there again. So we have to use our freedom every day.

The three dimensions of freedom I have named have to be balanced out. Taken by itself, freedom as the rule of subject over objects leads to the global market society of having. Taken by itself, freedom as community leads to a world of total community. Freedom as rule can be gathered up into freedom as community only if freedom as initiative and responsibility for a common future is in the foreground. For this purpose, the categories of having and being can be integrated without any adverse mutual effects into the comprehensive category of becoming and of a sustainable development.

(iii) Is the market to be the measure of all things?

The globalization of markets and production is seriously endangering all traditional communities, from the family and civil society right down to the nation as a community in solidarity.[12] The capacity of these communities for social integration is becoming weaker. They are also increasingly unable to compensate for the human costs of the global marketing of everything. I am not an economist. I am a Christian theologian, and think of the experiences of pastors and social workers with the people who drop out of the net of our economic system, or who never find a way into it. I am an ecumenical theologian, and listen to the voices – and to the speechlessness – of people in the countries of the Third World, particularly in Africa and

Latin America. My questions to the global market economy spring from this context.

1. There were already markets before there was any modern society: otherwise towns would never have grown up out of the little marketing centres. Market relationships were originally based on barter. People produced for their own needs, and took the surplus to market. In the modern world that has radically changed. The market has become an institution which penetrates all sectors of life. We speak of the money market, the market-maker on the stock exchange, the labour market, the food market, the drug market, the marriage market. We fetch our drinks from the 'cash and carry' market. We talk about the religions, morals and philosophies of life that are 'on offer'. It is no longer human needs which regulate production; it is the requirements of the market.

In the last twenty years, the Olympic Games have been transformed from an athletic contest into a marketing event. The participants are misused as living advertisement hoardings and advertising media, as we saw at the Coca Cola games in Atlanta.

The first question many people ask is consequently: is the market there for the sake of men and women, or are men and women there for the sake of the market? In families, neighbourhoods and free communities human relationships exist in mutual recognition and acceptance. If the market becomes the dominant power, then relationships of mutual recognition and acceptance come to an end. The self-respect experienced through the recognition gives way to the value assigned by the public market. People who look for a job on the labour market soon discover that their value is merely what they are able to offer as performers or purchasers. People who lose their jobs because of the rationalization or globalization of production, sense from their inner feeling of personal value the degree to which they have identified themselves with their value as performers. Because we are supposed to 'fulfil ourselves' through work and consumption, if we have no work and are poor we lose our own selves. 'He didn't give the performance we expected of him,' we are told, when footballers or trainers are sacked. It is not just the winners – the losers too adopt as their own the public scale of values which rests on competition in the public market, and condemn themselves as failures. Less money – less value – less self-confidence. Here the market society, which rewards only the competent performers and the successful, brings with it severe personal and family problems. It has done away with the old society based on rank, in which people found their identity through their birth, family and nation; it now assesses only performance and its success.[13] Every pastor and teacher among us knows that to belong to the new poor is the best-kept family secret.

Of course we know intellectually that a person is more than his or her market value. Of course we believe that human dignity is one and the same, whether it be the dignity of the person who 'sleeps rough' or the dignity of the Lord Mayor. But the human dignity which is a conscious creed does not have as regulative an effect on public life as the human being's market value. It acts on our public conscience, so that through unemployment benefit and social security payments we 'cushion' (as the phrase goes) the lot of the people who have dropped out of the labour market. But it no longer acts on society itself, which is given over to the market. The 'social' market economy functions quite well when we can afford it. But it is when we cannot afford it that people need it most. Market value or human dignity: what society do we really want? Is 'the social component' only supposed to alleviate the social damage caused by the market society and to reduce the human costs? Or can we plan a future in which the market benefits the whole human community?

One step on the way would be to stop making the global market either into an idol which has to have its victims, or into a demon which has to be feared, and to cut it down to human size. Competitive struggles and comparisons of market value are as adolescent as boys who knock each other down or girls who preen themselves in front of the mirror. Another stage in society's maturity is undoubtedly conceivable, a stage in which we would move from the principle of competition to co-operation, and grow as human beings beyond anything which the market can achieve. The long-term jobless man or woman who walks with head held high in unbroken dignity and the manager who turns down the next step up the career ladder for his family's sake know that there are more important things in human terms than the market.

2. The global market looks different when we no longer see it from within but from outside, and do not enjoy its benefits on the upper side of its history but suffer it on its downside. In the countries of the Third World, fatalism is spreading, and with it the feeling that this is the end of the road, the world's finale. The mega-cities in the Third World are sinking into anarchy and violence, and are becoming ungovernable.[14] The very genesis of the Third World is causally linked with the beginning of the modern world. The Third World countries first served the exploitation of gold, silver, cotton and coffee, and the enslavement of millions; later they were the source for shipments of cheap labour. Then the debt trap took the place of direct exploitation. Today countries which neither possess appreciable resources of raw materials nor can offer the prospect of worthwhile markets are ignored. They drop out of the global market. Millions become surplus people. No one can use them. They easily become the victims of violence, as in Rwanda, or of the plagues which are coming back again in the guise of epidemics, as in Latin America – not to speak of AIDS in Africa.

Mass movements are taking these people into the islands of prosperity. In the future we could well see poverty crusades against the rich countries. Even harsh laws designed to restrict emigration and political asylum will not protect 'fortress Europe' or 'fortress North America' or Japan. Without justice between the First World and the Third, there will be no lasting peace. But what do *we* want ourselves? More property or better community? The alternative to poverty is not property. The alternative to both poverty and property is community. Community with the people of the Third World involves the creation of bearable living conditions in their countries. What has been destroyed in those countries through unjust prices on the world market cannot be made good by way of 'development aid'. The world market itself must turn into development aid. But that requires long-term investments in place of short-term profits. The present globalization of production may unintentionally become a kind of development aid for eastern Europe, India and Africa. Here too, would it not make sense to change the goals of the world market, and to give precedence to the developing countries, because ultimately their development benefits everyone?

3. Finally, 'the ecological market economy' is good, but the feeble ecological measures are insufficient to repair the injury done to the natural environment, and to avoid new damage. The felling of the rain forests and the growth of the deserts show that the ruthless marketing of everything leads to ruin. Only bankrupts are out for short-term profits, and for the sake of these profits they are selling the foundations of life we all share. Up to now the global market has been one-sided in its orientation towards human beings, not the earth. If we think long-term and for coming generations, it is advisable to move from ecological damage-limitation to an economic 'policy for the earth', such as Ernst von Weizsäcker has demanded. Up to now, the earth's organism has hardly played any part on the global market. The earth has dumbly endured the exploitations of its raw materials and has been the silent recipient of the outpouring of human rubbish. But humanity has meanwhile become so numerous a species that its food requirements and its output of rubbish are threatening to destroy the planetary environmental system, which is the basis of human life itself. So in the coming century *the earth* is going to become the factor which will have to be respected everywhere in our economic and political calculations. This will change our spiritual attitude to the earth too. From being an object of our domination, we shall see it as a source of everything living which we have to revere. Here too values and goals will change. What was up to now a merely subsidiary concern – ecological consideration – will become the main thing; for if this world ceases to exist there will be no global market and no world religions any more.

The human race is a relatively late species in the evolution of the living. Perhaps we are still at the adolescent stage, intoxicated by our own power, wanting to test our strength in competitive struggles, and ruthlessly draining to the dregs the earth, which is our mother. We can take our bearings from older creatures and from the earth itself, so as to become more mature and, in the end, adult. We need science and better technology, but what we need most of all, if we want to survive, is more wisdom in our dealings with knowledge and technology. We need, not more profits and more expansion, but more wisdom in dealing with the dynamics of the global market. I believe that, now that the market has been globalized, we should reduce it to the dimensions which human beings and nature can endure, so that it can be integrated into the greater values of the human community with the earth. We shall learn this in one way or another, of that I am convinced: either through conviction, or through catastrophes. I am for learning through conviction.

III

Theology and Religion

I

The Pit – Where Was God?
Jewish and Christian Theology after
Auschwitz

On 23 August, 1941, in Belaya Tserkov, a town in the Ukraine not far from Kiev, ninety Jewish children were shot, thrown into a pit and buried there. Some of them were tiny babies. The oldest of them was seven or eight years old. Their parents were among the 3,000 or 5,000 Jews in the town, men, women and children, who had already been shot. The ninety children had been left over – a remnant.

August Häfner, who ordered the children to be shot, was at that time an officer in the SS, in Task Force IVa. In 1964, during an interrogation, he gave the following account:

'The army had already dug the pit. The children were brought in a tractor-drawn truck. I had nothing to do with the technical details. The Ukrainians stood around trembling. The children were taken down from the truck. They were stood up above the pit and shot so that they fell into it. The children just stood there, and where they were hit they were hit. They fell into the pit' (Documentation for the film *Die Grube* ('The Pit') by Karl Fruchtmann, Radio Bremen, 21 December 1995).

(i) The horror remains

I can only approach this question with fear and trembling. I am
overwhelmed by the same horror as I was the first time, when
in 1959 I went through what was left of the concentration camp
in Maidanek/Lublin, saw the gas chambers, the mountains of
children's shoes and the shorn hair, and for horror and shame
wished that the ground would open and swallow me up. Karl
Fruchtmann's film *Die Grube* transports one again into the
same horror: ninety Jewish children, babies, and all of them
under eight, were shot, thrown into a pit, and buried. The army
had dug the pit. The SS carried out the murder of the children.
And this was long before the Wannsee conference. It happened
on 23 August 1941, only three months after the attack on
Russia. This murder was part of the extermination of Judaism
and the Jewish people which was planned and carried through
to the end in Germany by the Third Reich.

The horror doesn't wear off with time. The remembrance
doesn't fade. Every attempt after more than fifty years to
historicize the mass murder of the Jews by us Germans founders
when it is confronted with the abyss of horror and brought face
to face with God. For before God there is no statute of limitations, either in the detachment of the past or through the alleged
'grace of a late birth'.* Before the Eternal One everything is
simultaneous and present. That is why the horror that lays hold
of us in the face of that crime is unplumbed, fathomless. We
cannot repress it, for we cannot grasp it. It is there, and goes
with us from one generation to another.

Nor is the horror lessened by any comparison. Every attempt
to set off Auschwitz against the Gulag Archepelago, or
Hiroshima, or Srebreniza, is stillborn when it is brought up
against the abyss of horror at ourselves. People belonging to our
own country, people no different from ourselves, were the
pepetrators – perhaps seduced, blinded, drunken perpetrators.
But are we sure today that it couldn't be us? What was a
reality once is always possible again. And we shall not rid our-

---

* The phrase applied to himself by the then chancellor Helmut Kohl.

selves of the horror by relativizing it either. Our burden will not be any lighter because we compare other mass murders and 'ethnic cleansings': on the contrary.

We shall never be able to understand Auschwitz and what happened in Belaya Tserkov, nor shall we be able to forget it. But we must open our minds to the questions with which they confront us.[1] Nothing is just as it was before: our relation to ourselves, our relation to God, or our relation to Israel, to the Jews. But what is it going to be?

I am a Christian theologian, and I have to address and wrestle with the question about God after Auschwitz. That is not just a question for believing men and women among the Jews and the Germans. The question about God was the question of the antisemites and the murderers of the Jews as well. There I agree with Dieter Koch.[2] Why did the mass murder of the Jews only really get under way when the war had already been lost? Why were Jews from all the Balkan countries still herded together and gassed in Auschwitz at the end of 1944, when the Russian front was already close, and was inexorably moving forward? Why did Eichmann have the right to use railway trucks for this purpose, although it weakened the German front? Wasn't that totally irrational? Of course there were the perverse 'plot' theories of the Nazis, according to which the real opponents in the war were not the Allies but 'Judah', the messianic 'Third Reich' having the historic destiny to bring about 'the final solution of the Jewish question', even if it itself perished in the process. But behind this apocalyptic messianism of 'the Reich' there was at the deepest depths something else as well: the hatred of God, and the will to exterminate not only the Jews but with them the God of Abraham, Isaac and Jacob and his eternal righteousness and justice, so as to establish the atheistic despot. The murder of the Jews was an attempt to murder God.

(ii) The question about God in suffering and God's question about guilt

The suffering of helpless children from which there is no way out, and which has no meaning, makes people cry out for God and despair of God. 'If there is a God, why this suffering?', ask some. 'Where was Israel's God when his children were thrown into the pit? Where was the Christian God when people belonging to Christendom turned into these cruel monsters who faithfully and in faith carried out the commands of the Antichrist? After Auschwitz can we go on believing in an almighty, good God in heaven? After Auschwitz, can even evil still work for good?

That is the way some people ask about God: their questions are theoretical questions. How can God permit this if he is just? They have the impression that God is a cold, blind force of destiny, for whom the dying and death of his human children is a matter of indifference. People think about God like this because they are afraid of becoming like that themselves – untouched, cold and cynical towards suffering. But isn't this so-called theodicy question wrongly framed? Why did God permit this? Given a negative slant, this is an onlooker's question, the question of onlookers who ask 'why' after the event, and yet know perfectly well that any answer that begins 'because' would make a mockery of the sufferers and would blaspheme God. Given a positive turn, this question of theodicy is not the question which the people involved ask. It is the question of the people who mourn for them: 'My God, why, why . . .?' We cannot answer that question in this world, but we cannot let it drop either. We have to exist in the question and with it, as with an open wound in our lives.[3]

The question asked by the sufferers themselves is not 'Why does God permit this?' It is more immediate than that. Their question is 'My God, where are you?', or, more generally, 'Where is God?'

The first question – why does God permit this? – is the question how God can be justified in view of the immeasurable suffering in the world. The second question – the question of the people involved – is the cry for God's companionship in the suffering of the world, a suffering which he condemns. The premise of the first question, the 'why', is an apathetic God who is supposed to justify himself in the face of human suffering. The second question, the 'where', seeks a God who shares our suffering and carries our griefs.

But then there is still a third question about God, which we often suppress with the help of the first. It is God's question about men and women. It is not the question about the victims. It is the question about the perpetrators and those who have to live in the long shadows of Auschwitz. This question is what we call the question of justification, meaning by that, not that God has to justify himself to the world for its suffering, but that the evil-doers, the murderers and those who have to live in their shadows, have to justify themselves before God. Can the godless become just? Is there reconciliation for the perpetrators and those who come after them? Is conversion to life possible? After Auschwitz, do we still have a human future worth living for? In this context we don't cry 'Where is God?'. We hear the eternal voice which cries 'Adam, where are you?' and 'Cain, where is your brother Abel?' and 'What have you done?'.

We shall now listen first to Jewish voices 'after Auschwitz' in order to learn from them. Out of the many I have picked out four: Richard Rubenstein and Emil Fackenheim, Eliezer Berkovits and Elie Wiesel. After that we shall listen to the first approaches to a Christian 'theology after Auschwitz'. Here I have taken Johann Baptist Metz and Dorothee Sölle, and have ranged myself beside them. But after that we shall go over to the other side, which has been so inexcusably neglected, and ask about the life of the people burdened by guilt, and about the future of Cain and those whose collective biography bears the mark of Cain. It is the question which Simon Wiesenthal has put to us all in the story he tells in *The Sunflower*: is there any reconciliation for whose who bear the burden of guilt?

(iii) Jewish theology after Auschwitz: is Israel's God 'the Lord of history'?

The shock of Auschwitz went so deep that it was decades before the few who escaped could talk about it; and a long time was needed before the first questions were put to theology in the Jewish community, and afterwards to Christian theology too. For Jews, building up the state of Israel and the struggle for its existence was in the foreground, and for Germans the assimilation of the displaced persons from the Eastern territories, and the reconstruction of the ruined cities. The fact that the discussion did not begin earlier is not a reason for reproach on the part of those born later.

The great 'after Auschwitz' discussion was probably started by Richard Rubenstein with his book *After Auschwitz. Radical Theology and Modern Judaism*, which appeared in 1966 (revised 1992).[4] I have met him personally several times, but have never understood why with that book he made common cause with the God-is-dead movement in the Protestant theology of the United States. But I took the questions which moved him very seriously indeed.

On the one hand his concern is the theological question whether the God of Israel is also the Lord of history, so that it was God who tried to exterminate his own people in the gas chambers.

And on the other he grapples with the practical question whether he should give his children a Jewish upbringing, so that they may live as Jews in this world in which Auschwitz was possible, and will be possible again, or whether he should save them from that fate.

He took over the first question from Dean Grüber in Berlin, for it was Grüber who expounded Germany's fate to him as being God's will. With the misery of the post-war era, God was punishing sinful Germany. 'Having commenced with his biblical interpretation of recent history, he could not stop until he asserted that it had been God's will to send Adolf Hitler to exterminate Europe's Jews' (261). Grüber was not antisemitic:

on the contrary. He had been imprisoned for years in a concentration camp because 'the Grüber office' protected persecuted Jews. But with Grüber's theology of history Rubenstein's crisis of faith began. Is Israel's God the Lord of history who acts 'all in all'? If we view 'the sorrows of Israel's history' as mere historical accidents, then we live in a preposterous universe, a universe of the absurd. If it was God's providence, then God is a sadist who inflicts pain, and he chose Israel only so that he could let it be exterminated in Auschwitz. Israel's election is then 'the most fearsome curse that God ever inflicted' (262). Rubenstein decided 'to live in a meaningless, purposeless Cosmos rather than believe in a God who inflicts Auschwitz on his people' (262). He saw quite correctly that Nazism was neither an old nor a new paganism, but that it was 'a kind of Judeo-Christian heresy' (267) – the black mass of the political Satan cult. As the Nazi ideology with its symbols 'the Third Reich', the 'Thousand Years' Empire', 'the Führer' and 'the Final Solution' shows, it was political messianism.

Rubinstein puts on record as his personal creed after Auschwitz: 'I am a pagan' (267). With this surprising phrase he means that he wants to leave the God of history, to whom Israel in exile had been delivered up, and to return home to 'the gods of earth'. These are 'the gods of space and place, not the gods of time'. They are 'the gods of home and hearth', no longer 'the gods of wandering'. By the return home he means the homecoming of the Jewish people from the *galuth* to 'the land' – Eretz Israel. 'Auschwitz was indeed the terminal expression of exile' (268).

What Richard Rubinstein says and wants to say is not always entirely clear, but he has lightning shafts of insight. As far as I know he does not live in Israel, but in the exile of Florida. He has not renounced his Judaism, and has not had his children brought up as secular pagans. But he has asked the two correct questions: Is Israel's God the Lord of history? and: Can one bring up children in Judaism after Auschwitz?

Emil Fackenheim (with whom I have often talked about this) has replied to Rubenstein's second question: 'Hitler failed to murder all Jews, for he lost the war. Has he succeeded in destroying the Jewish faith for those of us who have escaped? . . . And what of us . . . when we consider the possibility of a second Auschwitz three generations hence? Yet for us to cease to be Jews (and to cease to bring up Jewish children) would be to abandon our millenial post as witnesses to the God of history' (71).[5] 'In faithfulness to Judaism, we must refuse to disconnect God from the holocaust' (76). 'If all present access to the God of history is wholly lost, the God of history is Himself lost', he writes (79). But then all that remains is the cry of total despair: 'there is no judgment and no judge.' Hitler would then not only have murdered a third of the Jewish people, but the Jewish faith too – would have slain not just Israel but Israel's God. Anyone who after Auschwitz declares that God is dead, and renounces his Jewish faith, is giving Hitler the posthumous victory over the Jews and the God of Israel which he was unable to achieve during his lifetime.

At this point Emil Fackenheim speaks imploringly: 'The Jews are forbidden to hand Hitler a posthumous victory. They are commanded to survive as Jews, lest the Jewish people perish . . . Finally, they are forbidden to despair of the God of Israel, lest Judaism perish' (84). That is God's 'commanding voice' which speaks to the Jews and the other peoples through Auschwitz. In order to make the voice heard, it is our duty to hold those murdered in Auschwitz in remembrance and not to forget them. 'It is precisely because Auschwitz has made the world a desperate place that a Jew is forbidden to despair of it' (88). Citing Psalm 119.92, Fackenheim appeals to the Torah: 'If your law had not been my delight, I should have perished in my affliction.' That is the reason why hope after Auschwitz is for Jews the command to exist, to survive, to hold out, and to bear witness to God.

Emil Fackenheim's book *God's Presence in History* appeared in New York in 1970. A few years ago he left Canada and 'returned home' to Israel. But in this idea about God's presence in the voice of the categorical imperative is the God of Israel more than the God of the Torah? Does the command to be a

Jew in this world after Auschwitz already make him 'the God of history'? I do not believe that this is what Fackenheim means. But where, and who, then, is the God of history?

Eliezer Berkovits belongs to an older generation of rabbis. He sees Auschwitz in the wider context of Israel's history of suffering:[6] 'We have had innumerable Auschwitzes' (90), even if nothing equals the tragedy of the German death camps. 'Is it possible to take cognizance of the European holocaust in the light of Judaism's faith in a personal God?', he asks, and answers: it was not a divine punishment for Israel's sins. It was 'injustice absolute'. But because God permitted it, 'the ultimate responsibility for this ultimate in evil must be God's' (89). 'I am the Lord, and there is none else . . . I make peace and create evil; I am the Lord that doeth all these things,' says Isa. 45.7. Only if we admit this almighty power is it possible to believe in the God of history, the God who exercises Providence and executes justice. Only with this presupposition do the prophets and psalmists wrestle with God. Only with this premise does the righteous Job contend with God.

But then what about the evil and the undeserved suffering in history? There is suffering which derives from sin, but there is undeserved suffering too – an injustice which God tolerates and permits. For this the Talmud uses the telling phrase 'The hiding of the face' (*hester panim*). Because God 'hides his face', the sufferer cannot find God in his misery, and cries with Psalm 44.17–26: 'Awake, why sleepest Thou, O Lord? Arouse Thyself, cast not off for ever. Wherefore hidest thou thy face, and forgettest our affliction and our oppression? . . . Redeem us for Thy mercy's sake.'

God can 'hide his face' out of anger over something specific – 'because of sins committed', says Berkovits – but also out of general indifference. If God punishes someone, he has obviously not forgotten that person. The greater extremity is therefore the impression that God has forgotten us, that what happens to us is for him a matter of indifference – though the expression for this is indeed no longer God's 'hidden face' but his 'averted face'.

The God who 'hides' his face is present through his absence –
that is to say, we sense his presence through our missing of him;
his place, as it were, is unfilled.

But behind this there is also the fundamental absence of God
from human history. That does not provide an answer to the
question 'Why is there undeserved suffering?'. The question it
answers is 'Why are there human beings with the freedom to
do evil?'. Berkovits answers: 'If man is to be, God must be long-
suffering with him; he must suffer man. This is the inescapable
paradox of divine Providence. While God tolerates the sinner he
must abandon the victim; while he shows forebearance with the
wicked, he must turn a deaf ear to the anguished cries of the
violated' (106). Berkovits concludes from this: 'He who
demands justice of God must give up man. He who asks for
God's love and mercy beyond justice must accept suffering'
(106).[7] And yet that is the particular nature of God's 'omnipotence' in human history. He imposes shackles on his omnipotence and becomes powerless so that human history may be
possible. 'God is mighty in the renunciation of his might, in
order to bear with man' (109). Berkovits sums up his contribution to 'theology after Auschwitz' in the exulting word of praise:
'Who is like you our God, mighty in silence!'(113).[8]

This theological interpretation of the Auschwitz phenomenon
draws on the divine self-restriction implicit in the creation of
free human beings. But impressive though it is, the interpretation is – to put it simply – good for the evil-doers but bad for
the victims; and that is not just, and therefore not divine either.

Elie Wiesel's famous Auschwitz book *Night* appeared in 1958
in France, with a foreword by the Catholic philosopher François
Mauriac,[9] and from 1960 onwards it increasingly influenced the
'after Auschwitz' discussion in America and Germany. Here
we shall look only at the one, so often quoted, scene which no
reader can ever forget. Two men and a child are hanged in the
camp before the eyes of the assembled prisoners. The men cry
'Long live liberty!' and die quickly. The child is quiet.

' "Where is God? Where is He?" someone behind me asked.

At a sign from the head of the camp, the three chairs tipped over.

Total silence throughout the camp. On the horizon the sun was setting.

. . . The two adults were no longer alive . . . But the third rope was still moving; being so light, the child was still alive . . .

For more than half an hour he stayed there, struggling between life and death, dying in slow agony under our eyes . . .

Behind me, I heard the same man asking: "Where is God now?"

And I heard a voice within me answer him:

"Where is He? Here He is – He is hanging here on this gallows . . ."

That night the soup tasted of corpses'

(*Night*, 76f.).

Elie Wiesel describes a horrifying reality, but he describes it in highly symbolic terms. The child is described as 'an angel with sad eyes'. The three murdered victims and the setting sun remind us of the death of that other Jew on Golgotha. But the soup that tasted of corpses does not point forward to any Easter. The answer to the question 'Where is God?' comes through 'a voice within me', like the voice of God in a prophet. What does the voice disclose? God is not absent. He is present. God is not hidden. He is there, visible to everyone in the dying child.[10]

Is God himself the victim? Does God die there, once and for all, in the innocent child with the sad eyes? That is the way Elie Wiesel has often seen it: 'I shall never forget the moments which murdered my God and my soul. I shall never forget the flames which consumed my faith for ever.'

Or is God the one who suffers and dies with and in the children of Israel, and is yet the Eternal One? Elie Wiesel has frequently given this interpretation too. It goes back to the rabbinic idea of the Shekinah: 'God will dwell in the midst of the Israelites.' That is part of the old covenant promise to which

God's people owes its existence. God moved with his people out of bondage in Egypt. God dwelt in the Ark which they carried with them. God had his abode in the Holy of Holies of the Temple on Zion. When the Temple was destroyed in 587, God went into exile with those who were deported, and shared Israel's sufferings in exile as the God who is homeless in this godless world. What the children of Israel suffer, Israel's God suffers too, the God who dwells among them and wanders with them. Shekinah – that is God's indwelling in his people by virtue of his self-humiliation. Through this self-humiliation the Eternal One whom the heavens cannot contain becomes the companion on the way and the fellow-sufferer of his people on this earth.[11]

Where that child hangs on the gallows God hangs on the gallows too. Where that child suffers torment, God himself is tormented. Where that child dies, God himself suffers the child's death. 'Though I make my bed in hell, you are there,' says Psalm 139 about the omnipresent God; even in the hell of Auschwitz God was there – but not as the Lord of history: as the victim among millions of victims. Elie Wiesel took comfort from this rabbinic idea about God the fellow-sufferer – God himself shares our suffering and 'a trouble shared is a trouble halved'. But he discovered the double burden too, since with our human suffering we have to endure God's suffering as well. For that reason the answer of that 'voice within him' remains ambiguous for Elie Wiesel. 'He hangs there on the gallows' – that means that Jewish child is not alone, not forsaken by God; God suffers with him. 'He hangs there on the gallows' – but that also means that that child and we who have to look on endure the unending suffering of God on which every naive belief in God breaks down and shatters. Elie Wiesel's summing up is this: 'We cannot understand it with God. And we cannot understand without him.'[12] But the idea of God the fellow-sufferer is clearly good for the victims, and clearly bad for those who inflicted the suffering.

(iv) Christian theology after Auschwitz: is the God of Jesus Christ 'the Almighty'?

It was only late, very late, that we of the postwar generation became aware that 'after Auschwitz' the situation of theology had changed. And right down to the present day there are still only a few, a very few, in the Protestant and the Catholic tradition who in Germany seek for conversion because they perceive the long road that led to Auschwitz. Many people would rather go on as before, after this 'mishap', and believe that theology, with God, stands beyond this historical tragedy.

One of the most important admonitory voices in a theology which consciously thinks and speaks 'after Auschwitz' is my friend Johann Baptist Metz.[13] 'Auschwitz touches us all,' he says. 'The incomprehensible thing is not just the apotheosis of evil and not just the silence of God. It is the silence of human beings: the silence of all those who looked on, or looked away, and by doing so delivered up this people in its deadly peril to an unspeakable loneliness' (123). That is why, he goes on, we Christians can never go back again to the time before Auschwitz. 'But strictly speaking we can no longer get beyond Auschwitz by ourselves, but only together with the victims' (144). A future after Auschwitz 'with the victims' means first of all listening to these victims when they begin to speak.

I would add to this by saying that in Germany we unfortunately took the second step before the first. We began with Jewish-Christian dialogue at the *Kirchentage*, the lay church assemblies, and left the Holocaust conferences, where the victims themselves speak, to the Americans. Auschwitz was not the physical end of Judaism – but was it perhaps the spiritual end of Christendom, an end which we have not yet noticed?

In the 1960s Adorno caused a furore with his dictum that 'after Auschwitz there is no more poetry'.[14] All the same, there was poetry – the poetry of Paul Celan and Nelly Sachs. But we were brought face to face with the question: can we still talk about God after Auschwitz? The answer which came to Metz and to me at that time was this: in Auschwitz the Shema Israel was prayed, and the Lord's Prayer too. We can pray *after* Auschwitz because people prayed *in* Auschwitz (124). But what can we say about God after Auschwitz? For Metz, Auschwitz shattered every theology of history, because in the face of the murdered victims of Auschwitz there can be no Christian 'theodicy', no justification of God, and no 'meaning in history' either. To want to justify God in the face of 'the pit' and to seek a meaning in that appalling event would be blasphemy. So the question 'And where was God on that 23 August 1941?' is one that we cannot answer. But can we simply let the question go by default without forgetting the dead children?

Metz wants to liberate Christian theology from the triumphalist victors' history of 'the Christian West' and to throw it open again for 'the remembrance of suffering' and the bleeding wound of the question about God. The victors of history are untouched, apathetic, because they are almighty. They have no feeling for the sufferings of their victims because they are incapable of feeling guilt. Like their God, they are omnipotent and impassible. And if they are after all unable to be quite that, they suppress their own weakness and look for scapegoats for their helplessness. Metz has continually insisted on remembrance of the suffering of the victims of our world, has counselled 'theodicy sensibility', and finally expressed the not unfounded supposition that the deeper reason for the apathy of people in the Western world could be that God has forsaken them and withdrawn from them his life-giving presence. Our 'social frigidity' is grounded on the objective remoteness of God: God hides his face from us and leaves us to our self-chosen roads into the abyss.[15]

Adolf Hitler believed in a God too. He called him 'the Almighty', who was going to pin victory on our banners. Hitler idolized almighty power, and with it himself. The Almighty – that is 'the Lord of history' who is always on the side of the big batallions, and triumphs with the triumphant. 'The Almighty' – that is absolute potency without any virtue. 'The Almighty' can do whatever he wants. But what does he really want? 'The Almighty' – that is the apathetic deity who determines everything and is determined by no one, who rules everything and suffers nothing, who can always merely speak and never listen. All absolutist rulers in history have taken the stage on the model of this picture of God, from Genghis Khan to Hitler. It was therefore quite right when after Auschwitz the theological revision of the generally held picture of God began with God's omnipotence. Where was the God 'who o'er all things so wondrously reigneth' in Auschwitz?

The rethinking was begun by a theologian who was hanged in a concentration camp on 9 April 1945 because of his active resistance to Hitler: Dietrich Bonhoeffer. In 1944, in his Gestapo cell, he discovered that 'only the suffering God can help'.[16] Christ helps not by virtue of his omnipotence but by virtue of his suffering. It is true that generally accepted religious feeling points human beings in their necessity to God's power in the world. But the Bible points them to God's helplessness and suffering in that world. The human being is called to suffer with God's suffering over the godless world: 'Christians stand beside God in his suffering.' It is this which distinguishes Christians from pagans.

How did Bonhoeffer come to talk about God's helplessness and his suffering in the world, and to put this in place of religious talk about Almighty God? This other thinking has two roots. On the one hand there was the English discussion about the passibility of God, which went entirely unnoticed by theology in Germany, but which put a profound stamp on Anglican theology.[17] The other root is the rabbinic Shekinah theology, which talked about God's 'self-humiliation' and his participation in Israel's sufferings in exile, and in this way comforted the forsaken and persecuted people. 'In his "indwelling" (Shekinah) in the people he suffers with the people, goes with them into imprisonment, feels their pains with the martyrs.'[18] In 1972, in *The Crucified God*, I interpreted Elie Wiesel's Auschwitz story in the light of this Shekinah theology of the rabbis.

Dorothee Sölle followed me in this in 1973, in her book *Suffering*: 'So one can say that God, in the form of this

Shekinah, hangs on the gallows at Auschwitz and waits "for the initial movement towards redemption to come from the world . . ." Redemption does not come to people from outside or from above. God wants to use people in order to work on the completion of his creation. Precisely for this reason God must also suffer with the creation.'[19]

God is not the powerful tyrant. In the conflict between perpetrators and victims, 'the suffering God' is always on the side of the victims – indeed he himself is the victim in, with and among the victims of those who wield power. This world's history of suffering is the history of God's suffering too, the God who does not merely *permit* the evil act because he wishes men and women to be free, but also *endures* the evil act in the victims, and receives only the victims into eternal community with him. A God who cannot feel suffering cannot understand us. A God who cannot suffer cannot love either. Every loving man or woman who through love is capable of suffering is more than a God like that.[20]

At this point there are again two possible interpretations. If God is no longer the Almighty, who has everything under control, then we human beings are called to participate in God's suffering in the world and to collaborate – to be co-instrumental – in its redemption. Then 'the sanctifying of his Name' and 'the doing of his will' is in our hands, and hence 'the coming of his kingdom' too. I respect this humanist interpretation of our responsibility for God, as Dorothee Sölle maintains it. But I feel that it makes too great a demand on beings as ambiguous as us. God himself must help us. If, as Bonhoeffer said, God does not help through his omnipotence but through his powerlessness, not through his untroubled bliss in heaven but through his suffering on this earth, then God is still the determining subject of redemption, both his own redemption from his suffering with us, and the redemption of this unredeemed world too.

What does the redemption look like? It then means that God's Shekinah unites itself again with God. In his *Star of Redemption* (1921) Franz Rosenzweig saw it as follows: 'God himself cuts himself off from himself, he gives himself away to his people, he suffers their sufferings with them, he goes with them into the misery of the foreign land, he wanders with their wanderings.'[21] This divine self-differentiation is the divine suffering. It only finds an end when the separated Shekinah, together with the forsaken people and the lost creation, returns home to God. Believing men and women are co-instrumental in this homecoming of the Shekinah and its union with the waiting God. In 'the sanctification of the Name' and 'the doing of the will' of God, the Shekinah returns from the exile of the world, back to its divine origin. 'To acknowledge God's unity – the Jew calls it uniting God.'[22] It is the indwelling of God himself which gnaws at our conscience and does not let us come to terms with injustice, but makes us protest and cry out for the dumb and the silenced. This is what we might perhaps call the mystical interpretation of our responsibility towards the suffering God in 'the crucified peoples' of history.

If in place of God's almighty power in history we perceive God's sufferings in the victims of human violence, this means at the same time hoping for the coming of God in his almighty power, to judgment and to his kingdom. God is not yet so present that he is efficacious 'all in all', which is what Paul expects for God's coming kingdom (I Cor. 15.28). But God is already so present that he dwells among the victims and the sufferers, comforting them through his eternal companionship. In the history of this world, the lordship of God is still in dispute. It is the victims and the martys who testify to it, as the Book of Revelation describes. But when the glory of God itself enters into creation and his Shekinah fills everything and makes everything eternally alive, that lordship will be omnipotent and omnipresent. The challenges to faith and the theological difficulties arise because people believe that the omnipotence and omnipresent kingdom in which God 'o'er all things so wondrously reigneth' is already present here and now. That is a fallacy which by-passes the presence of God in history; for in history that presence takes the form of the cross.

(v) God's question: 'Cain, where is your brother Abel?'

Finally, we turn from our human questions about God to God's questions to us. It is good to learn theology from those who exist with the remembrance of the victims among their people. But it is necessary for us then to come back to ourselves, we who exist in the long shadows of the evil-doers and their appalling acts which were committed in the name of the German people, and have to seek for life. Solidarity with the victims of Auschwitz is important, but it does not yet help us out of the guilty liability which fetters us Germans to the evil-doers then. Is there such a thing as a conversion to life? Is there community with God, with a new confidence in living for us? How shall we be free?

Let me begin with a story which Simon Wiesenthal tells in his Auschwitz book *The Sunflower*. While he was a prisoner in a concentration camp, Wiesenthal was called to the death-bed of a man belonging to the SS, who wanted to confess to him, the Jew, that he had taken part in mass shootings of Jews in the Ukraine. He wanted to beg Wiesenthal's forgiveness so that he could die in peace. Simon Wiesenthal could listen to the murderer's confession. But he was unable to forgive him because, he says, no living person can forgive murderers in the name of the dead. He has neither the right nor the power. But Wiesenthal was so disturbed by this impossibility of forgiveness that he told his story to a number of European philosophers and theologians, and then published his own story together with the answers of these others.[23]

This story and Wiesenthal's own self-encounter in it make two things clear:

1. The crime has been committed. The pit has been dug. Nothing can make undone what was once done. Nothing can 'make good' the murders, because no one can raise the dead to life again, and that would be the only thing that could 'make good' what has happened.

2. The victims have been murdered. No one can go on living under the burden of guilt imposed by a story like this. It is still

crushing even for people born later. It destroys self-respect and blocks the will to live.[24] What can one do?

The murderers have always tried to blot out the remembrance of the mass murders which they cannot make undone. In 1944/45 Himmler had the bodies dug up out of the mass graves and burned, so as to destroy all traces of them. In Latin America, people who have been murdered become 'the disappeared', the purpose being to eliminate every trace that might be a reminder of them, and that could be used to indict the murderers. But people who blot out their past destroy themselves. And all the religious traditions we know tell us that to live with the load of a past like this, and neither to suppress it nor to be overwhelmed by it, calls for atonement, expiation. Only if injustice is atoned for do the unjust become free of their burden, so that they can live again. Without liberation from the burden of guilt no one, and no nation, can live. Yet without atonement there is no liberation from the burden. But who can make this necessary atonement? Is atonement humanly possible? Who can atone for Auschwitz or for 'the pit'? Isn't this only possible for God?

In the cults of many peoples, human crimes are atoned for through the death penalty, or vicariously through the sacrifice of animals. The sacrifices are supposed to pacify the wrath of the gods, which has been roused by the human wrong-doing. In the Torah too we find the possibility of liberation from the burden of guilt through expiatory sacrifice,[25] by way of the so-called scapegoat. The priests laid their hands on the goat, transferring to it the sins of the people. Then they drove it off into the desert, so that it might carry away the people's sins. This scapegoat is not offered to God by the people in order to pacify his wrath. *God himself* gives the scapegoat, in order to reconcile the people with himself again. God does not want to *be reconciled*. He himself *reconciles* human beings. That distinguishes Israel's practice from the sacrificial cults of the other peoples, and from human longings for self-punishment.

According to the great vision in Isaiah 53, God will send a new 'Servant'. Just as the first Servant of God, Moses, once led the children of Israel out of their enslavement in Egypt into the promised land of liberty, this new Servant of God will free the people from the enslavement of their sins, and lead them into the peace of the eternal righteousness. 'Upon him was the chastisement that makes us whole, and by his wounds we are healed' (53.5). This new Servant of God 'shall make many to be accounted righteous; for he bears their iniquities' (53.11).

The New Testament says that Jesus of Nazareth is this 'suffering Servant' and proclaims the crucified Christ to be the one 'who bears the sins of the world'. According to the biblical traditions, it is always God himself who 'bears' the burden of human guilt, and thus brings about reconciliation. God himself – the atoning God. How does this happen? God assumes our human guilt, making it his own suffering, and 'carries' the burden of it in our stead, so that we can breathe again. 'Thou who bearest the suffering of the world' – that is for the victims. 'Thou who bearest the sin of the world' – that is for the perpetrators. God's suffering is a double suffering.

In knowledge of the guilt already atoned for in the boundless suffering of God, it becomes possible, without denying ourselves and without destroying ourselves, to face up to the appalling happening of the past and to keep alive the remembrance of the victims, and of the perpetrators. Today reconciliation in the presence of the atoning God means holding this past in our remembrance. It must not be forgotten. But in the divine reconciliation the past is made inoperative, in the sense that it no longer determines the present, but lets the present be determined by that other future of righteousness and justice. Reconciliation means being absolved from the burden of guilt and being reborn to another life, so that there can be something new.[26] According to the biblical traditions, when God 'forgives' guilt he is anticipating in the midst of history that new creation in which this blood-soaked earth 'need not be remembered or taken to heart' (Isa 65.17; Rev. 21.1). Only if the forgiving of sins leads to a remembering, can it one day also lead to a 'no longer having to remember'. That has nothing to do with forgetting or suppressing.

In the face of our past, how can we shape the future with this hope?

According to the ancient penitential ritual of the church, three acts belong to conversion and a turning away from the shadows of the past into the light of liberty:

1. The *confessio oris*, private confession – today that means public confession of the collective past of our people. Truth is the first act of freedom. Only those who deal honestly with their past become free, are already free. 'The truth shall make you free,' says the Gospel of John.

2. The *attritio cordis*, the contrition of the heart. Today that means what German calls *Trauerarbeit*, the work of grief, which is needed if there is to be complete and utter freedom from the temptations and compulsions which led to those crimes. The change of heart is important, so that the rest does not remain a surface affair. And the examination of conscience that belongs here is not just a personal one; it is also a public examination of the ideologies which dominate our politics, culture and economy today.

3. The *satisfactio operum* – satisfaction through good works. Today that means acts of compensation, in so far as these are still possible, and also liberating initiatives carried out as 'signs of expiation' among the peoples who at that earlier time were the victims of our people.

Acceptance of guilt – the work of grief – first steps towards justice: these are the possibilities open to us human beings, if atonement is to be transformed into conversion. And yet there is still a sombre remnant. Or rather, there is still an insoluble mystery between God and the guilty. And this we ourselves and others too – even the victims and their children – must respect. It is the mark of Cain:

'The Lord said to Cain, "Where is Abel your brother?" He said, "I do not know; am I my brother's keeper?" And the Lord said . . . "The voice of your brother's blood is crying to me from the ground. And now you are cursed from the ground . . ." Cain said to the Lord, "My punishment is greater than I can bear . . ." And the Lord put a mark on Cain, lest any who came upon him should kill him' (Gen. 4.9–13, 15).

The mark of Cain is at once an admonitory, reminding sign and a protective one. No one may kill the person who bears that mark. Nor may that person take his own life. This sign is the mark of our collective German biography.[27]

2

Protestantism: 'The Religion of Freedom'

'It is not worth while pursuing the fate of German Protestantism any longer. Four hundred years of a glorious history are drawing to a close. Whatever still exists in Europe in the way of a *Volkskirche* – a church for the whole people – will be Catholic.' So wrote the well-known journalist Johannes Gross in May 1987 in the *Frankfurter Allgemeine Zeitung*, after he had read some studies published by the Evangelical Church in Germany.*

Is this melancholy prediction true, or is it Catholic wishful thinking? At all events it challenges Protestants to think about what they really are. The person who thinks about what he is also asks where he has come from, and addresses that past. He asks where he is going, and tries to explore his future. There is no other way of arriving at self-awareness.

Why do I love Protestantism? Why am I glad to be a Protestant? I believe that the reason is freedom – freedom before God in faith, freedom of religion in face of the state, and freedom of conscience in face of the church. But this freedom has its perils and burdens too. Of course everyone wants to be free, but many people shrink back from the dangers of freedom. Of course everyone wants to be free, but many people find the responsibility which is inextricably bound up with freedom too heavy a burden. So the longing for freedom is itself ambivalent,

---

* The Evangelische Kirche Deutschland is a federation of Lutheran, Reformed and United churches. The word 'evangelical' is therefore employed here as the equivalent of Protestant, and implies no more distinct theological direction than that.

for often enough it is linked with a flight from freedom. Do people in our society really crave for freedom of conscience and freedom of religion? Aren't a good many people afraid of the perils of freedom? Aren't they so sick of the torment of having to make their own choices that they are glad enough to let other people – or an authority – decide things for them? Do we really want 'freedom now'? Or would we prefer to shift our responsibility on to other shoulders, because it has become too heavy for us? Do we really want to 'come of age', as Dietrich Bonhoeffer put it, or would we perhaps after all if need be gladly become infantile and immature again, and find shelter under the cloak of 'Mother Church' or our 'Big Brother' the state? Progression and regression are often enough not far removed from one another. So it could well be that the fate of Protestantism in our future society and the fate of freedom in that society are one and the same. Where there is freedom there is Protestantism. If Protestantism relinquishes freedom, Protestantism will disappear.

Let us look at the essence of the evangelical faith and Protestant ideas of freedom in the context of their three formative epochs:

1. The Reformation of the sixteenth century,
2. The Protestantism of the eighteenth century,
3. The ecumenism of the twentieth century.

If we wished to characterize the differences, we might say that in the Reformation of the sixteenth century the point at issue was 'freedom of belief' and the fundamentals of freedom in the church; in the Enlightenment period – the eighteenth and nineteenth centuries – the argument centred on 'freedom of religion' and its personal dimension; while today, in the twentieth century, it is a question of ecumenical freedom in community, and the social dimension of freedom.

(i) 'Justified through faith alone'

It is easy to discover the guiding idea behind the Reformation. As in all great movements, it is a simple one. It is recognition of the justifying gospel. 'We become righteous before God by grace, for Christ's sake, through faith alone,' as Article 4 of the Augsburg Confession of 1530 says. The righteous God does not judge according to merits – good works and bad; he receives unjust men and women out of pure love, and for Christ's sake makes them just, righteous and good. That was Luther's 'reforming perception': God is righteous because he makes us righteous. His righteousness is not a righteousness given according to our deserts (*iustitia distributiva*); it is a creative righteousness (*iustitia iustificans*). It is revealed in Christ 'who was put to death for our trespasses and raised for our justification' (Rom. 4.25). For that reason, justifying faith alone is the true knowledge of Christ, and the true knowledge of Christ leads to justifying faith. The clarity of its doctrine of justification decides whether the church is the church of God's gospel or a Christian religious institution. And it is this that decides whether the real human being believes in the true God, or runs after his or her own idols.

The subject of Christian theology is therefore, according to Luther, 'the justifying God and the sinful human being'. The faith of the Reformers and those who come after them is again, as it was in earliest Christian times – the New Testament era – faith in Christ. Christ alone – the Christ crucified for us – is the foundation and criterion of true faith, the true church and true theology. He himself is 'the gospel', 'the evangel' from which the 'evangelical' churches take their name.

The consequences were far-reaching. Here I may name the most important of them. These are the four principles of Protestant theology:

(*a*) *Sola fide* (by faith alone). If someone assents to the God who loves sinners and has made them just through grace, that person believes. It is not we who decide for God. We perceive that God has decided for us, and joyfully say Yes and Amen. Believing means accepting for ourselves God's judgment, trusting in his promise, affirming his justifying grace. If my righteousness (identity, self-respect, self-awareness) were to depend not just on God's grace but also on what I do, there would be no assurance of salvation, because then I would never know whether I had done enough. Only if a person's righteousness depends simply and solely on God's grace is there the unequivocal assurance of salvation which the Apostle Paul talks about: 'I am sure that neither death, nor life . . . will be able to separate us from the love of God which is in Christ Jesus our Lord' (Rom. 8.38f.). At the time of the Reformation, this personal asssurance of salvation in life and death was the mark of Protestant Christians.

(*b*) *Sola gratia* (by grace alone). People who have become righteous solely through grace can live without fear. They have no further need to worry about their souls' salvation. All their concern is focussed on their neighbour. Faith alone saves, but faith is never alone; it is active in love as long as the believing person lives. The person who is righteous through grace alone has become God's child. Through good works and merits no one ever becomes a child of God; he or she always remains a servant. We become a child through birth. We become God's child through rebirth from God's Spirit. This aristocracy conferred by the divine birth is the seal of God's children. The renown brought by achievement, and judgment based on good or evil works, are the signs of servants. In Protestantism, the principle *sola gratia* never meant making a principle of idleness; it was always the wellspring of unresting labour, especially among Reformed Christians. The person who is freed from the compulsion to perform good works brims over with love, and does every good work spontaneously and unprompted, out of pure thankfulness, as the Heidelberg Catechism says. I might put it as follows: the person whom God has justified out of grace hungers for righteousness and justice in the world, and protests against injustice. The person to whom God gives peace of soul thirsts for peace on earth, and protests against the world's peacelessness.

(*c*) *Solus Christus* (through Christ alone). The Christian church is true to itself and can then speak with assurance if Christ and Christ alone is its Lord. The Christian church arrives at its proper freedom when it listens only to the gospel of Christ.

That is why all Protestant creeds require the edicts, rituals and symbols of the church's tradition and popular belief to be subjected to the standard of Christ.

When under the Hitler dictatorship the Evangelical church in Germany was also supposed to be brought into line, the Confessing Church declared in Barmen in 1934: 'Jesus Christ . . . is the one Word of God which we have to hear . . . We reject the false doctrine that the Church can and must acknowledge as a source of her proclamation, beside and in addition to this one Word of God, other events, powers, forms and truths as the revelation of God . . . We reject the false doctrine that there are spheres of our life in which we belong not to Jesus Christ but to other masters.' The Reformation applied this christocentricity critically to the church of its own time. The Confessing Church applied it critically to the totalitatian claim of a dictatorship and to its political religion. This exclusive faith in Christ marks the centre of Protestant faith. But because Christ is believed and confessed as Lord of the whole world, this faith is the centre for a horizon which reaches up to the clouds and encompasses the whole creation. Properly understood, christocentricity does not mean succumbing to tunnel vision; it leads to true openness for the world.

(*d*) *Sola scriptura* (through Scripture alone). This was contrary to the Catholic synthesis of scripture and tradition, tradition and the church's present consensus of faith. Scripture itself is the sufficient and, for everyone who can read, the comprehensible testimony of the gospel of Jesus Christ, which justifies sinners. But is scripture literally infallible? Is scripture 'the Protestant pocket paper pope'? Behind that question there is a genuine theological problem: the problem of the teaching ministry in the church. The Catholic view says that the doctrinal authority of the apostles has passed via Peter to the Bishop of Rome, or to the bishops as a whole. For that reason the bishops now speak with apostolic authority in the name of Christ. The Protestant view says: the authority of the apostles was passed on to no one. The apostles were eye-witnesses of the risen Christ, and for their part appointed no new apostles to be their successors. Instead their apostolic authority was passed on to their apostolic writings. They speak today in the church and through the church by way of the writings of the New Testament. The first view talks about a *successio apostolica*, an apostolic succession; the second about a *successio evangelica*, an evangelical succession. What use is the formal apostolic succession from one bishop to another if these bishops do not belong to the true succession of the proclamation of the gospel according to Scripture?

These four evangelical principles lead to a new understanding of the church and Christian existence in the world.

(*a*) Because God also calls every Christian whom he justifies through the gospel, in the community of Christ what obtains is the general *priesthood of all believers*. 'That man who has crawled out of baptism is consecrated priest and pope,' wrote Martin Luther in 1521. I would add 'that man and that woman'. With this principle Luther wanted to pull down the wall dividing clergy from laity in the church. All Christians who are called belong to the one people of God, which as a whole represents 'an elect race and a royal priesthood'. By tracing priestly ordination (*sacramentum ordinis*) back to baptism, Luther gave a higher status to baptism as the sacrament of vocation: every Christian, man or woman, is a witness of faith, called to preach and to the celebration of the Lord's Supper. Where this perception was taken seriously, the priestly hierarchy, or the pastors' church, was replaced by the congregational church, the actual, specific assembly of believers.

(*b*) The person whom God justifies he also calls. That is not just true in the community of Christ. It applies to everyday life too. Through a stroke of genius Luther carried the term 'calling' (*vocatio*) out of the religious sphere into the secular world, and called all honest work performed by a man or woman their divine 'calling'. By so doing he enlisted the principles attendant on a divine vocation – obedience, faithfulness, love, dependability and concerted work for the kingdom of God – for work in the world. Every job of work performed honestly is an act of worship. All work in human society is work for the kingdom of

God and acquires its higher significance because of this alignment. This was the idea behind the Protestant work ethic. In Lutheranism it was the world of the estates which was seen as the divine order. In Calvinism it was the world of the small and greater independent entrepreneurs, who worked for and invested for God's kingdom.

But at both points the weakness of the Reformation also emerged. In the sixteenth century it remained 'an incomplete Reformation':

First, *in the form given to the church.* Congregational churches grew up only in refugee communities, and in the 'congregations beneath the cross' on the Lower Rhine. Where the congregational church proved impossible of realization, the church's papally guaranteed freedom from state control gave way to the church of the Protestant princes. The ruler of a particular state was enlisted as 'emergency bishop'. He organized the Protestant church as the church of his own territory, on the principle *cuius regio, eius religio.* The Protestant churches lost their universality and became particularist, provincial and national churches. They fell into a new Babylonian captivity out of which they are being led only through the ecumenical movement in our own century.

Second, *in the form given to Christian existence.* If the society in which Christians live is 'a Christian world', then the sacred calling of Christians could be identified with their work in society or politics. But in a post-Christian world this is no longer possible. The spiritual calling of every Christian is something special, and it must show itself in the 'special righteousness' of Christians in this secular world. In the contradictions of secular society, this special righteousness shows itself when Christians enter into the discipleship of Christ, following the precepts of the Sermon on the Mount. They then demonstrate to this violent and unjust society the divine alternative, which leads to peace and to life.

What is freedom? Let me sum up theologically what the Reformation has to say about the fundamentals of freedom. The message of the Reformation was experienced by many people as an incomparably liberating message; and this is still so today. It was, and is, the experience of freedom in faith. According to Luther's treatise *On the Freedom of a Christian* (1521), freedom is thrown open to all who believe through the justifying and liberating Word of God. Faith makes them 'free masters of all things'. They are subject to no one. Love makes them 'the ministering servants of all things'. They are subject to everyone. What does the Word of Christ free those who believe *from*? According to the theology of the Reformers, it frees them from the compulsion to evil, from the law of self-justification, and from the fear of death, because sin, law and death are the great godless powers of this world. *For what* does the Word of Christ free those who believe? It frees them for unhindered, direct and eternal fellowship with God: in faith they all have unimpeded, immediate access to the Father. In faith they all become God's children. In faith they become God's friends, whose prayers God hears. In faith we are in God and have God in us.

Freedom in faith is a relational and theological concept of freedom: in his relation to men and women the justifying God becomes the liberating God. In their relation to God those who are justified become free. In God's covenant with human beings freedom is defined from God's side as righteousness, and from the human side as faith.

(ii) 'The religion of freedom': Protestantism

In the seventeenth and eighteenth centuries the Protestant faith entered into an especially close association with the new cult of Enlightenment and tolerance. For many people, the bourgeois world of the nineteenth century was 'the Protestant world': Great Britain, Holland, Prussia and the United States of America. The 'idea' of Protestantism becomes manifest in this modern form of the Protestant faith.

But what is 'Enlightenment'? Let me start from two definitions given by Immanuel Kant, the philosopher of Protestantism:

1. 'Enlightenment is the human being's emergence from his self-incurred tutelage.'

2. 'Nothing is required for this Enlightenment except the freedom to make public use of one's reason in all respects.'

Historically, we distinguish between the eras of the English and American Enlightenment, the French Enlightenment, and the German Enlightenment. The delay between them extended over about 50 to 100 years, counting from the seventeenth century. The English and American Enlightenment was Protestant in character, non-conformist, free-church and highly religious, as we can still see today in the United States every Sunday. The French Enlightenment, on the other hand, following the cruel Huguenot persecution, acquired in this Catholicized country an anti-clerical and laicized stamp; its humanism was a-religious through and through, and atheistic. The German Enlightenment was shaped by Protestantism, but it was directed against the state churches. It maintained the individual's right to personal religion, and clung to the utopian dream of the coming 'kingdom of the Spirit', in which no one will have to teach the other, because in the Spirit all will see God as he is.

The Christianity of the Enlightenment can be found in the new Protestant denominations of the time: among the Quakers the religious experience of 'the inner light' of the Spirit; among the Baptists the personal decision of faith; and among the Methodists the heart-warming experience of faith and personal sanctification through self-control and self-mastery.

'Soul liberty' (Roger Williams's phrase) was the new slogan. Modern Protestantism is dominated by the discovery of the individual and the right to subjectivity.

In Germany, after the Thirty Years' War of religion ended in 1648 with the Peace of Westphalia, denominational affiliation was made a matter for the state: *cuius regio – eius religio*. The only religious liberty permitted was the *ius emigrandi*, the right to emigrate. Consequently in Germany 'Enlightened' Christianity could develop in bourgeois Protestantism only as 'a private affair'. 'Religion is a private matter.' 'Let everyone be saved in his own fashion,' said the Enlightened Prussian king Frederick the Great.

In England and the United States Protestantism created the system of voluntary religion. Here religious liberty means that everyone has the right to worship and pray to God in the church of his or her choice. In Germany this proved impossible: there was an enduring cleft between religious affiliation and voluntary religion, between state religion and private faith, between institutionality and subjectivity. As always in Germany, what was lacking was the freedom to make 'public use' of one's personal faith 'in all respects'. Even today, over 80% of the German people 'belong' to one or other of the churches, but only 10–15% attend the church to which they 'belong'. Religious liberty in Germany always took the sole form of the right of 'inner emigration' from the institution of the church.

The principles of the Enlightment and of Protestantism are the principles of individual liberty:

1. *Religious liberty over against the state*. As long as the state lays down the religion or ideology which has to be followed, individual men and women have still failed to come of age. They can make use neither of their reason nor of their faith without the direction of another – the state or the church. The religious freedom of every individual is therefore the presupposition both of the Protestant faith and of reason. Religious freedom liberates religion from the state and the state from religion. It is the precondition for the secular, reasonable and, in religious matters, tolerant state. After religious liberty had been fought for and won in seventeenth-century England, it was introduced into France in 1789 and then hesitantly, with the relevant delay, in Germany; while in Vatican II it was finally recognized by the Catholic Church too, after it had still been condemned fifty years earlier.

2. *Liberty of conscience over against the church*. As long as the churches bind the consciences of individuals in ethical questions, these individuals are still dependent, and have not come of age. The Enlightenment therefore freed the conscience first of all. In their consciences, all individuals stand directly before God and must make their own personal decisions, because each individual is personally responsible before God.

Kant called conscience 'the God in us', with the purpose of thereby securing its inviolability. For many people Protestantism became what Karl Holl called it: 'the religion of conscience'. The church can make the conscience of the individual more sensitive, but it must not relieve anyone of his or her own decision in matters of conscience, either through encyclicals or through memoranda; for it is not the church which can or must be responsible before God for what the individual person does or fails to do. So the church must not encourage anyone to act against their conscience. Incidentally this has been the general Christian view from earliest times.

3. *Liberty of belief over against the authority of the Bible, tradition and the church.* I have a right to my own convictions and a right to my own doubts, as Lessing, the Protestant representative of the German Enlightenment, said: 'Miracles which I see with my own eyes and am able to test for myself are one thing; miracles of which I merely know historically that others claim to have seen and tested them are another' (*Werke* III, 9). Fortuitous truths of history and those passed down in good faith are one thing; truths of reason immediately comprehensible to me myself are another. 'It is one thing to believe truth out of some anterior judgment, another to believe it for its own sake' (III.127). 'It is one thing to do good out of fear of punishment, another to do good simply because it is the good.'

4. The freedom of conscience and freedom of belief of individual persons are the reason why people have *the right to congregation 'from below'*, over against the church, understood as a divine institution 'from above'. The church is nothing other than 'the gathered congregation' in a particular place at a particular time. 'Congregation' was the original promise of the Reformation, even though this was enduringly prevented in Germany through the rule over the church of the Protestant princes in the various German states. It is one of the ironies of history that – if we leave on one side the churches of the Independent tradition – it should be the Catholic base communities in Latin America which today are fulfilling this promise.

The determining subject of liberation through Enlightenment and Protestant belief is the human subject in the form of the civic subject.

The rights to freedom of religion, belief, conscience and congregational autonomy were fought for and won in the Enlightenment period at the same time as human and civil rights. Through these the dignity of the human person is publicly acknowledged. Even today, freedom of religion cannot be realized without, or apart from, the rights to personal freedom and individual human rights. The middle classes won these rights to freedom in the English, American and French revolutions, in opposition to feudalism and clericalism. The rights to freedom of religion, belief and conscience became the foundation of liberal democracy.

What is freedom? Let me sum up what Protestantism has to say about the personal dimension of freedom.

Out of the *freedom for God in faith* of the Reformers, modern Protestantism made *freedom of faith* – that is, liberty for the personal decision of faith. The *relational* concept of human freedom in its reference to the justifying God was complemented by the *subjective* concept of freedom of choice. The subjectivity of every individual human person came into its own and now characterized the human side of fellowship with God. The pressure for a personal decision of faith, personal experience of conversion, and the heart-warming, inward testimony of the Holy Spirit in the modern Protestant denominations could lead to a new righteousness of works, but it does not have to do so, as we can see from John Wesley, who went back to Luther himself. But we may say that in modern Protestantism the christocentricity of the Reformers has experienced a pneumatological complementation and concentration. Freedom through the Word of Christ is also freedom in the Spirit of God. No state and no church can deprive human beings of the personal experiences of the divine Spirit.

'Subjectivity is truth,' said the Protestant philosopher Kierkegaard. Protestant subjectivism has led religiously and culturally to all possible kinds of individualism, pluralism and egoism. But it has also brought into modern culture the dignity of every human person, and individual human rights, so that these can never again be forgotten. Without freedom of belief and personal responsibility, a humane society is not possible. All 'post-modern' attempts to surmount human subjectivity end up in nothing other than the abolition of the human being, whether it be through the bureaucratic conspiracy, or through the 'gentle conspiracy' of esotericism.

(iii) 'The religion of community': the ecumenical era

About eighty years ago, the Protestant churches entered upon the path leading from the denominational to the ecumenical age. On this path they are increasingly discovering the meaning of catholicity in the church of Christ, and are seeking in the ecumenical movement of the separated churches 'the religion of the fellowship of the Holy Spirit'. Today, for many Protestant Christians, ecumenical solidarity with their oppressed brothers and sisters in other countries and other denominations is greater than national loyalty or their own denominational identity. Ecumenism is the discovery of the other, and reciprocal acceptance of others in their otherness.

(a) Living ecumenically

The path to ecumenical understanding between the divided churches began with work on comparative ecclesiology. The churches learnt to know each other in the hope that – as the World Missionary Conference held at Edinburgh in 1910 said – a better understanding of the divergent views about faith and ecclesiology would lead to a deepening wish for reunion and to corresponding official resolutions on the part of the different denominations.

The result of this work, which is still by no means finished, is a kind of negative consensus, for it was discovered that the traditional distinguishing doctrines do not necessarily have to divide the churches. They can also be used for mutual complementation and enrichment. The different theological and ecclesiastical traditions therefore proved to offer no further reason for excommunicating separation, even though it has still as yet proved impossible to formulate the common ground that binds. It was at the General Assembly of the World Council of Churches held at Lund in 1952 that a move was made for the first time from *comparative* ecclesiology to *christological* ecclesiology. It was recognized at that time that we can make no real progress in the direction of unity simply by comparing our different ideas about the nature of the church and the traditions in which these ideas are embedded. It became plain that we come closer to each other by coming closer to Christ. We must therefore pierce through our divisions and get beyond them, so as to arrive at a deeper and richer understanding of the mystery of the unity given us by God in Christ with his church. This turn from a merely external comparative ecclesiology to the christo-logical ecclesiology which binds us together inwardly has ever since then determined the path of ecumenism: *the closer we come to Christ, the closer we come to one another.*

Ecumenism is realized only (but then also world-wide) where we find ourselves beneath the cross of Christ, and mutually dis-cover ourselves beneath his cross as brothers and sisters, as the hungry in shared poverty (Rom. 3.23), as people imprisoned in shared sin. Beneath his cross we all stand there with empty hands. We have nothing to offer God except the burden of guilt and the emptiness of our hearts. Beneath the cross, people are not accounted Protestants, Catholics and Orthodox. There the godless are justified, enemies reconciled, the imprisoned freed, the poor made rich and the grieving filled with hope. That is why beneath the cross we also discover ourselves as children living from the same freedom in Christ, and as friends in the same fellowship of the Spirit.

'*The closer we come to the cross of Christ, the closer we come to one another.*' How could we keep alive our divisions and enmities in the face of his bitter suffering and death? How, in the face of 'the open heart' of Christ, could we remain closed to one another, and be afraid for the church? Clasped by the arms of God stretched out in his suffering on the cross, how can we clench our fists, or cling fast with tenacious hands to what we possess in our different denominations?

(b) Thinking ecumenically

When Christians and whole churches emigrate from the narrow bounds of their particularist traditions and denominations, and perceive the ecumenical horizon that spans them all, a rethinking begins. One can observe this learning process in oneself. It is bound up with the pains and joys of conversion. We begin to surmount particularist thinking. Particularist thinking is an isolating, segmental and self-complacent thinking, a thinking which, because it knows only itself and desires only to endorse itself, comes forward with an absolute claim. We cannot endure our own particularity, limitation and relativity. So individuals and whole groups insist obstinately on what they themselves possess. They are obsessed by anxiety, and disseminate anxiety. Particularist thinking is at heart schismatic thinking. In the age of the church's divisions and of denominational absolutism, we have got so used to schismatic thinking that some people no longer notice it. We fence ourselves off, we anxiously define our own profiles over against others, we assert ourselves and our own heritage. Until quite recently this was still called 'controversial theology'. It was theology at the service of the church's divisions and denominational self-assertion. Thinking ecumenically means overcoming schismatic thinking. But this is only possible if particularist thinking is surmounted by a universal thinking. How?

We can view the testimonies of Christian faith and life with an eye to their denominational particularity. Then there are Orthodox, Catholic and Protestant testimonies, and others too; and understanding ends with the recognition: that is Orthodox, that is Catholic, that is Anglican, and that is Lutheran.

But we can also view these testimonies with an eye to their Christian universality. Then we understand them as expressions of the one, whole church. Then we examine them in this universal context, and respond in this community. That does not make theological thinking any easier. In fact it becomes harder, because then we can no longer foist the problems and controversies on the differences between the denominations. Thinking ecumenically means thinking about the whole – the whole of the one church.

If schismatic thinking means holding our own part to be the whole and making it absolute, then ecumenical thinking disperses this syndrome of anxiety and arrogance, and makes it possible to exist in conscious imperfection, in conscious limitation, open for others and dependent on others. Only truth's claim on us is absolute, not our claim to truth. Only the divine kingdom is all-embracing – not our own sectors. I believe that it is one of the strengths of ecumenical thinking to awaken longing for the other through recognition of one's own incompleteness. So thinking ecumenically also means: remember that you are only a part – one part of the one church!

To belong to the evangelical church in the ecumenical age does not mean fencing oneself off; it means carrying the gospel into ecumenism, and trusting the gospel to make its own impact.

What is freedom? Let me sum up what we have learnt in the ecumenical era about the *social* dimension of freedom.

In the ecumenical era, Protestants are discovering the social side of justification, and the communicative concept of freedom. They are discovering what the catholicity of Christianity means. They are comprehending what solidarity with the suffering and the oppressed means. They are learning to understand that true freedom cannot be domination, but means community, sociality. Nor is freedom of choice, according to which I can do and leave undone what I like, as yet human freedom. These formal concepts of freedom derive from the language of domination. Even modern individualism has not changed that, if it simply maintains that everyone is his own master and belongs to himself.

The specifically human concept of freedom is different; it stems from the language of sociality. Here freedom means the same as friendship. I feel completely free where I can be completely myself. I can only be completely myself where people know me and recognize me and accept me as I am. For my part, I shall be free when I open my life for other people and recognize them in their otherness, and like to be with them. Human freedom is realized through mutual recognition and acceptance – that is to say, in personal fellowship. Then the other person is no longer a restriction of my freedom but complements my own limited life. That is the social and communicative side of human freedom. We call it solidarity or friendship or love. It is only through this that the freedom *in* faith of the Reformers, and Protestant freedom *of* faith, is realized. 'Accept one another as Christ has accepted you, to the glory of God' (Rom. 15.7). Today we look for this reality of freedom, and experience it, in narrower and wider contexts: in the ecumenical fellowship of different Christians, in the fellowship of solidarity with the oppressed, and in community with the threatened creatures of this earth.

Summing-up

1. Evangelical faith is faith in the justifying gospel ('evangel') of Christ. This faith gives personal assurance of salvation. In this faith men and women are called to all ministries for the community of Christ, and to all ministries for the world, each according to his or her abilities, each according to his or her needs.

2. The idea of Protestantism is the modern, democratic form of the evangelical faith which by way of human rights extends to all humanity. The principle and the rights of subjectivity are in the foreground: one's own personal decision of faith, one's own conviction, one's own individual decision of conscience, reponsibility for one's own life.

3. The ecumenical form of the evangelical faith is to be found in the discovery of the supra-national and supra-denominational catholicity of Christ's church. This perception was come by in times of persecution – that is to say, beneath the cross. It leads us to press for eucharistic fellowship at the Lord's

Table. Living ecumenically means hungering and thirsting for the eucharistic fellowship of all Christians. Thinking and acting ecumenically means hungering and thirsting for God's righteousness and justice for the whole world. Today these two things belong together – ecumenism within the church and Christian ecumenism outwards, towards the world. For the church to enter the global age of humanity's history, an age which began at latest with Hiroshima in 1945, it must arrive at full ecumenical community.

3

Liberalism and Fundamentalism in the Modern Era

What fundamentalism is concerned about is 'the modern world'.[1] It is an opposition phenomenon, not an independent, innovative movement. It was only born together with its hostile brother, modernism or liberalism. Fundamentalism is a modern reaction to the modern world, but it has no hesitation about employing against that world every means of communication which the modern world offers, as a way of surmounting its perils. In Christian fundamentalism, the opponent is 'the modern world' itself, but even more than that, all the Christians who in the form of Christian modernism have fallen victim to that world. Islamic fundamentalism sees the Western world as the great Satan, and therefore fights first of all against all the Muslims who have accepted the Western world's principles and spread its poison in Muslim countries. This means that we cannot understand the phenomena of modern fundamentalism just by themselves. We have to see them as a reaction against the essence and values of the modern era and the world of Western civilization.

In the first part of this chapter I shall therefore try to work out principles and values which hold good in the modern Western world, and to understand them. In the second part I shall describe the reactions of Christian liberalism. It is only then, in a third step, that we can understand the reactions of Christian fundamentalists to Christian modernism, and hence to the modern world of the West. In the fourth part of the chapter, we shall then seek for movements and ways open to Christianity in the modern world which will take it beyond both liberalism and fundamentalism.

I am convinced that both Christian modernism and Christian fundamentalism are dead ends, and lead to the self-surrender of Christian existence. The modernist adaptation to what simply happens to be 'in' in the modern world is just as pointless as fundamentalism's 'great refusal'.

Modernist theology merely produces a religious mirror image of the modern world, and simply repeats what modern women and men know in any case. Of course this is fine for the church, but it is tedious for contemporaries, for the original is always more interesting than its theological copy, whether we are talking about Marx and Marxism, Popper and positivism, or Lyotard and postmodernism. For the theological modernists, this continual race to catch up is a risky game. The person who always rides on the crest of the last wave will soon find himself stranded. It has been said that a theology married to 'the spirit of the age' will be widowed in the next generation.

It is the justifiable fear of loss of Christian identity and Christian values which produces the fundamentalist option. This is termed 'what is distinctively Christian'. Threatened by the confusing complexity and pluralism of the modern world, the withdrawal into the unpolitical ghetto seems an obvious way out, for there one can live one's own faith undisputed, and 'all's right with the (Christian) world'. Theology becomes first a churchy theology, and after that fundamentalist theology, pursued within one's own churchy circles. This retreat into the 'safe stronghold' of true faith, inerrant Scripture and the infallible magisterium does certainly make this faith unassailable. But the stronghold can be starved out, like all besieged strongholds. Today fundamentalist faith is being starved out by lack of public interest. A faith which makes itself impregnable to attack is no longer in a position to attack on its own account. Its safe stronghold becomes its prison.

The task of Christian theology today is not exhausted by the renovation of ancient historical buildings. It has to create a new architecture for this endangered modern world, in recollection of God's kingdom and in anticipation of the new creation of all things. In saying this I have indicated the direction in which I see the responsibilities of Christian churches and theologies in their confrontation with the modern world. The church isn't there for its own sake. It is there for the sake of the kingdom of God. However small it may be, it must publicly maintain the universal concerns of God's coming kingdom. Christian theology is always kingdom-of-God theology first of all, before it becomes church theology or the theology of modernity or anti-modernity.

(i) Principles and values of the modern world

I shall confine myself to the principles and values which give rise to controversy in the dispute between modernism and fundamentalism, and shall look first at the separation between church and state, religion and politics, and at the development of individual religious liberty in the framework of universal human rights. Second, I shall consider scientific-technological civilization and the global market economy.

1. *The separation between church and state* is one of the essential characteristics of the modern world. Every comparison with other civilizations and cultures shows that this separation is something that is quite unusual, indeed unique, in human history. Elsewhere, religion – or, as its substitute, ideology – was, and is, always and everywhere understood as a legitimation of rule and as its inner unity: one religion – one sovereignty – one realm. Outside the modern world, there were and are no religionless politics. In Germany, the Reformation of Christianity as a whole was ended through the principle: *cuius regio – eius religio*. With this principle, denominational affiliation was declared to be a matter for the state, and to be the primary civic duty. The state unified under a single faith and denomination dominated Europe, whether that state was Protestant, Catholic or Orthodox.

Individual freedom of religion was first fought for and won in the Netherlands, then in England during the period of the Civil War, and from 1789 on the continent, as a result of the French Revolution. It became the supreme expression of a person's subjective freedom. Religion is no longer a matter over which the state can dispose; it is the individual citizen's private affair, and subject to free decisions of faith. Individual religious liberty frees the state from the church and the church from the state. It is the presupposition for the modern, reasonable, tolerant, constitutional country which prescribes no religion for its people but guarantees their religious liberty. The right to individual religious liberty was an outcome of the Protestant world and what Hegel called its 'religion of freedom'. It was only in the Second Vatican Council that the Roman Catholic Church acknowledged religious liberty for the first time, after having rejected it fifty years previously. The secularization of the modern state which Christian and Islamic fundamentalists lament is a religious achievement springing from the religious liberty of modern men and women; it is not an irreligious evil.

The first principles and supreme values of the modern world are to be found in *the self-determination of the determining human subject*. The great discovery of modern times is human subjectivity. All human rights are founded on human dignity, which is one, indivisible, inalienable, and hence universal. This dignity lies in a person's subjectivity. A person must never be turned into an object and treated as such. But if human dignity lies in individual self-determination, then the great collective powers of disposal lose their force – the family, the church, tradition and, not least, the biology of one's own body too. Every human being is the subject of understanding and will, and can freely confront the forces of his or her origin and nature. The authorities of the Bible and the church become subject to people's historical-critical awareness, and lose their unquestioned claim. They become what Lessing called fortuitous 'truths of history', communicated in good faith, and are not possessed of any direct, absolute truths of reason. The place of tradition is therefore taken by our own experience. The extent to which family ties and family care are also diminishing in the face of the increasingly spreading self-determination of individuals (now called 'singles') is something we have discovered only in the twentieth century, in modern cities. Even the nature of our own bodies is no longer something we have to put up with, as our fate. It becomes the object of medical and genetic intervention.

2. Whereas modern subjectivity is always termed a child of the Enlightenment, *the Western world* has at least two earlier significant sources: (*a*) the *conquista* – that is to say, the discovery and conquest of America from 1492 onwards; and (*b*) the seizure of power over nature by means of science and technology.

(*a*) In 1492 the European states were marginal, peripheral and insignificant compared with the giant Ottoman and Chinese empires and the Indian empire of the Moguls. It was the conquest and exploitation of America which initiated Europe's advancement to world power and the victorious march of the Western world. The Europeans 'discovered' the world and appropriated their discoveries for themselves. The enslavement of Africans and the exploitation of American resources created the economic presuppositions for the build-up of what is today the industrial West or, as it is sometimes called, 'the First World'.[2]

(*b*) The seizure of power over nature through the instruments of science and technology is the other foundation stone on which the new, modern world order rests. In the century between Copernicus and Isaac Newton, the new sciences stripped nature of her magic and took from her the divine mystery which up to than had been called 'the world soul'. 'Knowledge is power,' said Francis Bacon, and the natural sciences put 'Mother Nature' and her children in the power of human beings, who according to Descartes become her 'masters and possessors'. Scientific 'discoveries' also lead to appropriation. And with this human reason changes: instead of being an organ of perception and a tool of wisdom, it becomes the instrument of rule, and the knowledge of control. Through modern scientific and technological civilization, people became the determining subjects of the world they had appropriated, and of their own history.

(c) It was out of these two seizures of power that the messianic dream of the modern world developed: the dream of 'the New World' and 'modern times'. At the beginning, this dream of modernity was the Christian dream of the Thousand Years' Empire, in which Christ will reign with those who are his, and will judge the nations. Then it became the dream of a golden age for the whole of humanity. After that came the utopia of 'the realm of freedom' which was to follow 'the realm of necessity'. Finally, the nineteenth century saw the development of ideas about world history which envisaged 'the end of history' in a post-historical, non-historical paradise. For Francis Fukuyama, the adviser to the United States State Department, the end of human history, to which there is no alternative, has already dawned today in 'liberal democracy' and 'the global marketing of everything'.[3]

(ii) Christian modernism

Ever since the beginning of modern times, theology and the church have made great efforts to keep pace with the progress of the modern world, and to be present wherever women and men live today.[4] Because the modern world developed in the Protestant countries of Western Europe first of all, Protestant theology and the Protestant churches accepted the new principles and values very early on, and produced what is called liberal theology, or 'culture Protestantism', and – in a Catholic context – 'modernism'.

1. As early as the eighteenth century, Protestant theology adopted a historical-critical awareness towards tradition, and developed the historical criticism of the Bible. True faith does not depend on the biblical picture of the world and is not belief in the letter of Scripture; it takes into account the historical circumstances in which the biblical writings developed. Historical criticism does not destroy the foundations of true faith, but brings to light that faith's transcendent foundation.

Albert Schweitzer's *Quest of the Historical Jesus* (1906; ET 1910) shows that historical awareness certainly does not lay to rest historically the figure of Jesus; it makes Jesus live for the present in a way that christological dogma failed to do. Schweitzer called this research 'a uniquely great act of truthfulness'. The historical-critical relationship to the Bible and tradition is quite ambivalent. It can lead to historical relativism, but it can also actualize the truth and give it present force.

2. The Protestant faith of 'the cultured' in the modern world was always consciously in transition from the 'historical faith of the church' to what Kant called 'the true faith of reason'. It gave the soul's personal relationship to God precedence over church-determined faith. What Karl Holl called the Protestant religion of conscience strove for awareness of the God 'within us', and it was to this awareness that the testimonies of God 'for us' in history were supposed to contribute. If religion is no longer a matter for the state but is a private affair, then it is no longer a matter for the church either. Everyone must be personally convinced. All must decide for themselves. For only personal faith can sustain the individual. 'Subjectivity is truth,' said Kierkegaard. The modern awareness of human subjectivity led in Protestantism both to liberal 'culture Protestantism' and to modern Pietism. The modern Protestant denominations are religions of subjectivity. George Fox and the Quakers proclaimed 'the inner light' of the Holy Spirit and reverenced it in every human being. In Rhode Island the Baptist Roger Williams proclaimed 'soul liberty' and hence religious liberty too. John Wesley, understanding true faith as a 'heart-warming experience' and as the personal sanctification of life, founded Methodism.

3. Culture Protestantism was a Protestant form of the modern world's messianic dream. Christianity is on the move from its ecclesiastical phase to its moral and political era. The pious churchgoer is a thing of the past. Now there is only the Christian as a mature citizen in the realm of morality and culture. The moral commonwealth is the ultimate purpose of God's history with the human race. The mature Christian grows

beyond the church, and lives in culture and politics, said Richard Rothe in the nineteenth century. The shrinking church gives way to the expanding Christianity of world history. That is the positive meaning of secularization. This Christian 'culture messianism' was the mark of 'the Christian century' and 'the Christian world'. It mobilized a missionary movement throughout the world which was unique in the whole of Christian history, and allied itself with the modern world's belief in progress. The consummation of history seemed to be at hand in the realm of universal morality, generally accepted human rights, and eternal peace. The paradigm of global community and global peace was achievable. That is the dream of Christian liberalism and modernism.

(iii) Christian fundamentalism

However strangely Christian fundamentalists may behave, it is wrong to exclude them, ignore them, or brush them aside in intellectual arrogance. So we shall pick up their concerns positively, and shall incorporate our criticism in our reception.[5]

2. In opposition to the relativity of history and the subjectivity of faith, fundamentalists appeal to the *authority of God*. Faith is personal decision. But the assurance of faith is based solely on the firm foundation of the eternal divine authority. In the so-called religions of the book, this foundation is the divine authority of the document of revelation. God's Word, like God himself, is inerrant and infallible. For Protestant fundamentalists the foundation is the inerrancy of the Bible; for Muslim fundamentalists, the Qu'ran is the unfalsified, pure, divine revelation exalted above all error; for Catholic fundamentalists, the foundation is the Bible and the infallibility of the papal magisterium. Historical investigation is not rejected, any more than is scientific research, but their methods and results must be subordinated to the foundation of divine authority. Historical-critical research must show that 'the Bible is right after all', and scientific 'creationism' is intended to confute Darwin's godless theory of evolution. Fundamentalism is not

just a reaction to the dangers of modern thinking. It is also an attack on modern thinking, the aim being to subordinate that thinking to divine authority, like all other sectors of life – hence the campaigns for re-Christianization and re-Islamization.

Over against both the linear concept of time, which underlies historical thinking, and the modern belief in progress, fundamentalism sets the whole of life in the category of eternity, and therefore asks about 'the timeless truth' of faith in God and 'the absolute commandments' of morality. In the presence of eternity, the modernist pressure to 'keep up with the times' is absurd. In the presence of eternity, historical divergence from the book of revelation also becomes unimportant. It is not the historically limited stance of the witnesses that counts, but simply and solely the eternal content of the testimony. It is not the hermeneutical communication of the past to the present that is of interest; it is the communication of eternity to time.

Before the eternity of God, all times are simultaneous. So the divine document of revelation – the Bible or the Qu'ran – speaks directly to the present with the authority of eternity. In actual fact the historical levels of history and the vertical levels of eternity are not mutually contradictory. The contradiction arises only when fundamentalists confuse the time when the book of revelation came into being with the eternity of God's revelation, and when modernists make their own present absolute and the criterion of revelation. There is a pre-critical fundamentalism, and it is widespread. But there is a post-critical fundamentalism too.

The more the modern world produces its own contradictions and catastrophes, the less human beings trust it. After Hiroshima and Chernobyl, the *trust in time*, which underlies faith in progress, no longer provides a sustaining foundation. Only eternity gives security. *Trust in the earth*, which is the basis of scientific and technological domination, no longer provides a sustaining foundation either, in the face of the growing eco-logical catastrophes. All that remains and that can give security of soul is heaven. Finally, in the wake of two world wars and after Auschwitz, *trust in humanity* has been lost. It isn't God who is dead; it is the human being. So the only trust left is trust in the transcendent God. The modern world's losses of trust are the matrix for fundamentalism, even if fundamentalism doesn't provide any good and sustaining answers. The social strata of the once upwardly mobile and now economically declining middle classes are so open for the fundamentalist message because they have been thoroughly disappointed by the modern world.

2. Wherever the modern world spreads, people lose their traditional identity and with it their culture and morality. The social ties shaped by their tradition, such as the family, are dissolving. The freedom of the individual and his or her free associations are taking their place. But can a multiplicity of options, where 'anything goes', take the place of binding community and binding norms? Pluralism without community is undoubtedly anarchy, and a culture of narcissism in which everyone thinks only of himself destroys life. Fundamentalists, both Christian and Muslim, defend the endangered orders of family and the sexes, and try with the help of religion to enforce the values which are absolute because they are indispensable for life together. With the veil and the prohibition of contraception, they fight against the liberation of women. But the individual liberty of determining human subjects is the foundation of the modern world, its science, culture and economy. It develops of itself through the urbanization of the masses. By the year 2000 more than 40% of the world's population will be living in the mega-cities. In the mass cities of the modern world it is impossible to enforce pre-modern, agrarian ways of life, and family and patriarchal values.

At the same time there is no pluralism without community, that is to say without fundamentals. Whereas pluralism is obsessed by the plurality of individual possibilities in the modern world, fundamentalism is obsessed by the common fundamentals. However, there are no fundamentals which run counter to the diversity of life, but only those which contribute to it. A foundation which demands uniformity is a foundation not for life but for death. The Christian foundation for the exuberant variety of the gifts of the Spirit is Christ himself, not a pre-modern Christian lifestyle. The human foundation for the pluralist, multicultural society is provided by human rights, which in the different societies become civil rights – or must become so. Since today human beings themselves are threatening the survival of humanity, militarily and economically, the pluralism of possibilities must be limited to what is conducive to life, and must exclude everything that ministers to death. Neither the family itself nor private property is 'sacred', in the secular sense; it is life itself that is sacred.

3. Not least, fundamentalism is spreading in *the apocalypse of the modern world* and is disseminating a doomsday mood. Ever since modernism praised the rise of modernity as the new messianic era, there has been modern apocalyptic, which has seen in modernity nothing other than the 'end-time' in which everything will be destroyed. In place of the golden age of humanity which was supposed to be dawning, people have heard the hoofbeats of the four apocalyptic horsemen, and the noise of the battle of Armageddon. Whereas in the nineteenth century these fearful apocalyptic visions were evoked by the French Revolution and Napoleon, 'the Antichrist', in the twentieth century they are the realistic scenarios of a nuclear Armageddon which President Reagan envisaged, and 'the nuclear winter which will follow'.

It is no doubt true that in general, fears that the world is coming to an end are triggered off by the decline of a historical cultural world, such as the Byzantine empire, the Christian Middle Ages, Arab rule, the empire of the Tsars, and other worlds. But with the beginning of the nuclear age, the whole of humanity finds itself in the 'end-time' in which the end of humanity is possible at any time, an end-time which no other time can follow, because human beings can never again forget the formula for the nuclear annihilation of the world. Yet the reaction of American fundamentalists to this real challenge of the modern end-time is astonishing. The nuclear annihilation of the world which can be touched off by the nuclear superpowers is given the name Armageddon, God's great day, following Rev.

16.14; and responsibility for it is pushed off on to God. The necessary responsibility for peace is replaced by the empty promise of religious escapism: before that terrible end, true believers will be 'snatched away' into heaven ('the great rapture'). If people feel that the responsibility of power is more than they can bear, they gladly avoid it, and easily let themselves be 'snatched away'.

And yet fundamentalist apocalyptic points to the threatening self-destruction of the modern world, and is its challenging symptom. Christian eschatology must separate itself from the messianism of the modern world, and out of this world's ruins must rescue the categories of redemption.

(iv) Beyond modernism and fundamentalism

The church is not there for its own sake; it is there for the sake of God's kingdom. However particularist it may be, it maintains the universal interests of God's kingdom and his righteousness and justice in history. From this simple and really undisputed observation, it follows that Christianity can neither identify itself with the modern world nor cut itself off from it, for the modern world is not the kingdom of God – nor even an approach to it, as the pious men and women of the Enlightenment believed. But God does not exist without his kingdom either. And this means that the modern world with its potentialities and its limitations can be in accord with the kingdom of God or in contradiction to it. Those who hope for God's kingdom will contradict the contradictions of the modern world and will welcome those points in which it corresponds to the kingdom. They will work critically and prophetically on the reformation of the modern world. That was what the 1934 Barmen Theological Declaration of the Confessing Church had in mind. Thesis 5 says: 'The church calls to mind the kingdom of God, God's commandment and righteousness, and thereby the responsibility both of rulers and of the ruled.'

Today we must transfer this public reminder to the market economy, culture and the ecology of the earth. It remains the critically prophetic and hence public task of Christianity in the modern world. There can be no withdrawal from public life into the unchallenged space of the church, or the holy remnant of true believers, such as the fundamentalists seek; for that would also be to withdraw from the prophetic task in public life. God does not exist without his kingdom, which will fill heaven and earth with its splendour. Consequently, on the foundation of the Bible there can be no faith in God without hope for God's coming kingdom. This is true for Jewish and Islamic faith in God as well.

After Protestant culture theology had been shattered by the First World War, what dawned for many Protestant Christians was what Otto Dibelius called 'the century of the church'. Protestant theology became an emphatically 'church' theology. This meant that fundamentals were turned upside down. The church was no longer orientated towards the kingdom of God; the kingdom of God was centred on the church. Today we shall only arrive at a critical and prophetic relationship to the principles and values of the modern world when we take our bearings from the kingdom of God for which Jesus was publicly crucified. Then we shall leave behind us the mindless alternatives of modernism and fundamentalism.

1. Discovering the kingdom of God in the church means *discovering the mature congregation.*[6] The church is not an established major organization with local branches. Nor is it a sectarian circle. Properly speaking, everything in the institution of the 'church' ministers to the conversion, gathering and instruction of the mature congregation. It is in the congregation that Christianity is gathered. In the congregation there is no division between clergy and laity, for it is made up entirely of specialists, each of them in his or her own sphere and profession. The mature congregation can deal with most tasks by itself, for it has the gifts required. It doesn't have to delegate its charitable work to charitable organizations. It is itself a charitable congregation which looks after its sick and disabled members. It doesn't have to delegate mission to missionary societies, but discerns and pursues its own apostolate in the

areas of life and professions of its members. It doesn't have to delegate ecumenical relations to representatives for ecumenism or to committees; it lives in ecumenical fellowship with all Christians in its own locality. It doesn't have to delegate theology to professors either, but continually thinks about its own praxis in the light of the gospel. The principle of delegation made the Christian congregations immature, cut off from their best gifts and proper tasks, and turned Christians into the voluntary subordinate helpers of the office bearers who have 'the cure of souls'.

To discover the mature congregation is nothing less than to experience God's Spirit and the wealth of the Spirit's gifts. A mature congregation is a *charismatic* congregation. In it everyone has received the Spirit, not just the so-called 'spiritual pastors'. Even if today's charismatic movements and Pentecostal churches convey fundamentalism, that is no reason for dispensing with one's own experiences of the Spirit, or for denying them to other people. On the foundation of the Christ once crucified and eternally alive, an exuberant wealth of spiritual gifts develops, and these acquire their value when they are put to common use on behalf of the kingdom of God and his righteousness and justice in the world. The first thing is a *church reform in line with the kingdom of God*. We don't need a *Volkskirche* – an established church for looking after the whole people – nor do we need a church which is a self-sufficient club. We need Christian congregations for the kingdom of God: instead of a congregation *of* the church we need the congregational church; instead of the church for looking after people, the church in which people get involved. We saw an eloquent example in the prayers for peace held in small groups in the Leipzig churches on Monday evenings in 1989, which the mass demonstrations for freedom joined ('We are the people'). Here resolute minorities – critical, prophetic and non-violent – represented universal concerns, convincingly and successfully.

2. To discover *the kingdom of God in the modern world* is a subject for the imaginations of mature Christians. Let me mention here only three problem complexes where the critical

and prophetic 'calling to mind' of God's kingdom and his righteousness and justice is necessary.

(a) *Human dignity is more than market value.* After the end of the socialist alternative 'as it really existed', apparently all that remains to us, without any alternative at all, is the global marketing of everything. This used to be called capitalism.[7] If market value is made 'the measure of all things', then the market literally becomes the apocalyptic 'end of all things'. Religion too will no longer be a matter for the state, nor will it be a private affair. It will be a commodity on the global market in the services section headed 'service-centre for meaning in life'. The electronic churches of the fundamentalists in the United States are remarkably successful in marketing their religion as a commodity. Here liberals and modernists have inhibitions – or simply no money.

What the market does to religion is evident. Marketed religion, religion as a 'special offer' – or as a 'positively last offer' – doesn't go down very well, at least with us. Nor do we need a church 'on the cheap'. What the market does to men and women is more important. If human dignity is identified with market value, that dignity is enduringly destroyed, as the long-term unemployed discover for themselves, and as managers threatened by what they suppress learn from their psychiatrists. Human beings are more than the sum of their achievements, and more than the sum of their failures. Women and men must be respected as persons before God, and must be liberated from their market value – or non-value. What we need on the market is the pertinent message about the justification of men and women through grace alone, without any market values. We need communities in which people feel accepted and respected as persons, so that they do not founder in the market struggle of each against all. The difficult problem complex for the future is no longer church and state. It is church and market.

(b) *No freedom without equality.* The human project of modernity began with the promise that all human beings are created free and equal. In the liberal democracies of the West we have grasped what individual freedom is in confrontation with governmental power. But that all human beings are free? That is a promise that has not nearly been fulfilled as yet. We shall need a great many liberation and civil rights movements before it is fully implemented. And the truth that all human beings have been created equal has not yet been implemented at all. Now that the socialist experiment has come to grief, no one wants to talk about this equality any more. And yet there is no such thing as freedom for everyone without equality. Without equality, freedom cannot be universalized. Extreme economic inequality makes democracy impossible. The social concept of equality is *justice*. Without just social conditions there is no peace between people and nations. The ethical concept of equality is *solidarity*. If hundreds of thousands are not to move from east Germany to the west, equal living conditions must be created in east and west. That is expensive but possible. If millions are not to emigrate from eastern to western Europe, equal living conditions must be created in Europe as a whole. If Europe is not to turn into 'fortress Europe', equal living conditions must be created in south and north. Otherwise the poverty-driven movement which we call 'the flood of asylum seekers' will not stop.

The Christian churches which are 'catholic' or 'ecumenical' can show that for them what is universal is more important than what is particularist, that ecumenical solidarity has more value than national or class loyalty. They will resist the temptations of a global apartheid society, just as they have successfully withstood the local apartheid society in South Africa.

(*c*) Not least, we have to face up to an *ecological revolution of the modern world* if that world is to survive, and we in it. For this, an *ecological reformation of Christianity* is necessary. And for that we need a new theological architecture. Modern monotheism has robbed nature of its magic and delivered it up, with no holds barred, to the rapacity of human beings, in whom alone God's Spirit is supposed to be present. Even the modern idea of humanity was pursued at the cost of other living things. Only the human being is a determining subject – all other beings are objects. We are face to face with a 'rediscovery of the earth' and a 'return of the body'.[8] The suppressed sectors of creation are making themselves felt. They are making themselves felt through their silence and their death. Here a new Christian spirituality will discover the hidden immanence of God in the earth and in our own bodies. 'No creature is so far from God as not to have him within itself,' said Aquinas, and for Luther and Calvin this dignity of all God's creatures was a matter of course. The concern of Christian congregations should not be solely the salvation of souls or the redemption of men and women. Their concern should also be the salvation of the cosmos, especially the earth from which we live and which we are progressively destroying. Among all God's creations, it is only *the earth* which in Genesis 1 is called 'the bringer forth' of plants and animals. The modern earth sciences are working with the model of the Gaia hypothesis, according to which the earth itself is a single great organism which makes life within it possible and preserves it.

In order to acquire theological categories for a new, post-modern view of human beings and the earth, culture and nature, we have no need to make pilgrimages to India. We only have to drink from our own mystical wells. The oldest pre-modern ideas about the unity of everything living and the great community of creation (Psalm 104) can become the model for postmodern blueprints. The goal will be to integrate human culture once more into the nature of the earth, the human spirit into the nature of the body, and modern instrumental reason into the wider cohesions of wisdom.

4

Dialogue or Mission?
Christianity and the Religions
in an Endangered World

Let me begin with a personal experience and an honest doubt.

1. When I was in India, I was fascinated by the glorious
Hindu and Jain temples, with their crowd of praying and
sacrificing people. For thousands of years the same figures, the
same stories, the same rituals. What wisdom in suffering, what
experience of life, love and death is preserved here, kept alive
down to the present day! I think of the Vishnu temple in
Srinagar, and the Jain sanctuary on Mount Abu. When I was
there I often found myself asking: do I as a Christian really want
these religious marvels to disappear and to be replaced everywhere by Christian churches? And yet, does this mean that I
don't want all these people to hear the gospel of Christ, and
experience the Spirit of life, and hope for the new creation and
the fullness of life? I feel torn. On the one hand I am impressed
by the wonderful world of the Indian religions. On the other, I
am captive to faith in Christ, and to hope for his kingdom.
What ought I to do? Should I relinquish Christ's command to
go out and preach the gospel, and do my utmost through interfaith dialogue for religious tolerance and understanding
between the religions? Or should I reject the dialogue, and
devote myself entirely to mission? 'Go and make disciples of all
nations,' says the missionary charge according to Matthew, not
'Engage in conversations with all the religious groups!' Or are
dialogue and mission not contradictory after all?

2. When a new appointment had to be made to the Chair for Missionary Studies in our theological faculty in Tübingen, objections were raised in the senate by members of other faculties: mission was no longer in keeping with the times, it was said; what was needed were programmes for dialogue. So ought we to rename the Chair for Missionary Studies, and call it a Chair for the Study of Christian Dialogue – or simply pass it over to the Faculty for Religious Studies, and make it a chair for the study of religions in general, the Christian religion included? If we do that, ought we not then logically to turn the denominational faculties into departments for religious studies? But if we really come down to it: what *is* Christian mission? Is it the extension of the Christian empire, Christian civilization, or what today goes under the high-sounding title of 'the community of Western values'? Or does it aim to spread the Christian churches, or to convert people to the Christian faith? Or is mission perhaps something quite different? Is it perhaps the invitation to the future of life?

In this chapter I shall try first to take stock of our experiences of interfaith dialogue up to now. (What *is* a dialogue of this kind with people of different faiths and different philosophies of life? What ought we to be discussing? When we enter into a dialogue of this kind, what are our premises and what are our expectations? And what is the outcome?) Second, I shall try to develop a new interpretation of mission which presupposes dialogue, is continually engaged in dialogue, never breaks it off or pushes it aside, which makes dialogue possible because it is necessary – but uses it for more than just an encounter.

I am starting from two simple facts.

1. Without the religious and cultural dialogue between religious communities, no one will be able to understand anything – no Christian, no Jew, no Muslim, and no Hindu or Buddhist. People who just stay in their own little circles and stew in their own juice become stupefied, because wherever they are they always hear only the same thing, the thing which endorses them. But sooner or later, what is no different will become for the people who are no different a matter of

indifference. It is only from the other that we become aware of what we ourselves are, and sure of our identity.

2. No one has ever become a Christian or a Jew or a Muslim or a Hindu or a Buddhist through interfaith dialogue. The dialogue between the religious communities has a tranquillizing effect on things as they actually are, and is in tendency completely conservative. We all remain just what we were, but in dialogue we 'converse', or are simply nice to each other; otherwise we leave each other in peace, religiously speaking. Without peace between the world religions there will be no peace in the world, says my friend Hans Küng. He is right. If we don't talk to each other today perhaps we shall be shooting at each other tomorrow. And yet in view of the many deadly perils in the world in which the religious communities live, we can surely expect rather more of these communities than a cease-fire and a 'leave us in peace'.

So I shall ask critically: dialogue yes – but to what end? Mission, yes – but in what direction?

(i) The present state of interfaith dialogue

The history of the religions has seen abundant opportunities for encounter, and a rich variety of ways of living together. Dialogue is only one of them, and it is a specifically modern, originally Western possibility at that, for it presupposes the separation between religion and state power, as well as individual religious liberty.

1. The original and most widespread form was and is a unity of religion and state.[1] In antiquity, the states were religious states, and great religions were state religions. Worship was accounted the first civic duty, and the kings and emperors, Pharaohs and Caesars were the high priests of the territories over which they ruled. As the father of his country (*pater patriae*), the Roman Caesar was at the same time the *pontifex maximus* for Jupiter, the father of the gods. In the world of the Egyptian Pharaohs, the great Persian kings and the Chinese emperors, things were no different. The state religion legiti-

mated the absolutism of the rulers. Their rule therefore became a 'holy rule' which promised their subjects salvation. Anyone who refused to conform to the public state cult counted as an enemy of the gods and the realm. That person evoked the wrath of the gods, which brought misfortune to country and people, and he therefore had to be sacrificed. Countries in which Buddhism or Islam have been made the state religion still exist today. Countries in which Marxism-Leninism was made the state ideology existed earlier in the Eastern bloc, now a thing of the past. In the Holy Roman Empire, the Emperor Constantine and his successors Theodosius and Justinian made Christianity the imperial religion for their realm, with its many peoples.

In the Western world this unity of state and Christian religion existed right down to the present – in Germany until the Weimar Constitution of 1919, where Article 48 says for the first time: 'There is no state church.' The 'religious' state united under a single denomination was for long a political ideal: one king – one law – one religion. It was with this absolutist motto that the Protestant minorities were driven out of France, Austria, Italy and Hungary, and Catholics out of England.

If a religion becomes a political religion in this sense, then religious wars are more likely to result than religious dialogue. The other denomination of one's own religion will be persecuted as apostasy. The other state religion will be eradicated as idolatry and devil worship, and its adherents forcibly converted. The encounter between state religions usually led to the annihilation of the weaker one, and to the defection of its adherents, who ranged themselves on the side of the gods of the bigger battalions. Wars of religion, or wars in which the religions became the driving powers of aggression – as in Bosnia – always have to do with political religions.

But the political religions of the ancient world were not as totalitarian as the modern ones. The state cult was binding on everyone; but beneath that threshold the Roman empire, with its myriad peoples, was tolerant. Families could worship their private gods, the *penates*, in their own homes. The private associations could keep their Mithras cult, and the diverse military units their national gods. Things were no different in the Chinese empire and in Buddhist countries. On these levels – the levels below the state cult – religions spread, new ones sprang up, and there was dialogue and an easy-going co-existence among the different religious communities, which were made up of families, kinships, clans and castes.

If religious communities affirmed the right to elevation as the religion of the state – if, that is, they came forward with an absolute and universal claim – a public trial of power was, from time immemorial, open to the contestants, like the contest between Moses and Pharaoh's 'magicians' in Egypt, or – a rather more modern example – the public disputations between the priests and the missionaries, the representatives of the religious communities which were battling for cultic power in the state. The forum was the seat of central power – the king's court, or the city council. After the arguments for 'the true' religion and against the false one had been exchanged, the king or the city council decided which religion was to hold sway in the country, as the 'true' and 'beneficial' one, and which religion had to be banished, because it was 'false' and 'would bring misfortune'. The religious disputation was a dialogue leading to a public political decision, a kind of court proceeding, with indictment, defence and verdict. This was also the way the Reformation was introduced into the Holy Roman Empire in the sixteenth century. After the Leipzig disputation between Luther and Eck, the Reformation faith was established in Saxony by the Electoral Prince. After the Zürich disputation, for which Zwingli formulated the theses, the Reformation was introduced into the city by the city council.

What does this brief glance at the widespread unity of religion and state suggest to us about interfaith dialogue?

(a) In Asia and Africa (except for Ethiopia), a non-political – i.e., a non-Constantinian – Christianity has existed ever since the first century as a religious minority living tolerantly with other religious groups. Strong family ties ensure the survival of these Christian communities in India and Egypt. The only mission these churches know is non-violent mission, mission through conviction, simply through the process of co-existence. Of course there were and are dialogues with representatives of other religious groups, but they have no great importance. The Protestant church in China did not grow out of religious or ideological dialogue; it emerged out of martyrdom during Mao's brutal, anti-religious cultural revolution. It survived in house churches and in steadfast Christians, and today has between 60 and 80 million members. The Orthodox Church in the former Soviet Union never entered into dialogue with state representatives of the ruling Marxist-Leninist ideology, and even in 1967 refused to participate in our last Christian-Marxist dialogue in Marienbad; and yet it has outlived the Marxist state religion.

(*b*) In the Western world, religious pluralism, and with it interfaith dialogue, developed very differently, for here the foundation was the ancient *corpus christianum*. Until the Reformation, Christianity in its Roman Catholic form was the imperial religion. After the Reformation, denominationally unified 'religious' states were established according to the motto *cuius regio eius religio*. The denominational divisions of Christianity and the existence of Jewish communities promoted the modern type of the secular state, which is neutral towards religion. This developed in Holland first of all, then in Prussia, later in France, and so on. Initially, the secularization of the state means only that governmental power has no competence in religious questions and must let the religous groups settle their internal affairs by themselves, 'although within the limits of the law to which all are subject' – that law being the human and civil right to religious liberty. The separation of church and state, and the right to religious liberty, have made of the denominationally unified 'religious' states of the Christian world modern *multifaith societies*. What do we mean by that?

(i) In a state constituted in this way, all religious communities must be treated alike.

(ii) The state ensures the individual's religious liberty: everyone is free to enter a religious group orto leave it, and is also free while he or she belongs to it. The state cannot allow any religion to dispute the right to religious liberty.

(iii) All religious communities are free within the limits of the rule of law which is valid for all. No secular state can permit groups in the name of their religion to torture witches, burn heretics, mutilate girls, burn widows, sacrifice children, torment animals, train suicide squads, or terrorize and execute members who have defected. It is only if this frame of reference is clear to the different religious communities in the secular society that they can enter into dialogue with each other. The state must reject as attacks on its free constitutional structure any attempt to abolish the separation between religion and state, and to set up a theocracy, as well as efforts to subjugate adherents of a religious group psychologically; for the state is responsible for the multifaith society's frame of reference. The religions are subordinate to religious freedom, not religious freedom to a religion.

But this frame of reference modifies quite considerably the life of the religious communities that accept it. They automatically lose their total claim, and become relative to the personal religous liberty of the people. If religion is no longer 'a matter for the state', it becomes 'a private affair'. We respect the liberty of other people in religious matters, and require them to respect ours. Personal decisions of faith are not really open to discussion, because they are not open to dispute. Everyone can believe what he or she likes, and no institution has the right to lay down rules for them; only, they must not make an absolute claim for what they believe, and take this to radical lengths. Because decision in religious questions is shifted from the state to the individual, religions change their character. They are no longer a civic duty; they are a spiritual offer in the service sector of the market society's supermarket economy.[2] They offer 'spiritual resources' for 'the mastery of contingencies', to use the language of secular sociologists – meaning by that the mastery of such critical situations as disablement, sickness, loss, or death. The religions which are processed for the religious market of the Western, multifaith society are therefore no longer what they once were, or what they are elsewhere. What emerges is a Christianity without expectation of the kingdom of God, a Judaism without the land of Israel, and an Islam without a geographical 'house of Islam'.

The earlier absolute, in our case the Christian claim in a Christian world, has been replaced by the secular world's claim to religious pluralism, which is maintained just as exclusively. It is impermissible to make anything absolute – except pluralism. In 1968, in his criticism of the bourgeois world, Herbert Marcuse called this 'repressive tolerance'. If we add the modern marketing of religions in the modern world, it is then the repressive tolerance of the consumer society. Modern interfaith dialogue is evidently meant to minister to the establishment of religious peace in religious pluralism. This is something new in the history of religion. Up to now this modern religious peace has not had a particularly enlivening effect on the faith communities: rather, it has put them out of commission socially and politically, turning them into a personal 'do as you please'.

In the three biblical religions, Judaism, Christianity and Islam, the general opinion would seem to be that one must have a monogamous relationship to one's religion – one person, one religion. But in Asia, the pluralism of the religions can be lived polygamously too. In Japan there is the Three Religions Movement, in Taiwan the Five Religions Movement. In India one can also live the religions successively, according to the stage in life one has reached. In Japan one can be married in a Christian ceremony, celebrate the New Year in a Shinto temple, and meditate among the Buddhists. So there is no need to take such a narrow view of religion as we are accustomed to do. Of course one can also dispense with all religious offers, on the ground that they make no difference to life as it is actually lived.

2. The programme of modern interfaith dialogue is really a conservative programme. It completely leaves out all the criticism of religion made by Feuerbach, Marx and Freud.[3] Through conversations, the religious communities are supposed to dismantle their prejudices, get rid of their bogey-man images and their aggressions, and arrive at peaceful co-existence in

mutual respect. This is vitally important. Multifaith societies can be incomparably fruitful and lively, but they can also explode and be deadly, as history shows. But if peaceful co-existence is the goal of dialogue, then in contrast to the religious disputations we mentioned earlier, dialogue has no higher goal than itself: dialogue is the goal of dialogue. Dialogue doesn't lead beyond dialogue, but only to a deepening of dialogue. In interfaith dialogue the common path is also the goal. It is understandable that in the countries of the Western world interest in these dialogues is considerable, for here multifaith societies are supposed to develop, and yet social peace has to be maintained. But it is equally understandable that in Islamic countries and among Hindus in India and Buddhists in Burma interest in the Western offer of dialogue is relatively slight.

If interfaith dialogue is directed towards the ethical goals of tolerance and freedom, what the communities have in common is generally speaking put in the foreground; and all the hitherto absolutist religions therefore now vie with each other to be accounted the most tolerant. If the religious concern is in the foreground, the unbridgeable differences surface. In Iran the mullahs didn't want to talk with Christian 'pluralists', but only with convinced Christian theologians, who take their own religion seriously to the point of making an absolute claim for it. We would do the same thing with Muslims and Buddhists and Marxists.

Experiences of dialogue on an international level up to now show a number of imbalances. I am mentioning them, not in order to hinder the dialogue, but so as to make it more serious. We all know the dialogues which run according to the following pattern: a Christian theologian puts questions – a rabbi, a mullah or a swami readily replies. But they ask nothing on their own account, because they aren't interested in Christianity. At most they may make critical remarks about the decadence of the Western world, which they take to be the Christian world. Many mullahs reject interfaith dialogue, because self-criticism is foreign to them, and they are therefore not prepared to allow any criticism of Islam; instead they simply give propaganda speeches everywhere on behalf of the Qu'ran. They prefer to talk about a 'cultural dialogue' such as was held at the Islam conference in Cairo in 1996. A well-known pioneer of Christian-Jewish dialogue in Germany noticed the one-sidedness after twenty years, and said to me rather sadly: 'The Jews never asked me anything.' The result is that some dialogues turn into discussions between Christian theologians in the presence of astonished and silent rabbis, swamis or Buddhist monks. 'Of course you can ask us anything at all,' they say – and see that as their contribution to the dialogue.

Another imbalance is that minorities are always very interested in public dialogue, but majorities are not. Representatives of Islam have no interest in dialogues with Coptic Christians in Egypt, or with Christian minorities in Iran or Turkey, Iraq or Syria; but in the Christian countries of Europe they gladly finance Muslim-Christian dialogues as a way of presenting themselves. I experienced this myself in Turin and Naples. When I suggested that the next Christian-Muslim dialogue should be held just as publicly in Cairo or Riad, the Muslims quite coolly waved the proposal aside. In Christian countries which are now multifaith, they demand tolerance for Islam, a tolerance which they notoriously deny to Christians, Jews and Hindus in their own 'house of Islam'. Religious freedom is fine when it permits Christians to become Muslims, but it would be a bad thing if it allowed Muslims to become Christians. At the centre of Catholic Christendom in Rome, a costly and lavish mosque was built with Saudi-Arabian money. In Riad, not even Christian crosses can be worn round the necks or on the clothing of Christian clergy. The Archbishop of Canterbury told me that he had to change on the plane. But the minimum requirement for dialogue is reciprocal hospitality and mutual respect.

3. There are two different forms of interfaith dialogue: direct dialogue about the different religious ideas of the participants, and indirect dialogue, about ethical, social and ecological topics of common concern.

The *direct dialogue* is the religious dialogue between different so-called world religions – religions, that is, which are not confined to a single people and a single culture, but appeal to each and every human being, and are therefore to be found everywhere in the world. Among these, of the Abrahamic religions Christianity and Islam may be mentioned especially; of the Asian religions, Hinduism, Buddhism and Confucianism. Over against the allegedly primitive animist religions, these used once to be called the 'advanced' religions.

In spite of all the political impediments imposed by antisemitism, the Christian-Jewish dialogue is the most fruitful, for we share 'a single book and a single hope', as Martin Buber put it. The dialogue is a dialogue over an open book, so to speak – the Tenach/Old Testament – and a dispute about interpretation in the spirit of the Torah or the spirit of the gospel.

The Christian-Muslim dialogue is burdened not only by a painful political history on both sides, but also by the fundamentalism which elevates the Qu'ran or the Bible into the infallible divine Word, and forbids all historical criticism or self-criticism as Western or modern decadence. As the publications show, it is difficult to get beyond mutual missionizing or propaganda speechifying. But for this dialogue too there is a shared pre-history in the Tenach/Old Testament, and in Abraham a shared father in faith.[4]

Christian-Buddhist dialogue is exceedingly difficult, once one gets beyond the initial exchange of superficial courtesies. An American-Japanese dialogue group has therefore drawn up a long-term programme which indicates possible approaches. The Buddhist interpretations of Christian texts by Masao Abe and Christian interpretations of Buddhist texts by David Tracy are extremely helpful.[5]

Chinese Confucianism seems at first quite convincing as a family ethic, but if it is used for the purposes of Asian educative dictatorships opposed to allegedly Western human rights (as was earlier the case in Korea and is still so in Singapore), Confucianism ceases to be available as dialogue partner.

Taoism is much more exciting. Ever since Leibniz in the seventeenth century, Laotse ('Tao te King') has been famed as a 'natural theology', while today it is extolled as an ecological cosmology. The parallels to Jewish Wisdom literature and to Christian cosmos mysticism are certainly astounding. But there are very few Taoist scholars in the world today.

The idea of interfaith dialogue is that the world religions should arrive at peace with each other, and should be brought to co-operate in efforts for world peace. But this is of course a Western idea, for 'book' religions are better equipped for spoken dialogue and logical argumentation than meditative or ritual ones. This is already evident from the fact that in all the different dialogue programmes, the animist religions of Africa, America and Australia do not crop up at all.

Indirect dialogue takes place today on Earth Day, for example, at global forum conferences, and at conferences on the environment held under the aegis of the UN and UNESCO. The purpose here is not the exchange of religious ideas, or a theological dispute about 'the truth'. The underlying concern is a shared perception of the perils in which the world stands today, and the common search for ways out of those perils. How, up to now, have the major religions of the world helped to justify the spoilations of the world – and what can they do to save it? Where do the religions harbour a resignation hostile to life, or forces – apocalyptic forces, for example – which are destructive of the world and prepared for violence? And what changes are necessary if the religions are to become forces which affirm humanity's life and preserve the world?

This dialogue is indirect because we are all talking, not about ourselves or each other, but about a third factor. Hans Küng's programme for 'a global ethic' is really also a call to a general, indirect dialogue of the religions about an ethic which will preserve the world from devastation and ruin. This, at least, was the message of the Parliament of the World's Religions held in Chicago in 1994.[6]

The ecological crisis or catastrophe from which the Third World particularly is suffering requires the 'advanced' religions to return to the earth. Up to now these religions have had little to say at the environmental conferences I have mentioned except for generalities, whereas representatives of the despised 'primitive', animist religions disseminate profound wisdom about the cycles and rhythms of the earth. At a conference of this kind in Moscow in 1990 we heard the 'indigenous' children of the earth – the Mayas of Central America, Africans from the Cameroons, and Aborigines from Australia – talk about 'mother earth' and our 'grandmother the moon', and their harmony with the spirit (Tao) of the cosmos; and we were moved. The ancient wisdom of these peoples in their dealings with the organism of the earth is certainly pre-industrial; but in a post-industrial age it is going to become highly relevant. We only have to translate this past into our future. Today it is not just a question of peace between the world religions which dominate the world of men and women. It is also a question of rediscovering 'the religion of the earth', which the human religions must approach in sympathetic understanding, if the organism of the earth is to survive, and we with it.[7]

(ii) Mission is the invitation to life

Having thus summed up the present position of dialogue between the religions today, we may pass on to the second part of our discussion, and look at ideas for a new concept of mission. Here a fresh approach would seem to be called for.

1. Earlier, Christian mission meant the spread of the Christian *imperium*. The salvation of the nations was supposed to lie in their subjugation to the 'holy rule' of the Christian emperor, for his rule was nothing less than the Thousand Years' Empire of Christ on earth, the empire at the end of history, in which Christ will reign with his own, and they will judge the nations. Under these auspices, Charlemagne 'missionized' the Saxons, Otto the Great the Slavs, Columbus the Caribbean, Hernando Cortés the Aztecs, and Pizzaro the Incas. Baptism or death was the apocalyptic motto. In the nineteenth century, the violent Christian *imperium* was replaced by 'Christian civilization' and by the cultural mission of Christianity in Africa and Asia. This found the support of European economic

imperialism. In our own century 'the community of Western values' bears only faint traces of that earlier political and cultural Christian messianism.

2. Later came Christian mission as the spread of Christian churches from Rome *urbi et orbi*, from Wittenberg, Geneva and Canterbury. The salvation of men and women is to be found in their subjection to 'the holy rule' of the Christian church, for its rule is nothing other than the Thousand Years' Empire of Christ, in which Christ will reign with those who are his, and will judge the nations. The church is 'the mother and pre-ceptress of the nations', as a papal encyclical asserts. Mission and the spread of the church have led to the world-wide dissemination of Roman Catholic, Anglican, Methodist and Lutheran churches, and of all Europe's other Christian denominations. We may safely say that to the degree to which self-styled 'Christendom' disintegrated in Europe, the churches as churches – not as European state religions – became present all over the world. The European secularization of state and culture made the churches, through their mission, 'secular' in the original sense of the word, that is to say world-wide.

3. Finally, ever since the nineteenth century we have been familiar with mission as the evangelization of humanity. That means awakening personal experiences of faith in God's Spirit, and bringing people to make their own personal decisions of faith. Salvation lies in the acknowledgment of Christ's 'holy rule'. 'Accept Christ as your personal Lord and Saviour, and you will be saved.' This kind of mission too is deeply influenced by the expected future of God and his presence in the Spirit.

Common to these three forms of Christian mission is the fact that they are messianically and apocalyptically motivated. They all start from something which in the present exists only in particularist form, and try to globalize it, whether it be the Christian *imperium* or the Christian church or the Christian experience of conversion.

I would suggest proceeding in the reverse direction. If we understand mission, not as an aggressive appropriation of the whole, but as an invitation to God's future, then we begin with that universal future of the nations and the earth, and give it present force in the gospel of hope and in the service of love. We invite people of other religions and ideologies to work together for that future which we try to imagine in the symbols of the kingdom of God, eternal life, and the new creation of heaven and earth. The religions and cultures of other people will not thereby be destroyed; they will be interpenetrated by the Spirit of hope, and opened for the future of the world. This corresponds very well to the invitation to that indirect dialogue about the present dangers to the world, and ways of surmounting them. Why, one must finally ask, should we alone worry about life and survival in this self-destructive world? But how is that to be theologically interpreted?

Mission in the original theological sense of the word is *missio Dei* – God's sending. But what does God send? According to biblical understanding (both Jewish and Christian) he sends nothing less that his *Spirit* into this world, through the Christ, the Messiah.[8] This is the Spirit who is the life-giver and who is therefore called *the Spirit of life,* or *the source of life.* According to the Gospel of John, what God brings into the world through Christ can be summed up in a single word, *life.*[9] 'I live and you shall live also' (John 14.19). What is meant is the fulfilled life – the wholly and entirely living life – the shared life – the eternal life – the fullness of life. It is experienced in the new livingness of love. Nor is it just human life that is meant, for according to the prophetic message this living power of God will be poured out 'on all flesh', which in the language of the Old Testament means everything living. God's sending is biocentrically orientated, not anthropocentrically. It is not concerned with the political or religious rule of human beings over the world, and not merely with the salvation of human souls, but with the liberation, salvation and final redemption of the life shared.

Its goal is therefore 'the new creation of all things'. The eternal life which is the gift of the Spirit who is the life-giver is not a life other than this life here and now; it is the power through which this life here will be different. This mortal, temporal life gains a share in the divine life, and through that becomes life that is eternal: '*This* perishable nature must put on the imperishable, and *this* mortal nature must put on immortality', stresses Paul (I Cor. 15.53). So Nietzsche was right: 'Eternal life is eternal livingness.' If God's sending embraces the whole of life, the shared life of all the living, it must not be reduced to religion and inwardness and 'the salvation of our souls', important though our 'souls' are.

Jesus didn't bring a new religion into the world. He brought new life. He didn't found 'Christianity', nor did he set up an ecclesial rule over the nations. He brought life into this violent and dying world, the life 'that was from the beginning, which we have looked upon and touched . . . and the life was made manifest, and we saw it, and testify to it, and we proclaim to you the life that is eternal . . .' (I John 1.1–2). Christ is the divine Yes to life. That Yes leads to the healing of the sick, to the acceptance of the marginalized, to the forgiveness of sins, and to the saving of impaired life from the powers of destruction. This is the way the Gospels tell about Jesus's mission. And according to the Gospels this is also the character of the mission of the women and men who live in his Spirit (Matt. 10.7–8).

If we apply this sending – this mission – to the situation of life as it is today, then we come to at least three points of intersection.

1. It is not only our human life that is in deadly danger. Ever since Hiroshima in 1945 this has been true for life itself. Tens of thousands of nuclear weapons are lying ready for 'the final solution' of the question of the human race. In the nuclear winter that will follow their deployment, all higher life on earth will die. The nuclear end of life is possible at any time, even if at present it is not probable; so in this sense we are living in an 'end-time'. Through political efforts for peace we can extend our time limit – but no time is conceivable in which human beings will no longer be capable of doing what they can do today. The formulae for the weapons of mass annihilation can never again be forgotten once they have been discovered. The mission for life requires unconditional service for peace, and

work for the abolition of war as a means of settling conflicts. Humanity is intended for life, for God is a 'God of life'. In this context, or at this point of intersection, mission is the invitation to life.

2. Ever since Chernobyl in 1986, all life has been in deadly danger, not just human life. A whole region was contaminated by radioactivity, and made uninhabitable for centuries. Two hundred times more radioactivity was released in Chernobyl than in Hiroshima and Nagasaki. Up to now about 150,000 people in the area have died from radiation-related illnesses. And children are still dying, for example from leukaemia.

For the invitation to life, the conclusion from this has to be a new 'reverence for life', as Albert Schweitzer put it. At this point of intersection, mission is the invitation to joint resistance against technologies hostile to life, and the development of a way of dealing with energy which will be nature-friendly.

3. Over-population means more and more 'surplus people' whom nobody wants and nobody needs. Violence against life is on the increase, even in the name of religion. The abandonment of the street children, child prostitution, the unemployment of both women and men, the squeezing out of the old from the health services: these are only some aspects of the cynical way our society deals with young, old, and sick or impaired life. The production of 'surplus life' and the acts of violence perpetrated against this 'surplus life' are also among the deadly dangers of the modern world, just as are the weapons of mass destruction and the ecological crimes against nature. Here mission is the invitation to responsible dealings with life itself.

In distinction from the religious pluralism of our society, these threats to life permit no pluralism – at least no alternatives to life. The seriousness of the situation forbids the post-modernist free-for-all. 'Anything goes' has long since given way to 'nothing goes at all any more'.[10]

In this context, the question is not whether other religions can also be 'paths to salvation': whether in religions other than Christianity people are also searching for God, and can perhaps find God; whether, that is, there are 'anonymous Christians'

among members of other religious communities too, as Karl
Rahner conjectured – or however the questions about the theological significance of other religions may be formulated. In this
context the question is rather the question about *life* in other
religions, and also, of course, the question about life in the non-
religious, secular world. The mission to which God sends men
and women means inviting *all* human beings, the religious and
the non-religious, to life, to the affirmation of life, to the protection of life, to shared life, and to eternal life. Everything which
ministers to life in other religions and cultures is good, and must
be absorbed into the coming 'culture of life'. Everything which
among us and other people is a hindrance to life, destroys it, or
sacrifices it is bad, and must be overcome as a 'barbarism of
death'.

Earlier, the significance for Christianity of the plurality of the
religions was treated theologically under the heading of original
sin, and the myth of the Tower of Babel. Today some theologians think that religious truth itself is pluriform, and must
therefore manifest itself in a plurality of religions. For me, the
theological 'site' at which people of other religions come into
view is pneumatology and, within the doctrine of the Holy
Spirit of life, the teaching about the protean variety of life's
potentialities and life's powers – the potentialities and powers
we call charismata. Which forms and concepts in the world of
the religions minister to life? Can a religion or a culture become
a charisma of God's Spirit for people once they become
Christians and begin to love life with the love of God?

Earlier, when the religions fell under the doctrine of original
sin, people who became Christians had to cut themselves off
radically from the 'superstition' of their forefathers and the
'idolatry' of their people. According to the new pluralistic theology of religions, people don't have to become Christians at all
if they have found the divine truth in their own religion. In my
own view, everything a person is, and everything that has
moulded that person culturally and religiously, can become a
charisma, if he or she is called by Christ, and loves life,
and helps to work for the kingdom of God. 'Everyone as the

Lord has called them' (I Corinthians 7). So there are Jewish Christians and Gentile Christians, each with their own dignity. There are many different gifts, but one Spirit (I Cor. 12.4). There are many, many forms of life, but it is one life.

Lastly, conditions won't change *unless people change*. How else can they change? People must be different if the world is to be different. If we want peace on earth, we must become peaceable men and women. If we want a future for our children and our children's children we ourselves must overcome our lethargy and our egoism and be born again to a living hope for the future. If life is to survive, and if its deadly dangers are to be surmounted, faith must be awakened in us and other people, a 'faith that moves mountains'. The unconditional love for life must awaken in us. There is no future without hope. There is no life without love. There is no new assurance without faith. It is the task of evangelization and of the witness of Christian life to proclaim the living Christ and to awaken in us the Spirit of life.

5

Theology for the Church and the Kingdom of God in the Modern University

(i) From a confessionally unified state to the multifaith society

People from other faculties sometimes ask us whether theology still has a place in a modern university. After all, the university exists for everyone who wants to study there and is in a position to do so, while Christian theology is for Christians only – and, when all is said and done, Christians are a minority in modern society. So why don't we withdraw, and keep ourselves to ourselves in church seminaries? Does Christian theology have any function outside the church, in the public forum of our modern society? Our title indicates how much society has changed; and this change has made the position of Christian theology so uncertain, and so unsure of itself, that we have to discover afresh what that position is.[1] What we have seen up to now are no more than tentative attempts.

The stages of the social change are quickly told:

1. Under Constantine, the persecuted and merely tolerated Christian minority became the religion of the state, serving the unity of the Roman empire: one emperor – one law – one empire – one religion. Ever since the thirteenth century, state universities have included theological faculties pursuing theology as a form of scholarship. The term *facultas theologica* turns up for the first time at the university of Paris.

2. The schism in the Western church after the Reformation prolonged the notion of a state unified under a single denominational faith. *Cuius regio – eius religio* was the formula for the Peace of Augsburg and the Peace of Westphalia. That meant a single sovereign – a single territorial church – a single state university – a single theological faculty, Protestant or Catholic. The eighteenth century saw on the one hand the growth of absolute states, which drove out their religious minorities on the ground of their tenet *un roi – une loi – une foi* (one king, one law, one faith), while on the other hand there were countries where religious toleration was developing, such as England, Holland and Prussia, where Protestant and Catholic churches, and in some cases university faculties, were allowed to exist side by side. That is the stage to which the university I come from, Tübingen, belongs. In 1815 the Protestant king of Württemberg acquired Upper Swabia, which was Catholic. For his Catholic subjects the king established a Catholic theological faculty side by side with the already existing Protestant one, in the state university of Tübingen.

3. But what happens when immigration turns denominationally mixed Christian countries into multifaith societies? Then religion cannot be a state religion any longer. The separation of religion and state must free the way for a number of different religious communities. But if the state becomes religiously neutral, then the religions have to surrender the claims of a state religion.

Up to now three possible answers have been found for this new situation.

1. The theological faculties in state universities continue to exist, and continue to represent the religious condition of the country, which, since it is now multifaith, is in tendency presented in the descriptive terms proper to a science of religion and comparative religion. Theology is then transformed into an 'empirical science of belief and the philosophy of life', as with the chair for dogmatics at the Swedish university of Uppsala. Or Christian theology is transformed into a post-Christian 'pluralistic theology of religion', of the kind propagated in

the United States by John Hick and Paul Knitter, and will be directed to common features which can be construed in the framework of the philosophy of religion, or can be empirically observed, and which are 'above' denominational and religious differences.[2]

2. The theological faculties continue to exist, but parallel to Christian studies they offer courses for Islamic, Jewish and Buddhist communities, and for any other sizable religious groups existing in their particular society. This is now the practice at Cambridge University in England. But this turns the old theological faculties into what are quite professedly faculties for the science of religion, and the venerable divinity schools become modern departments of religious studies, as in many places in the United States.[3] The different study courses need no common spiritual basis to hold them together. The courses of theological study within these faculties can now easily change their character, in the direction of Model 1; but they do not necessarily have to do so. They can remain denominationally influenced too.

3. Special theological training reverts to the Christian churches and the religious communities themselves. These set up their own theological seminaries for the purpose, and no longer concern themselves about scholarly work in the universities. Their study courses and examinations no longer have to meet a university standard. These are the Bible colleges, Qu'ran and Torah schools. At the moment atheists and fundamentalists, joined by a number of Catholic bishops in Germany, have entered into an unholy alliance to split the theological faculties into the science of religion on the one hand, and specifically 'church' studies on the other. The one party wants to get rid of theology altogether; the other wants to bring theology under its own control.

At first sight, only the argument from tradition would seem to speak in favour of the preservation of the theological faculties at our universities: before we became a multifaith society we were a Christian country. It is only Christianity that can permit this modern society, which separates religion and state, and guarantees its citizens individual religious liberty. The secularized state lives from religious presuppositions which it did not itself create. This argument from tradition is deserving of respect, but in the course of time it becomes progressively weaker.

After the First World War, Protestant theology prepared the ground for the following development: *theology is a function of the church*. That was the unanimous declaration of the new theologians: Barth, Brunner, Bultmann, Tillich and others. It was a declaration made after the breakdown of bourgeois culture in the First World War and was directed against what these theologians criticized as 'culture Protestantism'.[4] At the same time, conservative bishops such as Otto Dibelius proclaimed 'the century of the church'. If theology is merely 'a function of the church', then it has to take its leave of the university, and withdraw from that public forum to its own community of faith, in church colleges and seminaries, so as to subject itself to the church's doctrinal authority, whether that be 'the inerrant Bible' or the 'infallible' magisterium of the pope. An attempt can be made to keep a degree of independence for theology by distinguishing between theology and the church's governing body in such a way that the one reminds the other of its own particular function. But in actual practice this is hardly possible in the long run, once theology ceases to be institutionally independent of the church's governing bodies. In Germany this development meant that people came to reduce what was Christian to 'the church', and 'the church' to the church in its official form; while they themselves ceased to think themselves capable of having any theological insights of their own.

The separation of religion and state is the presupposition of every modern society, and it is therefore sharply attacked by the fundamentalists in all religions. In many Western countries, this separation has led to the misunderstanding that because of it, religion is no longer 'a matter for the state' at all. It is a private affair, left to the individual as a question for his or her personal choice. The optional, do-as-you-please character of religious decisions fits in well with the individualistic trend of modern society. Religious pluralism becomes one component in the supply economy of the free market of modern society. But who creates and shapes the common basis, the general legal and moral conditions that provide a framework for modern, pluralist society? There can be no religious pluralism without shared foundations, any more than there can be a multicultural society without a common language and a common calendar.

What is left over for the state once it has cut itself free from church and religion varies; it has a different aspect according to the church or religion from which that state has separated itself.

1. In the English-speaking countries, and in Protestant Germany, what came into being was a pro-religious neutrality towards religion on the part of the state; religious liberty is exercised positively as far as a multiplicity of religious decisions is concerned. According to the preamble to the German Federal Republic's Basic Law (its constitution), the religious freedom named in Article 4 is guaranteed to every citizen by 'our responsibility before God'. In the United States, the separation between church and state already took place very early on, because it was recognized that the government had no competence in religious questions which were under dispute between the different denominations. This form of separation guaranteed the free-church principle of voluntary religion. The churches freed themselves from the state in order to settle their own affairs for themselves. It was not that the state freed itself from the domination of the church.

2. In France, Spain and Italy, on the other hand, what came into being after the French Revolution of 1789 was an a-religious secularity on the part of the state. What was guaranteed there was a negative religious liberty, because in these Catholic, feudalistic countries the state's freedom from the church and the people's freedom from clericalism was fought for and won by anti-clerical laicism. It was the state which freed itself from the church in order to be able to settle its own affairs, not the churches which freed themselves from the state. Even today, this laicist secularism shapes the cultural policies of these countries. There are no theological faculties at the state

universities, and no Christian religious instruction under the aegis of the church in the state schools. Strasbourg is an exception, because earlier on it belonged to the German empire. The conflict between free-church Protestant secularism and laicist Catholic secularity is going to keep the cultural policy of the European union in suspense for many a long day.

3. In the Orthodox, Eastern European states the socialist and atheistic separation of church and state led to the banishment of the theological faculties from the state universities and to the elimination of Christian religious instruction from the state schools. Marxist-Leninist ideology became the substitute for religion in universities and schools, and was now the atheistic religion of the state. After the disintegration of the Eastern bloc, and the disappearance of the Marxist-Leninist state ideology, the autocephalous Orthodox churches took up their old position once more, as the religion of people and nation. From Estonia to Romania, the theological faculties have returned to the state universities, and Christian teachers are once again giving religious instruction in state schools. The theological faculties are again training priests and teachers, as they are in the state universities in Protestant Europe.

If religion is made a private affair instead of a matter for the state, then it is inescapably relegated to the private sphere. It can then only be lived privately, no longer publicly. It must then be lived purely spiritually, and must no longer be lived politically. Then symbols and rituals have to disappear from public life, as crucifixes are officially banned from Bavarian schools and prayers from American ones. Religion must be restricted to reverence for God and to personal conduct. That means Christianity without the Sermon on the Mount and the discipleship of Jesus. It means Judaism without the Torah, and Islam without the Sharia.

The privatization of religion has as its presupposition its *de-politicization* and as a consequence its *marketing*. What is called modern multifaith and multicultural society is nothing other than the total market society. Religions and cultures are on display in this market in just the same way as political options, commodities and services. Religions become the spiritual services on offer in the religious supermarket of the modern world. Individual religious liberty is certainly a powerful protection for every person's own human dignity, but because of the typical Western concept of the consumer's freedom to choose or dispose, that same freedom has turned religion into a *commodity*, where the customer is allegedly always right. Marketed religions take on the characteristics of goods on sale. They are on offer optionally, without obligation, and with discount as 'religion light', like the offers on the shelves for esoteric literature in the bookshops. Everything is possible, nothing is taken seriously.

The road has led from religion as 'the first duty of every citizen' by way of 'religion as a private affair' to 'religion as a commodity'. In the multifaith consumer society, peace reigns between the religious communities. That is a fact. But this religious peace is achieved through the political shut-down on religion, its privatization and marketing – not through recognition and esteem, but by reducing religion to insignificance. One does not have to be a fundamentalist to see this as practised atheism.

(ii) Kingdom of God Theology

'Christ proclaimed the kingdom of God, and what came was the church,' said Alfred Loisy, the well-known Catholic modernist. But by saying this he wasn't just expressing disappointment; for the church is not a substitute, intended to make up for the non-appearance of the kingdom of God. It is the anticipation of the kingdom under the conditions of history. But if the church sees itself as *one form* of the kingdom of God in the history of this God-estranged world, its concern is always more than the church.[5] The proclamation of the gospel, the community of faith, and the diakonia or service of love all have to do with *the world in the kingdom of God* and *the kingdom of God in the world*. The future of God which is symbolized by the term 'kingdom of God' includes the future of the world: the future of the nations, the future of humanity, the future of all living things and the future of the earth, on which and from which everything that is here lives. In the biblical writings 'the kingdom of God' is the broadest, most comprehensive horizon of hope for the *general well-being* of the world.

If the church is only *one* historical form of God's coming kingdom, then theology cannot be merely a function of the church, and must not confine itself to offering what Schleiermacher (in the German title to his book) called 'the doctrine of the Christian faith', Karl Barth 'church dogmatics', and George Lindbeck 'the grammar of faith'. If the church takes theology seriously, it must, like the church, become a function of the kingdom of God in the world. As a function of the kingdom of God, theology belongs within all the different sectors of a society's life too – political, cultural, economic and ecological. This is demonstrated in political theology and the theology of culture, in the theology of education, in ecological theology and the theology of nature. In all these sectors, kingdom-of-God theology is *public theology*, which participates in the *res publica* of society, and 'interferes' critically and prophetically, because it sees public affairs in the perspective of God's coming kingdom. Of course by doing so theology also exposes itself to public criticism, which is what the church memoranda and papal encyclica notoriously avoid doing. Kingdom-of-God theology is a public reminder of God, a complaint to God, and a hope for God. As *public theology*, Christian theology is relatively independent of the church, for it too has political, cultural, economic and ecological mandates, parallel to the mandate of the church.[6] For these, it needs to be institutionally independent of the church, as it is, for example, in theological faculties at state universities.

In 1934, in resistance to Hitler, the Confessing Church issued the Barmen Theological Declaration, Thesis 5 of which states: 'It (i.e., the church) calls to mind the kingdom of God, God's commandment and righteousness, and thereby the responsibility both of rulers and ruled.'[7] The horizon of the kingdom of God is important here, for the Declaration does not say that the church reminds the government of the churches' interests as these are codified in agreements and concordats between government and churches. According to the Barmen Theological Declaration, the church does not come forward in opposition to the state for its own sake, but for the sake of something universal.

Is religion a private affair? Religion may be. But the Christian faith is not. Christ didn't preach a private religion. He proclaimed the kingdom of God. For the sake of God's coming kingdom, which he proclaimed to the poor and sick in Israel, he was publicly crucified in the name of the Roman imperium as a rebel, as the inscription over the cross proves. It was for the kingdom of God that the martyrs went to their deaths, from Stephen to Dietrich Bonhoeffer and Oscar Arnulfo Romero. In the Roman empire Christianity could quite well have survived unchallenged as a private or house religion, or as the religion of a private society or group, for that multifaith and multicultural empire was extremely tolerant. But by way of the Christian martyrs Christianity refused to go along with the cult of the emperor, which was necessary for the unity of the empire, and overarched the different religions and cultures. And this refusal made it politically dangerous. The person who does not stand up for the kingdom of God also has no need to flee to the catacombs.[8]

What kind of public life is established by way of kingdom-of-God theology? If we go back to Christ's proclamation of God's kingdom, we see clearly that, as the Beatitudes in the Sermon on the Mount show, the kingdom focusses on the poor, the sick and the weaker members of any given society. All kingdom-of-God theology becomes for Christ's sake a theology of liberation for the poor, the sick, the sad and the outcasts. So kingdom-of-God theology doesn't just enter the already existing public forum of its given society. It brings to light publicly the people whom society pushes into the underground or into private life.[9] It brings the eschatological light of coming redemption into public life as it exists, and reveals the human need for redemption.

The separation of church and state doesn't mean that religion has to become a private affair, and that the church turns into a kind of club. Religious freedom doesn't just mean the personal choice of a religion; it also means the freedom of the church's institutions and of Christian organizations. Creches and nurseries, schools, universities, newspapers, television, further education, and the various forms of charitable service all carry into society the universal kingdom-of-God concerns of the churches which are now free of the state.

In a multifaith society, too, the church has the task of bringing the gospel, faith and love to all human beings. It is not just individual private people who are the addressees of the church's message about the kingdom of God; it is society itself as well. No church which appeals to Christ and hopes for God's kingdom can dispense with this 'public character' of the concern it represents and maintains without forfeiting its own self. The point here is not to churchify the world. It isn't the church which has a word to say about every problem, nor the pope either. It is rather a question of focussing all sectors of life on God's coming kingdom and the changes that have to be made in all facets of life if life is to accord with that kingdom. The 'laity' are the Christian specialists who have the whole say here. In all sectors of life there are conditions which are in contradiction to the kingdom of God and his righteousness, and conditions which are in harmony with it.[10] The correspondences and harmonies in the conditions of history are our concern. They can often be more effectively achieved by resolute Christian minorities, if they maintain universal concerns, than by unbending Christian majorities who are simply caught up in their own administration and bent on securing their own survival.

(iii) The theological faculties and the common good

Does Christian theology have a place at state universities? If what I have said up to now is correct, then a Christian theology of the kingdom of God has a place in all the universal sectors of human culture. No militant secularism can prevent it from making its voice heard there. No militant fundamentalism must be allowed to seduce it into withdrawal from this public forum. But in that forum its voice will enjoy no special protection, and will convince only through the truth of what it has to say.

Today, however, Christian theology in the university theological faculties is itself sharing the fate of the universities, either willingly or perforce, as their fellow-sufferer.[11] The movement towards the *specialization* of science and scholarship has reached the theological disciplines, too, so that for some students it is difficult to perceive theology as a unity. The *pluralism* of the different theological positions means that some theologians can now detect the unity of theology only in critical reflections on method. In the theology sector, as in other faculties, the flood of students has meant that theology has turned into a *training school* for pastors and religious instructors, while inter-faculty dialogue on the university level has had to be neglected: for that there is no longer either time or energy. But that means that the common bond of 'the life of the mind', which fuses the university as such together, has weakened, and the university has turned into a conglomerate of diverse training schools. And as a consequence, the *uni*versity is giving way to a *di*versity.

The more theology has turned into a training school for pastors and teachers, the more it has become a merely churchified study. The relationship of the theological faculties to their churches has become closer than their relationship to other faculties. So if the theological faculties are to go on existing in the universities, it is not just for themselves that it is important to look beyond the horizon of the churches and to be aware of social, overall-human and global affairs in the light of God's kingdom and his righteousness and justice. This is *also* important for the continued existence and function of the universities in our society, among human beings, and on this earth. If the theological faculties succeed in their own way in once more discerning what is universal, and winning acceptance for it, the other faculties will do the same thing in *their* own way, too. Theology does not even have to lead the way. On this road from what is particularist to what is universal, and out of its self-inflicted isolation, theology will find itself in the wider community of the other faculties, with which it exists side by side.

What can society expect of the theological faculties? What, that is to say, can the universal whole expect of this 'particular'?

1. It can expect the theological faculties to have an eye to *the common good* of the whole of society in its wider ramifications, and not just to look to their own religious communities; for even the particularist religious communities participate in the common good, and contribute to 'the good life' of the community. What this common good is, can never be pinned down once and for all (if we except human and civil rights). It is developed in open discourse. The specific contribution of theology cannot be to reiterate secular options. Taking the categories of what is in correspondence and harmony with God and what is in contradiction to him, it has to set the common good in the light of the kingdom of God and his righteousness and justice. That is to say: the contribution of theology must be a theological contribution. What else could society expect of theology?

2. Society can expect the theological faculties to subject *the religious values* of society to critical investigation, and to present its own truth apologetically – that is to say, as reasoned explanation. By the religious values of society I do not mean private options. I mean the ultimate social and personal certainties which function as premises at the pre-rational level, and are accepted as a matter of course without further question. A society's religious traditions and the contributions they make to a society's weal or woe belong here. As ultimate certainties, religious values always play an immense part in moulding a society's life. But even they seldom remain static. Even their 'absolutes' are historically relative and in a state of flux. The ocean of uncertainties above which they rise, like islands or lighthouses, is always greater still. So in this sphere, too, public discourse is indicated, on the one hand between the various religious groups and communities of faith, and on the other hand with the a-religious, secular world.

3. Society can expect the theological faculties to have in view

the *moral values* of the social ethos, and not to look merely to their own Christian morality and the ethics of their own religious community. Christian theology's justification of these ethical values must be specifically Christian, and will inescapably be so. But the values nevertheless acquire general relevance in the social ethos of a society. The values of the person, his or her identity and authenticity, are certainly derived from the biblical belief that all and every human being is the image of God. But in Western societies these values have become part of the general heritage. The same is true of reverence for the life which God has created. The reverence derives from the biblical belief in creation, but it enjoys validity even apart from that, where life is endangered.

4. The universities can expect the theological faculties to reflect critically on the fundamental values of *academic freedom and responsibility*, and to defend these values publicly. The ethics commissions in the medical faculties – and recently in the faculties for the natural sciences, too – provide fields where theological faculties can pursue these assignments, but of course not these assignments alone. In addition we must mention a task which hardly anyone has noticed up to now. Until recently, what was in the foreground was the defence of scholarly and scientific freedom against the tutelage of the state ideologies of National Socialism and Marxist Lenininism, although at state universities this defence was hardly possible except through the emigration of the scholars and scientists concerned. Today what is on the agenda is the defence of scholarly and scientific freedom over against the claims and bids of industry and commerce. In the sphere of applied research there has always been co-operation between universities and the various branches of industry, and this will always be the case if whole sectors of research are not to emigrate from the university altogether. But the sphere of basic research must and can be kept free of exploitative economic interests as well. For these sectors, it is valuable that in the universities there should be faculties which seek for *truth*, without having to enquire about the utility or exploitability of that truth.

Finally, let me mention some characteristics which the theological faculties must preserve and which the universities to which these faculties belong must bear in mind.

1. Theology is one of the Christian faith's own proper tasks. It is the understanding of faith and the perspective of hope. Theology is not identical with a Christian philosophy of religion, and a study of Christianity as religion provides no substitute. So there is no Christian religious instruction without Christian theology.

2. Theology has its place at the university because, and in so far as, it supports universal concerns with a particularist reasoning. It would surrender its responsibility for creation and humanity, and its hope for God's kingdom, if it were to withdraw from the public discourse of universal concerns, or let itself be pushed out of this discourse. Christian theology is particularly well equipped for this universality because it does not just represent a religious community in its own particular country, or a national religion. It represents the *ecumenical church* for the human *ecumene*, the inhabited earth. *The universal church* and *Christianity all over the world* continually lead Christian theology out of the universities of a given country beyond the frontiers and particular interests of that country. There is no such thing as German theology. There is only Christian theology in Germany. And the same is true for all the other countries. This ecumenical solidarity often enough brings Christian theology into a degree of critical detachment from the national loyalty which is given and expected when theologians at state universities receive their salaries from the state, as is the case in Germany.

3. In this unique position, theological faculties can be expected to reflect critically about 'the common good' and to maintain it publicly, first in the framework of their own nation and continent, then globally, in the context of humanity, and for the sake of earthly life in general. Christian theology must avoid the pluralism trap, if only out of ecumenical solidarity. The critical awareness and public defence of the religious and moral values of the university, of one's own society, of human

civilization and of earthly life in general: these things belong essentially to the public responsibility of Christian theology and the Christian churches, just as they are part of the responsibility of all human beings in all life's different spheres.

Notes

I. Theology and Politics

1. Theology in the Project of Modernity

1. G. Gutiérrez, *A Theology of Liberation*, trans. from Spanish by C. Inda and J. Eagleson, Maryknoll, NY 1973, London 1974; ²1985; revised London and New York 1988.

2. G.W.F. Hegel, *Die Vernunft in der Geschichte*, ed. G. Lasson (PhB 171a), Hamburg 1955, 189ff., 200: 'America is thus the land of the future where, in times lying before us, . . . importance for the history of the whole world will be manifested . . .' (see *Lectures on the Philosophy of World History, Introduction: Reason in History,* trans. H.B. Nisbet, Cambridge 1975). Just how unimportant in 1492 the European peoples were in global terms compared with the Ottoman empire, the Indian empire of the Moguls and China has been impressively described by P. Kennedy, *The Rise and Fall of the Great Powers*, New York 1987.

3. I am here following B. Dietschy, 'Die Tücken des Entdeckens. Ernst Bloch, Kolumbus und die Neue Welt', *Jahrbuch der Ernst-Bloch Gesellschaft*, 1992/93, 234–51.

4. A.W. Crosby, *Ecological Imperialism. The Biological Expansion of Europe 900–1900*, Cambridge 1986; E. Dussel, *The Invention of the Americas*, ET (from Spanish) New York 1995.

5. T. Todorov, *La conquête de l'Amerique: la question de l'autre*, Paris 1982; E.E. Standard, *American Holocaust. The Conquest of the New World*, New York and Oxford 1992.

6. On the notion of the 'world soul', cf. H.R. Schlette, *Weltseele, Geschichte und Hermeneutik,* Frankfurt 1993; C. Merchant, *The Death of Nature. Women, Ecology and the Scientific Revolution*, San Francisco 1989.

7. M. Horkheimer and T.W. Adorno, *Dialectic of Enlightenment*, trans. J. Cumming, London 1973; M. Horkheimer, *Critical Theory*, trans.

M.J. O'Connell *et al.*, New York 1972; J. Habermas, *Knowledge and Human Interests*, ET London 1972.

8. E. Bloch, *The Principle of Hope*, trans. N. and S. Plaice and P. Knight, Cambridge, Mass., and Oxford 1986, 746ff.: 'Eldorado and Eden: The Geographical Utopias'. See here B. Dietschy, 'Tücken des Entdeckens' (n.3), 238ff., who terms these ideas 'the inner-worldly eschatology of modernity'.

9. G. Gutiérrez, *Gott oder das Gold* (German trans. of *Dios o el oro en les Indias*, 1989), Freiburg 1990.

10. J. Moltmann, *The Coming of God*, trans. Margaret Kohl, London and Minneapolis 1996, Chap. III: The Kingdom of God. Historical Eschatology.

11. E.L. Tuveson, *Redeemer Nation. The Idea of America's Millennial Role*, Chicago 1968; M.D. Bryant and D.W. Dayton (eds), *The Coming Kingdom. Essays in American Millennialism and Eschatology*, New York 1983.

12. That is shown by the reverse side of American millennialism: the modern apocalyptic of doomsday literature. To name one example, I may mention H. Lindsay's bestseller *The Late Great Planet Earth*, Grand Rapids, Mi. 1970.

13. See J. Taubes, *Abendländische Eschatologie* (1947), Munich 1991; R. Bauckham, *Tudor Apocalypse. Sixteenth-Century Apocalypticism, Millenarianism and the English Reformation: From John Bale to John Foxe and Thomas Brightman*, Oxford 1975. A considerable influence was exerted by *Spes Israel* (1650), written by the Chief Rabbi of Amsterdam, Manasseh ben Israel (1604–1657). It was dedicated to the Lord Protector of the Commonwealth, Oliver Cromwell, and brought about the readmittance of the Jews to England. Marjorie Reeves, *Joachim of Fiore and the Prophetic Future*, London 1976, shows how strongly English Protestantism and the English Enlightenment were also influenced by the spirit of Joachim.

14. L. Niethammer, *Posthistoire. Has History come to an End?*, trans. P. Cammiller, London and New York 1992; F. Fukuyama, *The End of History and the Last Man*, New York and Toronto 1989.

15. Evidence that Lessing was influenced by the pietistic chiliasm of the philosopher C.A. Crusius was provided by F. Gerlich, *Der Kommunismus als Lehre vom Tausendjährigen Reich*, Munich 1921.

16. I. Kant, *Ideen zu einer allgemeinen Geschichte in weltbürgerlicher Absicht* (1793), Eighth Proposition.

17. I. Kant, *Critique of Pure Reason*, A 804: 'The whole concern of my reason, both speculative and practical, comes together in the following three questions: 1. What can I know? 2. What must I do? 3. What can I

hope for?'

18. Still fundamental here is E. Galeano, *Open Veins of Latin America*, New York 1974. On the history of slavery see D. Mannix and M.J. Cowley, *Black Cargoes. A History of the Atlantic Slave Trade*, New York 1962.

19. R.D. Kaplan, 'The Coming Anarchy', *The Atlantic* Monthly 273/2, Feb. 1994, 44–76.

20. W. Leiss, *The Dominion of Nature*, New York 1972; B. McKibben, *The End of Nature*, New York 1989.

21. For a completely pessimistic judgment see G. Fuller, *Das Ende. Von der heiteren Hoffnungslosigkeit im Angesicht der ökologischen Katastrophe*, Leipzig 1993.

22. J.B. Metz, 'Die Gotteskrise', in his *Diagnosen zur Zeit*, Düsseldorf 1994.

23. H.E. Richter, *Der Gotteskomplex. Die Geburt und die Krise des Glaubens an die Allmacht des Menschen*, Reinbek 1979.

24. We are indebted to E. Peterson for showing the self-evident fact that the 'secret revelation' has nothing to do with the end-time speculations of salvation-history theology, but that it is the 'book of the martyrs'. Cf. E. Peterson, 'Zeuge der Wahrheit', in his *Theologische Traktate*, Munich 1951, 165–224.

25. P. Kuhn, *Gottes Selbsterniedrigung in der Theologie der Rabbiner*, Munich 1968; A.M. Goldberg, *Untersuchungen über die Vorstellung von der Schekhinah in der frühen rabbinischen Literatur*, Berlin 1969.

26. J. Moltmann, *The Way of Jesus Christ. Christology in Messianic Dimensions*, trans. Margaret Kohl, London and San Francisco 1990.

27. O.A. Romero, *Die notwendige Revolution*, with a contribution by Jon Sobrino on the martyrs of liberation, German trans. from Spanish by E. Pagán, Munich and Mainz 1982.

28. G. Gutiérrez, *The God of Life*, trans. from Spanish by M.J. O'Connell, Maryknoll, NY 1991; J. Moltmann, *The Spirit of Life. A Universal Affirmation*, trans. Margaret Kohl, London and Minneapolis 1992.

29. E. von Weizsäcker, *Erdpolitik. Ökologische Realpolitik an der Schwelle zum Jahrhundert der Umwelt*, Darmstadt ³1992.

2. Covenant or Leviathan? Political Theology at the Beginning of Modern Times

1. E. Wolf, 'Das Problem des Widerstandsrechts bei Calvin', in A. Kaufmann (ed.), *Das Widerstandsrecht*, WuF 173, Darmstadt 1972, 152–69. The earlier study by K. Wolzendorff, *Staatsrecht und Naturrecht in der*

Lehre vom Widerstandsrecht des Volkes gegen rechtswidrige Ausübung der Staatsgewalt (1916), is weak on Calvin's theology and Calvinism. See also J. Bohatec, *England und die Geschichte des Menschen- und Bürgerrechte*, ed. O. Weber, Graz 1956.

2. R. Nürnberger, *Die Politisierung des französischen Protestantismus*, Tübingen 1948.

3. T. Beza, *De jure magistratum et officio subditorum erga magistratus*, ed. K. Sturm, Neukirchen-Vluyn 1965, 12.

4. *The Scots Confession* (1560), ed. with introduction by G.D. Henderson, rendered into modern English by J. Bulloch, Edinburgh 1960; see also K. Barth, *The Knowledge of God and the Service of God according to the teaching of the Reformation. Recalling the Scottish Confession of 1560*, The Gifford Lectures 1937/38, trans. J.L.M. Haire and Ian Henderson, London 1938.

5. C.B. Hundeshagen, *Calvinismus und staatsbürgerliche Freiheit*; also H. Languet, *Wider die Tyrannen*, ed. L. Wyss, Basel 1946; G. Oestreich, 'Die Idee des religiösen Bundes und die Lehre vom Staatsvertrag', in *Zur Geschichte und Problematik der Demokratie. Festschrift für Hans Herzfeld*, Berlin 1958, 11–32; C. McCoy and J. Wayne Baker, *Fountainhead of Federalism. Heinrich Bullinger and the Covenantal Tradition*, Louisville 1991, 45ff.

6. Oestreich, 'Die Idee des religiösen Bundes' (n. 5), 22.

7. Languet Wyss (n. 5), 65f.

8. Ibid., 67.

9. Oestreich, 'Die Idee des religiösen Bundes' (n. 5), 25, draws attention to this point.

10. McCoy and Wayne Baker, *Fountainhead of Federalism* (n. 5), 25.

11. P. Miller, *The New England Mind*, Cambridge, Mass., Vol. 1, ²1954; vol. II, 1953.

12. McCoy and Wayne Baker, *Fountainhead of Federalism* (n. 5), 94ff.

13. *Leviathan or the Matter, Forme and Power of a Common Wealth Ecclesiasticall and Civil*, ed., with introduction, by M. Oakeshott, Oxford 1957 (page references in the text are to this edition). Cf. also C. Schmitt, *Der Leviathan in der Staatslehre des Thomas Hobbes. Sinn und Fehlschlag eines politischen Symbols*, Hamburg 1938; D. Braun, *Der sterbliche Gott oder Leviathan gegen Behemoth*, Zürich 1963; P.C. Mayer-Tasch, *Thomas Hobbes und das Widerstandsrecht*, Tübingen 1965; W. Förster, *Thomas Hobbes and der Puritanismus. Grundlagen und Grundfragen seiner Staatslehre*, Hamburg 1969; J. Taubes (ed.), *Der Fürst dieser Welt. Carl Schmitt und die Folgen. Religionstheorie und Politische Theologie*, Vol. 1, Munich 1983.

14. T. Hobbes, *Dialogue between a Philosopher and a Student of the*

Common Laws of England (unfinished; printed 1681); see *English Works of Thomas Hobbes*, London 1839–, Vol. VI.

15. See Taubes (ed.), *Der Fürst dieser Welt* (n. 13), 9.

16. See Schmitt, *Der Leviathan* (n.13), 25f; Taubes (ed.), *Der Fürst dieser Welt* (n. 13), 12f.

17. Taubes (ed.), ibid., 13.

18. On political chiliasm or millenarianism, cf. N. Cohn, *The Pursuit of the Millennium. Revolutionary Millenarians and Mystical Anarchists of the Middle Ages*, London 1957, revised and expanded 1970; E.L. Tuveson, *Redeemer Nation. The Idea of America's Millennial Role*, Chicago 1968.

19. E. Bloch, *Naturrecht und menschliche Würde*, Frankfurt 1961, 60f.

20. WA 39/II, 34–91; see the comment by E. Wolf, 'Leviathan. Eine patristische Notiz zu Luthers Kritik des Papsttums', in his *Peregrinatio* I, Munich 1954, 135–45.

21. WA 39/II, 42.

22. J. Heckel, 'Widerstand gegen die Obrigkeit? Pflicht und Recht zum Widerstand bei Martin Luther, in Kaufmann (ed.), *Das Widerstandsrecht* (n.1), 114–34; 132f.

23. Cf. here H. Meier, *Carl Schmitt, Leo Strauss und 'Der Begriff des Politischen'. Zu einem Dialog unter Abwesenden*, Stuttgart 1988; J. Taubes, *Ad Carl Schmitt. Gegenstrebige Fügung*, Berlin 1987.

24. This was my thesis in 'Theologische Kritik der Politischen Religion', in J.B. Metz, J.Moltmann and W. Oelmüller (eds), *Kirche im Prozess der Aufklärung*, Munich and Mainz 1970, 11–51, 36ff. (ET 'The Cross and Civil Religion', in *Religion and Political Society*, New York 1974, 9–48). On this C. Schmitt wrote: 'Incidentally Moltmann is right when he stresses the intensively political significance which the worship of a crucified God like this contains indestructibly in itself and which cannot be sublimated into "something theological"' (*Politische Theologie* II, *Die Legende von der Erledigung jeder Politischen Theologie*, Berlin 1970, 118).

25. Quoted in B. Nichtweiss, *Erik Peterson. Neue Sicht auf Leben und Werk*, Freiburg 1992, 735 n.119.

26. N. Chomsky, *Media Control. The Spectacular Achievements of Propaganda*, Open Magazine Pamphlet Series 19, Kentfield, Ca. 1991; cf. also his *Deterring Democracy*, New York and London 1991. Mayer-Tasch already voiced a similar suspicion in *Hobbes und das Widerstandsrecht* (n.13), 296.

27. J.B. Metz, *Theology of the World*, trans. W. Glen-Doepel, London and New York 1969; J. Moltmann, 'Political Theology', *Theology Today* 28, 1971, 6–23; id., *Politische Theologie – Politische Ethik*, Munich and Mainz 1984 (ET *On Human Dignity. Political Theology and Ethics*: selections trans. D. Meeks *et al.*, Philadelphia 1984).

28. Metz, ibid., 101.

29. Moltmann, *Politische Theologie – Politische Ethik* (n.27), 124ff. (see also id., 'Luther's doctrine of the Two Kingdoms', in *On Human Dignity* [n.27], 61ff.).

3. Political Theology and the Theology of Liberation

1. E. Feil and R. Weth (eds), *Diskussion zur 'Theologie der Revolution'*, Munich and Mainz 1969; J. A. Garcia and C. Restrepo Calle (eds), *Camillo Torres. His Life and Message. The Text of his Original Platform and All his Messages to the Colombian People*, trans. V. M. O'Grady, Springfield, Ill. 1968; J. Gerassi (ed.), *Revolutionary Priest. The Complete Writings and Messages of C. Torres*, trans. J. de Cipriano Alcantara *et al.*, New York and London 1971.

2. G. Gutiérrez, *A Theology of Liberation*, trans. C. Inda and J. Eagleson, Maryknoll, NY 1973, London 1974; ²1985; revised ed., London and New York 1988.

3. J.B. Metz, *Theology of the World*, trans. W. Glen-Doepel, London and New York 1969; H. Peukert (ed.), *Diskussion zur 'politischen Theologie'*, Munich and Mainz 1969; J. B. Metz, J. Moltmann, W. Oelmüller, H. W. Richardson and M. D. Bryant, *Religion and Political Society*, ET New York 1974; D. Sölle, *Political Theology*, ET Philadelphia 1974; J. M. Lochman, *Perspektiven politischer Theologie*, Zürich 1971; J. Moltmann, *Perspektiven der Theologie. Gesammelte Aufsätze*, Munich 1968 (ET *Hope and Planning*: selections trans. M. Clarkson, London 1971); id., *Politische Theologie – Politische Ethik. Gesammelte Aufsätze*, Munich and Mainz 1984 (ET *On Human Dignity. Political Theology and Ethics*: selections trans. D. Meeks *et al.*, Philadelphia 1984). Good introductions are provided by S. Wiedenhofer, *Politische Theologie*, Stuttgart 1976, and I. Ellacuria, *Teologia politica*, San Salvador 1973.

4. E. Kogon, J.B. Metz *et al.*, *Gott nach Auschwitz. Dimensionen des Massenmords am jüdischen Volk*, Freiburg 1979.

5. E. Kellner (ed.), *Schöpfertum und Freiheit in einer humanen Gesellschaft. Marienbader Protokolle*, Vienna 1969.

6. R. Garaudy, J.B. Metz and K. Rahner, *Der Dialog*, Hamburg 1966.

7. E. Bloch, *Das Prinzip Hoffnung*, Frankfurt 1959 (*The Principle of Hope*, trans. N. and S. Plaice and P. Knight, Cambridge, Mass. and Oxford 1986). For Bloch's influence in the 1960s see S. Unseld (ed.), *Ernst Bloch zu Ehren. Beiträge zu seinem Werk. Festschrift zum 80. Geburtstag*, Frankfurt 1965.

8. H. Gollwitzer, *Werkausgabe*, Kaiser Taschenbücher 42–51, Munich 1988.

9. *Das Bekenntnis zu Jesus Christus und die Friedensverantwortung der Kirche. Eine Erklärung des Moderamens des Reformierten Bundes*, Gütersloh 1982.

10. B. Klappert and U. Weidner (eds), *Schritte zum Frieden. Theologische Texte zu Frieden und Abrüstung*, Wuppertal 1983.

11. J. Moltmann (ed.), *Friedenstheologie – Befreiungstheologie*, Munich 1988.

12. G. Altner (ed.), *Ökologische Theologie*, Stuttgart 1989.

13. J.M. Lochman and J. Moltmann (eds), *Gottes Recht und die Menschenrechte. Studien und Empfehlungen des Reformierten Weltbundes*, Neukirchen 1977; L. Vischer (ed.), *Rights of Future Generations – Rights of Nature. Proposal for Enlarging the Universal Declaration of Human Rights*, Studies from the World Alliance of Reformed Churches 19, Geneva 1990.

14. E. Moltmann-Wendel, *Menschenrechte für die Frau*, Munich 1974; D. Williams, *Sisters in the Wilderness. The Challenge of Womanist God-Talk*, New York 1994; A.M. Isasi-Diaz, *Mujerista Theology*, New York 1996.

15. In the following passage I am drawing on the great compilation edited by I. Ellacuria and Jon Sobrino, *Mysterium Liberationis. Fundamental Concepts of Liberation Theology*, Maryknoll, NY 1993.

16. The first beginnings of this are documented in *Teologia India. Primer encuentro taller latinoamericano*, Mexico 1992; M.M. Marzal (ed.), *El rostro de Dios*, Lima 1991.

17. L. Boff, *Ecology and Liberation*, ET Maryknoll, NY 1995.

18. E. Cardenal, *Cantico Cosmico*, Managua 1989 (ET *Cosmic Canticle*, Willimantic 1993).

19. See J. Sobrino, *Mysterium Liberationis* I (n. 15).

20. H.-P. Martin and H. Schumann, *Die Globalisierungsfalle. Der Angriff auf Demokratie und Wohlstand*, Hamburg 1996.

21. H. Noormann, *Armut in Deutschland. Christen vor der neuen sozialen Frage*, Stuttgart 1991; E.U. Huster, *Armut in Europa*, Leverkusen 1996.

II. Theology and Politics

1. Christian Faith in the Changing Values of the Modern World

1. S. P. Huntington, *The Clash of Civilizations?*, Foreign Affairs, Summer 1993, published by the Council on Foreign Relations, Vol. 72,

No. 3, New York 1993.

2. M. Horkheimer and T.W. Adorno, *The Dialectic of Enlightenment*, trans. J. Cumming, London 1973.

3. See I. 1 above, 'Theology in the Project of Modernity'.

4. G. Picht, *Die Erfahrung der Geschichte*, Frankfurt 1958; W. Pannenberg (ed.), *Revelation as History*, trans. D. Granskou and E. Quinn, London and New York 1969.

5. K.-J. Kuschel, *Abraham. A Sign of Hope for Jews, Christians and Muslims*, trans. John Bowden, London and New York 1995.

6. L. Mumford, *The City in History. Its Origins, its Transformations, and its Prospects*, New York 1961.

7. As well as Robert Jay Lifton, G. Müller-Fahrenholz has pointed this out particularly emphatically; see his *Erwecke die Welt. Unser Glaube an Gottes Geist in dieser bedrohten Zeit*, Gütersloh 1993, 78ff., 'Globale Gefahren als seelische Lähmung'.

8. See *Our Common Future. The Brundtland Report of the World Commission on Environment and Development*, London 1987.

9. A.J. Heschel, *The Sabbath. Its Meaning for Modern Man*, New York [7]1981; J. Moltmann, *God in Creation. An Ecological Doctrine of Creation*, trans. Margaret Kohl, London and San Francisco 1985, Chap. XI, 'The Sabbath: the Feast of Creation', 276–96.

10. Teresa of Avila, *The Interior Castle* (1577), trans. E. Allison Peers, London 1974; W. Herbstrith, *Theresa von Avila. Die erste Kirchenlehrerin*, Bergen-Enkheim 1971; Thomas Merton, *The Seven Storey Mountain*, New York 1948; id., *Contemplation in a World of Action*, New York 1965; J. Moltmann, *Experiences of God*, trans. Margaret Kohl, London 1980.

11. A. Milano, *Persona in Teologia. Alle Origini del significato di Persona nel Christianesimo Antico*, Naples 1986; A.I. McFadyen, *The Call to Personhood. A Christian Theory of the Individual and Social Relationships*, Cambridge 1990.

12. Giovanni Pico della Mirandola, *De dignitate hominis* (1486): 'We have lent you, O Adam, neither an especial dwelling place, nor any visage of your own, nor any particular gift, so that you may have and possess any dwelling place you like, any visage you like, and all the gifts you surely wish for, these too according to your own will and own opinion . . . I have set you in the midst of the world so that from thence you may look round easily at all the things this world possesses . . . so that as your own, completely free and active sculptor and poet you may yourself decide the form in which you wish to live' (for an English version of the whole oration, see *On the Dignity of Man*, trans. C.G. Wallis, Indianapolis 1965).

13. Cf. H. Kessler, *Das Stöhnen der Natur. Plädoyer für eine*

Schöpfungsspiritualität und Schöpfungsethik, Düsseldorf 1990.

14. M. Grabmann, *Die Grundgedanke des Heiligen Augustinus über Seele und Gott*, Darmstadt 1957.

15. R. Descartes, *Discourse on Method, etc.*, trans. J. Veitch, London 1948, 65, *Dedication*: 'I have always been of [the] opinion that the two questions respecting God and the soul were the chief of those that ought to be determined by [the] help of philosophy rather than of theology.'

16. J. Moltmann, *God in Creation*, Chap. IX, 'God's Image in Creation: Human Beings', 215–43.

17. P. Singer, *How Are We to Live? Ethics in an Age of Self-Interest*, London 1993.

18. Here the new social communitarian movement begins. Cf. A. Etzioni, *Die Entdeckung des Gemeinwesens. Ansprüche, Verantwortlichkeiten und das Programm des Kommunitarismus*, Stuttgart 1995; P. Selznick, *The Moral Commonwealth. Social Theory and the Promise of Community*, Berkeley 1992.

19. M. Gronemeyer, *Das Leben als Letzte Gelegenheit. Sicherheitsbedürfnisse und Zeitknappheit*, Darmstadt 1993; G. Schulze, *Die Erlebnisgesellschaft. Kultursoziologie der Gegenwart*, Munich 1993; R. Wendorff, *Zeit und Kultur. Geschichte des Zeitbewusstseins in Europa*, Opladen ³1985; id., *Der Mensch und die Zeit. Ein Essay*, Opladen 1988.

20. S. Toulmin and J. Goodfield, *The Discovery of Time*, New York 1965.

21. For the experience of time in other religions and cultures, see E.T. Hall, *The Dance of Life. The Other Dimension of Time*, New York 1983.

22. A postscript. In some branches of industry, the stagnation in 'the acceleration trap' has been noticed, and a change in the direction of long-term durability has been initiated. The development of ever-new technologies and ever-new products swallows up such immense sums that it is only possible to make a profit with them on the market if they are sold over as long a period as possible. If the marketing phase becomes shorter and shorter, profits then become smaller and smaller, and no longer cover the development costs. That is 'the acceleration trap'. The way out of it is to turn to what is long-term. The sale of the complete product is replaced by the sale simply of its use – i.e., leasing. Servicing and repairs preserve the durabilitiy and longevity of the product. There are laser printers for computers which function without any time-limit. There are long-life cars. The longer a car can be used, the more important the skilled servicing carried out in local repair shops and garages becomes. Increased cost in production is made up for by the durability. So long-life products help to create work, and are environmental-friendly in addition, because less energy and fewer raw materials are used. Cheap cars use up a lot of

energy and raw materials, and produce more waste products, and put more people out of work, because they are manufactured by robots. 'The discovery of slowness' is of the utmost importance for the future of human beings and nature. Cf. W. Stahel, *Die Beschleunigungsfalle oder der Triumph der Schildkröte*, Stuttgart 1995.

2. The Destruction and Liberation of the Earth: Ecological Theology

1. The annual reports of the World Watch Institute, Washington, ed. Lester Brown, speak an unequivocal language.

2. R. Arce Valentin, 'Die Schöpfung muss gerettet werden. Aber für wen? Die ökologische Krise aus der Perspektive lateinamerikanischer Theologie', *EvTh* 51, 1991, 565–77.

3. This can clearly be seen, for example, in Nicaragua, which has been bled white by the Contra War. The forests are being destroyed by the Taiwanese and Korean lumber industry, and are afterwards used for the deposit of United States and Canadian nuclear waste.

4. See E. von Weiszäcker, *Erdpolitik. Ökologische Realpolitik an der Schwelle zum Jahrhundert der Umwelt*, Darmstadt ³1992.

5. Cf. J. Habermas, *Knowledge and Human Interests*, trans. J.J. Shapiro, second revised ed., London 1978. He coined the phrase 'knowledge-constitutive interests' (195ff.).

6. L. White Jr, 'The Historical Roots of our Ecological Crisis', in F. Schaeffer, *Pollution and the Death of Man. The Christian View of Ecology*, London and Wheaton, Ill. 1970, 95–115. He was followed by C. Amery, *Das Ende der Vorsehung. Die gnadenlosen Folgen des Christentums*, Hamburg 1972; E. Drewermann, *Der tödliche Fortschritt. Von der Zerstörung der Erde und des Menschen im Erbe des Christentums,* Freiburg 1991. For a critical view of White's thesis, cf. P. N. Joranson and K. Butigan, *Cry of the Environment. Rebuilding the Christian Creation Tradition*, Santa Fe 1984; C.S. Robb and C.J. Casebolt, *Covenant for a New Creation. Ethics, Religion and Public Policy*, New York 1991.

7. Max Weber, *The Protestant Ethic and the Spirit of Capitalism*, trans. T. Parsons, with foreword by R.H. Tawney, London 1930, ⁹1965, 105.

8. A. Gehlen, *Urmensch und Spätkultur*, Bonn 1956, 295.

9. R. Descartes, *Discourse on the Method of Rightly Conducting the Reason*, in *The Philosophical Works of Descartes*, trans. E.S. Haldane and G.R.T. Ross, revised ed, Cambridge 1931, reprinted 1979, 119.

10. A free version, following an adaptation of the original speech by the

American writer W. Arrowsmith.

11. B. McKibben, *The End of Nature*, New York 1989, 91.

12. Quoted from *The Global Forum on Environment and Development for Survival. Conference Report, Moscow, 15–19 January 1990*, 193ff.: 'We are all the children of the Earth. The earth is governed by the great laws of the universe, and we human beings are responsible for the neglect and violation of these laws . . . There is a crisis of life upon this planet because we, the human beings, have upset the balance of the life-giving forces of the natural world and have interfered with the structures and cycles of air, land and water . . . Our reponsibility is to protect Mother Earth. Nature is a seamless web of life in which all forms of life are related to all others. All are our relatives – the birds, the fishes, the trees, the rocks – we are all connected to that web. Indigenous people are nature's representatives to the modern human community. That which destroys nature destroys indigenous life. We are the people of the Earth.'

13. J. Moltmann, *The Trinity and the Kingdom of God*, trans. Margaret Kohl, London 1981 (= *The Trinity and the Kingdom*, New York 1981).

14. L. Boff, *Trinity and Society*, trans. P. Burns, Maryknoll, NY and Tunbridge Wells 1988.

15. A. Deneffe, 'Perichoresis, circumincessio, circuminsessio', *ZkathTh* 47, 1923, 497–532.

16. Basil, *De Spiritu Sancto*. Cf. also *The Book of St Basil the Great on the Holy Spirit*, revised text with notes by C.F.H. Johnston, Oxford 1892.

17. G. Schimanowski, *Weisheit und Messias. Die jüdische Voraussetzungen der urchristlichen Präexistenzchristologie*, Tübingen 1985.

18. J. Jeremias quoted this logion in part in *Unknown Sayings of Jesus*, trans. R.H. Fuller, London 1957, 95, taking it from Oxyrhynchus Papyrus 1.

19. Timothy Rees: 'God who laid the earth's foundation, / God who spread the heavens above, / God who breathes through all creation: / God is love, eternal Love' (Abbots Leigh, Carol Stream, Ill., 1978).

20. G. Strachan, 'The New Jerusalem – Temple of Creation', *Shadow*, Vol. 1, No. 2, December 1984, 45–58.

21. P. Gregorios, *The Human Presence. An Orthodox View of Nature*, Geneva 1977.

22. Since about 1972, almost all church synods and ecumenical global conferences have brought this cry of tormented creation to public notice. As a survey is impossible, I may refer to my article on ecology, in TRE, XXV, Berlin ³1995, 36–46, with its extensive bibliography.

23. E. Cardenal, *Love*, trans. D. Livingstone, with a preface by T. Merton, London 1974, 24.

24. J. Calvin, *Institutes of the Christian Religion*, ed. J.T. McNeill, trans. F.L. Battles, London and Philadelphia 1980, Vol. 1, Book 1, 51f., 68.

25. Cf. *EvTh* 53, 1993, 5, with contributions by E. Moltmann-Wendel, J. Moltmann, L. Boff, S. Bergmann and C. Rehberger.

26. On the Gaia hypothesis see J.E. Lovelock, *Gaia – A New Look at Life on Earth*, Oxford 1979, reissued 1995; cf. also E. Sahtouris, *Vergangenheit und Zukunft der Erde*, with a foreword by James Lovelock, Frankfurt and Leipzig 1993.

27. R. Radford Ruether, *God and Gaia. An Ecofeminist Theology of Earth Healing*, New York and London 1993. However, she makes no reference to J. Lovelock's Gaia hypothesis.

28. S. Schreiner, 'Partner in Gottes Schöpfungswerk – Zur rabbinischen Auslegung von Gen 1, 26–27', *Judaica* 49, 1993, 3, 131–41.

29. J.M. Lochman and J. Moltmann, *Gottes Recht und Menschenrechte. Studien und Empfehlungen des Reformierten Weltbundes*, Neukirchen 1976, esp. 44ff.

30. L. Vischer (ed.), *Rights of Future Generations – Rights of Nature. Proposal for Enlarging the Universal Declaration of Human Rights*, Studies from the World Alliance of Reformed Churches 19, Geneva 1990.

31. Ibid., 62ff.

32. On animal rights cf. C. Hartshorne, 'Rechte – nicht nur für die Menschen', *ZEE* 22, 1978, 3–14; A. Lorz, *Tierschutzgesetz. Kommentar*, Munich [3]1987, 1ff.; O. Reinke, *Tiere. Begleiter des Menschen in Tradition und Gegenwart*, Neukirchen 1995; G.M. Teutsch, *Mensch und Tier. Lexikon der Tierschutzethik*, Göttingen 1987.

33. Seoul 1989. 22nd General Council of the World Alliance of Reformed Churches, Section II: Justice, Peace and the Integrity of Creation, Geneva 1988.

34. A. Heschel, *The Sabbath. Its Meaning for Modern Man*, New York [7]1981; J. Moltmann, *God in Creation. An Ecological Doctrine of Creation*, trans. Margaret Kohl, London and San Francisco 1985, chap. XI, 'The Sabbath: The Feast of Creation', 276ff.; S. Bacchiocchi, *Deine Zeit ist meine Zeit. Der biblische Ruhetag als Chance für den modernen Menschen*, Hamburg 1988.

35. Cf. my critical argument with A. Auer, 'Ist der Mensch die Krone der Schöpfung?', *Publik Forum*, 31 May 1985, VI–VII.

36. On the new mysticism of the earth cf. L. Boff, *Cry of the Earth, Cry of the Poor*, ET Maryknoll 1997.

3. *Human Rights – Rights of Humanity – Rights of the Earth*

1. I am taking as my starting point the declarations of the World Alliance of Reformed Churches; see J.M. Lochman and J. Moltmann, *Gottes Recht und Menschenrechte*, Neukirchen 1976; also the statements of the Lutheran World Federation recorded in W. Huber and H.E. Tödt, *Menschenrechte. Perspektiven einer menschlichen Welt*, Stuttgart 1977. There is a good historical survey and collection of material in W. Heidelmeyer (ed.), *Die Menschenrechte. Erklärungen, Verfassungsartikel, Internationale Abkommen*, Paderborn 1973.

2. Outlines for the further development of human rights in the direction of 'the rights of future generations and the rights of nature' may be found in *EvTh* 50, 1990, no. 5, 433–77, with contributions on constitutional and international law, as well on theological aspects, by Elisabeth Giesser, Peter Saladin, Christoph Zenger, Jörg Leimbacher, Christian Link, Lukas Vischer and Jürgen Moltmann.

3. Cf. Giovanni Pico della Mirandola, *De dignitate hominis* (1486). For an English version of this oration see *On the Dignity of Man*, trans. C.G. Wallis, Indianapolis 1965.

4. Cf. here H. Küng, *Global Responsibility*, trans. John Bowden, London 1991, and the discussion in J. Rehm (ed.), *Verantwortlich leben in der Weltgemeinschaft. Zur Auseinandersetzung um das 'Projekt Weltethos'*, Munich 1994 ('Projekt Weltethos' being the German title of Küng's book).

4. *The Knowing of the Other and the Community of the Different*

1. J. Moltmann, *The Crucified God*, trans. R.A. Wilson and John Bowden, London 1974, 25ff.: 'Revelation in Contradiction and Dialectical Knowledge'; M. Welker (ed.), *Diskussion über Jürgen Moltmanns Buch 'Der gekreuzigte Gott'*, Munich 1979, 188ff. Cf. the controversy with W. Kasper, 'Revolution im Gottesverständnis?' and ' "Dialektik die umschlägt in Identität" – Was ist das? Zu Befürchtungen W. Kaspers', in Welker (ed.), ibid., 140ff. and 149ff. See also J. Sobrino's continuation of the discussion, 'Theologisches Erkennen in der europäischen und der lateinamerikanischen Theologie', in K. Rahner (ed.), *Befreiende Theologie*, Stuttgart 1977, 123ff. I was really merely pursuing a question which Ernst Bloch raised: 'Whether only like can grasp like or whether, conversely, the unlike is not better suited to do so.' See his *Tübinger Einleitung in die Philosophie*, Frankfurt 1964, 16. E. Lévinas, *Humanisme et l'autre homme*, Montpellier 1972, tries to find an ontological approach to the problem.

2. *Metaphysics* II, 4, 1000 b.

3. *Nicomachean Ethics*, VIII, 4, 1155 a.

4. Talking about Paul's doctrine of the charismata, Ernst Käsemann rightly says: ' "The body [of Christ] consists not of one member, but of many." . . . For while like entities can only cancel each other out and render each other superfluous, unlike entities can perform mutual service and in this service of *agape* can become one' (*Essays on New Testament Themes*, trans. W. J. Montague, London 1964: 'Ministry and Community in the New Testament', 70).

5. See W. Capelle, *Die Vorsokratiker*, Berlin 1958, 217f., 236.

6. *Nicomachean Ethics*, VIII. 4.

7. K. Popper, *The Open Society and its Enemies* (1945), London ⁵1966.

8. Cf. M. Horkheimer, *Zur Kritik an der instrumentellen Vernunft*, Frankfurt 1967; T.W. Adorno, *Negative Dialectics*, trans. E. B. Ashton, London 1973.

9. I. Kant, *Critique of Pure Reason,* trans. Norman Kemp Smith, London 1929, 20. 'Reason, holding in one hand its principles, according to which alone concordant appearances can be admitted as equivalent to laws, and in the other hand the experiment which it has devised in conformity with these principles, must approach nature in order to be taught by it. It must not, however, do so in the character of a pupil who listens to everything the teacher chooses to say, but of an appointed judge who compels the witnesses to answer questions which he himself has formulated. Even physics, therefore, owes the beneficent revolution in its point of view to the happy thought, that while reason must seek in nature, not fictitiously ascribe to it, whatever as not being knowable through reason's own resources has to be learnt, if learnt at all, only from nature, it must adopt as its guide, in so seeking, that which it has itself put into nature.'

10. See W. Leiss, *The Domination of Nature*, New York 1972; C. Merchant, *The Death of Nature. Women, Ecology and the Scientific Revolution*, San Francisco 1980.

11. B. McKibben, *The End of Nature,* New York 1989.

12. This has been more closely investigated by E. Spranger, 'Nemo contra Deum nisi Deus ipse' (1949), in *Philosophie und Psychologie der Religion*, Tübingen 1974, 315ff. See also C. Schmitt, *Politische Theologie* II, Berlin 1970, 116, 123ff., and Moltmann, *The Crucified God* (n. 1), 152f. and n.75.

13. K. Barth, *The Epistle to the Romans*, trans. by E. C. Hoskyns from the sixth edition, London 1933, reissued 1968, 240ff.

14. R. Otto, *The Idea of the Holy: An Inquiry into the Non-Rational Factor in the Idea of the Divine and its Relation to the Rational*, trans.

J. W. Harvey, sixth expanded ed., London 1931. This work carries Goethe's motto: 'Das Schaudern ist der Menscheit bestes Teil./ Wie auch die Welt ihm das Gefühl verteure; / "Ergriffen fühlt er tief das Ungeheuere." '

15. M. Horkheimer, *Die Sehnsucht nach dem ganz anderen*, Hamburg 1970, 56ff.

16. T. Todorov, *La conquête de l'Amerique: la question de l'autre*, Paris 1982.

17. *Nicomachean Ethics*, VIII, 2, 1155 b.

18. Theophrastus, *De sensibus*, 27ff., quoted in G. M. Stratton, *Theophrastus and the Greek Physiological Psychology before Aristotle*, New York and London, 1917, 90ff.

19. F.J.J. Buytendijk, *Pain*, trans. E. O'Shiel, London 1961. Cf. also his monograph *Über den Schmerz*, Berne 1948.

20. F.W. Schelling, *Über das Wesen menschlicher Freiheit* (1809), Reklam ed. 8913–15, 89 (*Of Human Freedom*, trans. J. Gutmann, Chicago 1936).

21. E. Fink, *Spiel als Weltsymbol*, Stuttgart 1960.

22. G. Béky, *Die Welt des Tao*, Munich 1972.

23. H. Nohl (ed.), *Hegels theologische Jugendschriften*, Tübingen 1907, 345ff.: *Systemfragment* of 1809.

24. J. Moltmann, *Creating a Just Future. The Politics of Peace and the Ethics of Creation in a Threatened World*, trans. John Bowden, London and Philadelphia 1989, 42f.

25. F. Capra, *The Turning Point. Science, Society and the Rising Culture*, London 1982.

26. Ernst Bloch, *Das Prinzip Hoffnung*, Frankfurt 1959, 224ff. (*The Principle of Hope*, trans. N. and S. Plaice and P. Knight, Oxford and Cambridge, Mass. 1995).

27. E. von Weizsäcker (ed.), *Offene Systeme I. Beiträge zur Zeitstruktur von Information, Entropie und Evolution*, Stuttgart 1974; K. Maurin (ed.), *Offene Systeme II*, Stuttgart 1981.

28. I. Prigogine and I. Stengers, *Dialog mit der Natur. Neue Wege naturwissenschaftlichen Denkens*, Munich 1980 (German trans. from English MS); also I. Prigognine, *Order Out of Chaos. Man's New Dialogue with Nature*, London 1984.

29. Moltmann, *The Crucified God* (n. 1), 200ff.

30. Sobrino, 'Theologisches Erkennen' (n.1), 138.

31. Moltmann, *The Crucified God* (n. 1), 27f.

32. Fourth Lateran Council of 1215; see H. Denzinger, *Sources of Catholic Doctrine*, trans. R.J. Deferrari, St Louis and London [13]1957, No. 432, p.171. Cf. here E. Przywara, *Religionsphilosophie katholischer*

Theologie, Munich 1926.

33. K. Barth, *Church Dogmatics* I/1, ET Edinburgh 1975, 5, 47ff.

34. *PG* 44, 377 B.

35. Augustine, *Confessions*, Book III, 6, 11; see here M. Grabmann, *Die Grundgedanken des Heiligen Augustinus über Seele und Gott* (1929), Darmstadt 1957, 10–12.

36. E. Bloch, *Das Prinzip Hoffnung* (n. 26), 343ff. (*The Principle of Hope*). Originally Bloch talked about 'the darkness of the lived God'; see his *Geist der Utopie* (1918) 1923, Frankfurt 1964, 254.

5. Freedom in Community between Globalization and Individualism: Market Value and Human Dignity

1. H.-P. Martin and H. Schumann, *Die Globalisierungsfalle. Der Angriff auf Demokratie und Wohlstand*, Hamburg 1996.

2. F. Fukuyama, *The End of History and the Last Man*, New York and Toronto 1989.

3. Apparently the hierarchical ethics and religion of Confucianism keeps the family intact in the Japanese and Chinese world as a form of social security. But the continual struggle against 'immoral Western individualism' shows that this individualism is making inroads in Asian cities too. In the results described above, modern Confucianism is not very far from the consequences in the Western world. Cf. A. Terzani, *Die Erben der Samurai. Japanische Jahre*, Hamburg 1994.

4. C.B. Macpherson, *The Political Theory of Possessive Individualism*, Oxford 1962, reprinted 1969.

5. D. Riesman, *The Lonely Crowd. Individualism Reconsidered*, New York 1954.

6. G. Freudenthal, *Atom and Individual in the Age of Newton*, trans. P.McLaughlin, Dordrecht 1986.

7. Martin Buber, *Dialogisches Leben. Gesammelte philosophische und pädagogische Schriften*, Zürich 1947.

8. E. Etzioni, *The Active Society*, New York 1971. The best analysis of the social-philosophical foundation of communitarianism can be found in P. Selznick, *The Moral Commonwealth. Social Theory and the Promise of Community*, Berkeley 1992.

9. See Chap.2 (i).

10. For a more detailed analysis of the term, see W. Huber, *Folgen christlicher Freiheit*, Neukirchen 1983, esp. 113ff.

11. R. Garaudy, *The Alternative Future: A Vision of Christian Marxism*, trans. from French by L. Mayhew, New York 1975, Harmondsworth 1976.

12. R. Weth (ed.), *Totaler Markt und Menschenwürde*, Neukirchen 1996.

13. T. Litt, *Das Bildungsideal der deutschen Klassik und die moderne Arbeitswelt*, Bonn 1955.

14. R.D. Kaplan, 'The Coming Anarchy', *The Atlantic Monthly* 273/2, February 1994, 44–76.

III. Theology and Religion

1. The Pit – Where was God? Jewish and Christian Theology after Auschwitz

1. A.H. Friedlander, *Riders Towards the Dawn. From Ultimate Suffering to Temperate Hope*, London 1993.

2. Cf. *Jesus Christus zwischen Juden und Christen*, theme number, *Evangelische Theologie* 55, 1995, 1.

3. W. Oellmüller (ed.), *Theodizee – Gott vor Gericht*, Munich 1990; id. (ed.), *Worüber man nicht schweigen kann: neue Diskussionen zur Theodizeefrage*, Munich 1992.

4. The following quotations, however, have been taken, not from this book but from a later article by Richard Rubinstein, 'Some Perspectives on Religious Faith After Auschwitz', in F.H. Littell and H.G. Locke (eds), *The German Church Struggle and the Holocaust*, Detroit 1974, 256–68. It is to this article that the page numbers in the text refer. Cf. also C. Münz, *Der Welt ein Gedächtnis geben. Geschichtstheologisches Denken im Judentum nach Auschwitz*, Gütersloh 1995.

5. Emil L. Fackenheim, *God's Presence in History. Jewish Affirmations and Philosophical Reflections*, New York and London 1970, Chap. 3, 67–104: 'The Commanding Voice of Auschwitz'. The page numbers in the text refer to this book.

6. Eliezer Berkovits, *Faith after the Holocaust*, New York 1973, Chap. IV, 86–113: 'The Historical Context of the Holocaust', esp. 94ff.: 'The Hiding of the Face'. The page numbers in the text refer to this book.

7. Martin Luther, in his writing *De servo arbitrio* [The Bondage of the Will] (1525), came up against a corresponding paradox between 'the revealed God' Jesus Christ and 'the hidden God', the almighty Lord of history: 'God must therefore be left to himself in his own majesty, for in this regard we have nothing to do with him, nor has he willed that we should have anything to do with him. But we have something to do with

him in so far as he is clothed and set forth in his Word, through which he offers himself to us and which is the beauty and glory with which the psalmist celebrates him as being clothed. In this regard we say, the good God does not deplore the death of his people which he works in them, but he deplores the death which he finds in his people and desires to remove from them. For it is this that God as he is preached is concerned with, namely, that sin and death should be taken away and we should be saved . . . But God hidden in his majesty neither deplores nor takes away death, but works life, death, and all in all. For there he has not bound himself by his word, but has kept himself free over all things' (*Luther's Works*, ed. H.T. Lehmann, Vol. 33, trans. P.S. Watson and B. Drewery, Philadelphia 1972, 139–40).

8. This idea – that God's almighty power consists in the very fact that he imposes restrictions on his power so that those he has created can exist with him and before him in their relative freedom, derives from Isaac Luria, who belonged to the tradition of the Spanish Kabbalah. This self-restriction on God's part is called 'zimzum'. Hans Jonas was the first to take up this idea in order to link belief in creation with evolutionary theory; see his *Zwischen Nichts und Ewigkeit. Zur Lehre vom Menschen*, Göttingen 1963. But he then also used it in order to formulate 'a concept of God after Auschwitz'. See O. Hofius (ed.), *Reflexionen finsterer Zeit*, Tübingen 1984, 81–6. Eberhard Jüngel has tried to find a Christian theological answer in Luther's sense; see his 'Gottes ursprüngliches Anfangen als schöpferische Selbstbegrenzung. Ein Beitrag zum Gespräch mit Hans Jonas über den "Gottesbegriff nach Auschwitz"', in *Gottes Zukunft – Zukunft der Welt. Festschrift für Jürgen Moltmann*, Munich 1986, 265–75.

9. E. Wiesel, *Night*, trans. S. Rodway, London 1960. Cf. also R. McAfee Brown's biography, *Elie Wiesel. Messenger to All Humanity*, Notre Dame 1983.

10. This idea accords with the young Luther's theology of the cross. In his theses for the Heidelberg Disputation of 1518 (*Luther's Works*, ed. H.T. Lehmann, Vol. 31, 40–1 [see n.5]) he did not call the God of history the hidden God, but the God who is present 'under the cross and in suffering' (Theses 20–23). The *Deus absconditus* is the *Deus crucifixus* . . . 'and no other God'; cf. J. Moltmann, *The Crucified God. The Cross of Christ as the Foundation and Criticism of Christian Theology*, trans. R.A. Wilson and J. Bowden, London 1974 (first German edition Munich 1972).

11. For the biblical origin, cf. B. Janowski, 'Ich will in eurer Mitte wohnen. Struktur und Genese der exilischen Schekina-Theologie', in *Biblische Theologie*, Vol. 2, Neukirchen 1987, 165–93. For the rabbinic tradition cf. P. Kuhn, *Gottes Selbsterniedrigung in der Theologie der*

Rabbinen, Munich 1978; A.M. Goldberg, *Untersuchung über die Vorstell-ung von der Schekina in der frühen rabbinischen Literatur*, Berlin 1969.

12. E. Wiesel, 'Der Mitleidende', in R. Walter (ed.), *Die hundert Namen Gottes. Tore zum letzten Geheimnis*, Freiburg 1985, 70–5, esp. 73.

13. J.B. Metz, 'Ökumene nach Auschwitz – Zum Verhältnis von Christen und Juden in Deutschland', in E. Kogon and J.B. Metz (eds), *Gott nach Auschwitz*, Freiburg 1979, 121ff. (the page numbers in the text refer to this contribution); id., 'Facing the Jews: Christian Theology after Auschwitz', *Concilium* 175, *The Holocaust as Interruption*, October 1984; id. (ed.), *Landschaft aus Schreien. Zur Dramatik der Theodizee-frage*, Mainz 1995.

14. J.A. Zamora, *Krise – Kritik – Erinnerung. Ein politisch-theolo-gischer Versuch über das Denken Adornos im Horizont des Krise der Moderne*, Münster and Hamburg 1994.

15. J.B. Metz, 'Gotteskrise', in *Diagnosen zur Zeit*, Düsseldorf 1994, 76–82.

16. D. Bonhoeffer, *Letters and Papers from Prison*, ed. E. Bethge, [4th] enlarged ed., trans. R.H. Fuller *et al.*, London 1971, letter of 16 July 1944, 361ff.

17. J.K. Mozley, *The Impassibility of God. A Survey of Christian Thought*, Cambridge 1926. It was in this tradition that Alfred North Whitehead, after the death of his twenty-one-year-old son in an accident, included in his metaphysics *Process and Reality*, New York 1929, the sentence: 'God is the great companion – the fellow-sufferer who under-stands' (532).

18. Cf. Moltmann, *The Crucified God* (n. 10), 273.

19. D. Sölle, *Suffering*, trans. E. R. Kalin, London 1975, 146.

20. It is remarkable that Karl Rahner and, following him, Hans Küng and Johann Baptist Metz, have rejected this step in today's theology of the cross, and still adhere to the omnipotent, impassible God – whether in order not to change the scholastic doctrine of God, or in order to be able to maintain the theodicy indictment against that God. In his last interview, Rahner maintained that a God who 'is having just as rotten a time as I am cannot help me. 'I am from the outset fixed in this hideousness, whereas God is the *Deus impassibilis*, the *Deus immutabilis*, and so forth, in a real and true and for me consoling sense.' See P. Imhoff and H. Biallowons, *Karl Rahner im Gespräch*, Munich 1982, 245f.

21. F. Rosenzweig, *Der Stern der Erlösung*, Heidelberg ³1954, III/3, 192f. (*The Star of Redemption*, trans. W. W. Hallo, London 1971).

22. Ibid., 194.

23. S. Wiesenthal, *The Sunflower*, trans. H. A. Pichler, London 1970.

24. That is the truth. And yet it is in contradiction to the untrue reality

of the people concerned, as A. and M. Mitscherlich already established in *The Inability to Mourn*, trans. B.R. Placzek, New York 1975. They maintain that 'the mechanism of denial' led to the 'defence of unendurable melancholy'. The confrontation with the insight that the tremendous efforts of the war and the appalling crimes of a mad inflation of self-feeling had served a narcissism increased to grotesqueness, ought to have led to the complete deflation of self-value, and would have been bound to result in melancholy, if this danger had not already been nipped in the bud by the work of denial. Cf. here also H.E. Richter, *Die Chance des Gewissens*, Düsseldorf 1995, 58ff.: 'Gegen, ohne, mit der Vergangenheit leben.'

25. See H. Gese's essay on atonement in *Essays on Biblical Theology*, trans. K. Crim, Minneapolis 1981; B. Janowski, *Sühne als Heilsgeschehen*, Neukirchen 1982; P. Stuhlmacher, *Versöhnung, Gesetz und Gerechtigkeit*, Göttingen 1981; R. Schwager, *Brauchen wir einen Sündenbock? Gewalt und Erlösung in den biblischen Schriften*, Munich 1978; N. Hoffmann, *Zur Theologie der Stellvertretung*, Einsiedeln 1981.

26. G. Müller-Fahrenholz, *Vergebung macht frei. Vorschläge für eine Theologie der Versöhnung*, Frankfurt 1996.

27. The assertion that 'anti-Judaism' in Christianity led to Auschwitz sounds on German lips like the attempt to hide one's own guilt in the collective guilt of a great institution. But it was not Scandinavian, West European, American, African or Asiatic Christianity that was responsible for Auschwitz, but simply and solely German Christianity – and there not so much Christianity as the 'national Germanism' maintained by the Nazis and believed in by a majority of Germans.

3. Liberalism and Fundamentalism in the Modern Era

1. T. Meyer (ed.), *Fundamentalismus in der modernen Welt*, Frankfurt 1989.

2. P. Kennedy, *The Rise and Fall of the Great Powers. Economic Change and Military Conflict from 1500 to 2000*, New York and London 1989; T. Todorov, *La conquête de l'Amérique: la question de l'autre*, Paris 1982.

3. F. Fukuyama, *The End of History and the Last Man*, New York and Toronto 1989.

4. J. Moltmann (ed.), *Religion der Freiheit. Protestantismus in der Moderne*, Munich 1990, with contributions by J. Moltmann, W. Huber, E. Moltmann-Wendel and K. Raiser.

5. H. Küng and J. Moltmann (eds.), *Fundamentalism as an Ecumenical Challenge*, *Concilium* 1992.

6. W. Huber, *Kirche*, revised ed., Munich 1988; J. Moltmann, *The Church in the Power of the Spirit*, trans. Margaret Kohl, London and New York 1977; with a new preface, San Francisco 1991; London ²1992.

7. M.D. Meeks, *God the Economist. The Doctrine of God and Political Economy*, Minneapolis 1989; H. Assmann and F.J. Hinkelammert, *Götze Markt*, Düsseldorf 1992; J. Moltmann, 'Ist der Markt das Ende aller Dinge?', in W. Teichert and E. von Wedel (eds), *Die Flügel nicht stutzen. Warum wir Utopien brauchen*, Düsseldorf 1994, 85–108.

8. J. Moltmann (ed.), *Gott und Gaja. Zur Theologie der Erde*, theme number, *EvTh* 53, 5, 1993, with contributions by E. Moltmann-Wendel, J. Moltmann, L. Boff, M. Okino, S. Bergmann and J. Baumgarten.

4. *Dialogue or Mission? Christianity and the Religions in an Endangered World*

1. For more detail see J. Moltmann, 'Dient die "pluralistische Theologie" dem Dialog der Weltreligionen?', *EvTh* 49, 1989, 528–36.

2. M.E. Marty already remarked on this; see his Introduction to W. James, *The Varieties of Religious Experience*, New York ⁴1985, XX: 'Religion is now a consumer item for a nation of spiritual window-shoppers.'

3. The deficit is particularly evident in P. Knitter, *The Myth of Christian Uniqueness. Towards a Pluralistic Theology of Religions*, London 1987, which he and John Hick edited, with contributions by twelve authors.

4. See K.-J. Kuschel's excellent book, *Abraham. A Sign of Hope for Jews, Christians and Muslims*, trans. John Bowden, London and New York 1995.

5. Cf. J.B. Cobb Jr and C. Ives, *The Emptying God. A Buddhist-Jewish-Christian Conversation*, New York 1990, with a foundational contribution by Masao Abe, 'Kenotic God and Dynamic Sunyata', and responses by T. Altizer, E. Borowitz, J. Cobb, Catherine Keller, J. Moltmann, S. M. Ogden and D. Tracy.

6. H. Küng, *Global Responsibility: In Search of a New World Ethic*, trans. John Bowden, London 1991; H. Küng and K.-J. Kuschel (eds), *A Global Ethic: The Declaration of the Parliament of the World's Religions*, London and New York 1993; *Weltfrieden durch Religionsfrieden. Antworten aus den Weltreligionen*, Munich 1993.

7. By the religion of the earth I mean 'the sabbath of the earth' which the Hebrew sabbath laws in Leviticus 26 respect, not the neo-pagan religion of 'blood and soil'. See here J. Moltmann (ed.), *Gott und Gaja. Zur Theologie der Erde*, *EvTh* 53, 1993, 5 (theme number), with contribu-

tions by E. Moltmann-Wendel, J. Moltmann, L. Boff, M. Okino, S. Bergmann, J. Baumgarten and C. Rehberger.

8. J. Moltmann, *The Spirit of Life. A Universal Affirmation*, trans. Margaret Kohl, London and Minneapolis 1992.

9. J. Moltmann, *The Source of Life. The Holy Spirit and the Theology of Life*, trans. Margaret Kohl, London and Minneapolis 1997.

10. The theories for interfaith dialogue which propound the pluralistic view of religions overlook the fact that in serious situations there is a *status confessionis* in which dialogue comes to a stop. Cf. the 1934 Barmen Theological Declaration of the Confessing Church, arrived at in Germany under the Hitler dictatorship, and the 1987 Kairos Document, issued during South Africa's apartheid dictatorship.

5. *Theology for the Church and the Kingdom of God in the Modern University*

1. See J.L. Waits, *Theology in the University. A Study of University Related Divinity Schools*, Pittsburgh 1995, who gives an excellent account of the American discussion.

2. J. Hick, *God and the Universe of Faiths*, London ²1975; J. Hick and P. Knitter (ed.), *The Myth of Christian Uniqueness. Toward a Pluralistic Theology of Religions*, New York and London 1987.

3. Cf. C. Cherry, *Hurrying toward Zion. Universities, Divinity Schools, and American Protestantism*, Indiana University Press 1995. Surprisingly enough, the names 'divinity schools' and 'faculty of theology' are used almost exclusively by Christian institutions.

4. O. Weber, *Grundlagen der Dogmatik* I, Neukirchen 1955, 11: 'No less a one than Schleiermacher set up the thesis that dogmatics as a theological discipline "is related solely to the Christian Church" (*Der christliche Glaube*, ²1830, 2), and contemporary dogmatics especially have adopted this thesis throughout in their own way (K. Barth, *Kirchliche Dogmatik* 1/1, 1; E. Brunner, *Dogmatik* 1, 3; P. Tillich, *Systematische Theologie* I, 9).'

5. D. Bonhoeffer early on reversed the usual Lutheran doctrine of the two kingdoms, and talked about church and state as the two forms of the one divine rule in our world. Cf. *Dein Reich komme* (1932), Hamburg 1958, 14ff.

6. In his *Ethics*, put together and edited in 1949 by E. Bethge (ET London and New York 1955 ²1965), Bonhoeffer therefore divided up the one 'reality of Christ' in this 'worldly reality' into four mandates: work, marriage, authorities and church; he occasionally added culture, thus

fanning out reality into five mandates. These mandates are 'not a second divine authority side by side with the God of Jesus Christ; but they are the place at which the God of Jesus Christ secures obedience to himself. The word of God is not concerned with the institutions themselves but with obedience in faith within these institutions' (322).

7. A. Burgmüller and R. Weth, *Die Barmer Theologische Erklärung. Einführung und Dokumentation*, Neukirchen 1983; J. Moltmann (ed.), *Bekennende Kirche wagen. Barmen 1934–1984*, Munich 1984, especially H. Simon, 'Die zweite und die fünfte These der Barmer Erklärung und der staatliche Gewaltgebrauch', 191–222.

8. J. Moltmann, *The Crucified God*, trans. R.A. Wilson and John Bowden, London and New York 1974, 53ff.

9. Latin American liberation theology has demonstrated and practised this excellently.

10. I am taking over these categories from K. Barth, 'The Christian Community and the Civil Community', in *Against the Stream. Shorter Post-War Writings 1946–52*, ET London 1954. He calls these 'correspondences' 'parables of the Kingdom of God' (56). I would call them real promises of God's coming kingdom. Cf. *The Crucified God* (n.8), chap. 8: 'Ways towards the Political Liberation of Mankind', 317ff.

11. For more detail here see D.H. Kelsey, *To Understand God Truly: What's Theological about a Theological School?*, Louisville 1992.

Bibliographical Details of Chapters

The chapters of this book were first presented as lectures, or appeared earlier, as follows:

I.   1. *Theology in the Project of Modernity*

Lecture held at a plenary session of the American Academy of Religion, Chicago, 21 November 1994; offprint published by the Association of Theological Schools in the United States and Canada, Pittsburgh 1995; *Evangelische Theologie* 55, 1995, 402–15; *Revue de Théologie et de Philosophie* 128, Lausanne 1996, 49–65.

2. *Covenant or Leviathan? Political Theology at the Beginning of Modern Times*

Lecture held at the Carl Siemens Stiftung, Munich, 21 January 1993; printed in part as 'Im Bund gegen den Leviathan', *Evangelische Kommentare* 1, 1994, 24–8; also 'Covenant or Leviathan? Political Theology for Modern Times', *Scottish Journal of Theology* 47, 1994, 19–42; *Zeitschrift für Theologie und Kirche* 90, 1993, 299–317.

3. *Political Theology and the Theology of Liberation*

Printed in part as 'Teologia politica y Teologia de la Liberacion', Universidad Iberoamericana, Mexico City 1991; *Carthaginensia* VIII, 1992, 489–502; *Union Seminary Quarterly Review* 45, 1991, 205–18; 'Die Zukunft der Befreiungstheologie', *Orientierung* 59, 1995, 207–10; 'Die Theologie unserer Befreiung', *Orientierung* 60, 1996, 204–6.

II. 1. *Christian Faith in the Changing Values of the Modern World*

'Entfremdungen moderner Menschen von der Natur, vom Körper, von der Zeit', lecture held at the 30th Montecatini Congress with psychotherapy weeks, 16 May 1996; in altered form under the present (German) title as lecture in Ulm, 11 September 1996, and in Hanover, 8 January 1997 (unpublished); *Theology. News and Notes*, Fuller Theological Seminary, October 1996, with responses by E. Cherry and N. Woltersdorff.

2. *The Destruction and Liberation of the Earth: Ecological Theology*

Printed in part as 'The Ecological Crisis: Peace with Nature?', *Scottish Journal of Religious Studies* IX/1, Spring 1988, 5–18; *Colloquium. The Australian and New Zealand Review* 20, 2, 1986, 1–11; *Questione ecologica e con scientia cristiana*, Brescia 1987, 137–54; *Washington Cathedral Papers*, 1991, Vol. 2, 23–35; *Pacifica* 5, 1992, 301–13; *Carthaginensia* XI, 19, 1995, 1–22.

3. *Human Rights – Rights of Humanity – Rights of the Earth*

With Elisabeth Giesser, 'Human Rights, Rights of Humanity, and Rights of Nature', in L. Vischer (ed.), *Rights of Future Generations – Rights of Nature*, Studies from the World Alliance of Reformed Churches 19, Geneva 1990, 15–25; *Evangelische Theologie* 50, 1990, 437–44 (not identical with the present article.

4. *The Knowing of the Other and the Community of the Different*

Evangelische Theologie 50, 1990, 400–14; 'Knowing and Community', in L. Rouner (ed.), *On Community*, Notre Dame 1991, 162–76; also in J. Andretsch (ed.), *Die andere Hälfte der Wahrheit*, Munich 1992, 173–91.

5. *Freedom in Community between Globalization and Individualism: Market Value and Human Dignity*

Lecture held at the Communitarian Summit in Geneva, 12 July 1996; hitherto unpublished.

III. 1. *The Pit – Where was God? Jewish and Christian Theology after Auschwitz*

Lecture on the occasion of the showing of Karl Fruchtmann's film *Die Grube* in Bremen, 21 December 1996. Also in *Festschrift for Milan Opocensky, Stand Firm and Take Action*, Studies of the World Alliance of Reformed Churches 34, Geneva 1996, 257–74.

2. *Protestantism: 'The Religion of Freedom'*

In J. Moltmann (ed.), *Religion der Freiheit. Protestantismus in der Moderne*, Munich 1990, 11–28.

3. *Liberalism and Fundamentalism in the Modern Era*

In J. Willms (ed.), *Fundamentalismus – verstehen und mit ihm umgehen*, Jahrbuch Mission 1995, Hamburg 1995, 144–59.

4. *Dialogue or Mission? Christianity and the Religions in an Endangered World*

Lecture given in Berlin, 16 September 1996; also in M. Welker (ed.), *Brennpunkt Diakonie. Festschrift für Rudolf Weth*, Neukirchen 1997, 185–200.

5. *Theology for the Church and the Kingdom of God in the Modern University*

Printed in part in *Evangelische Kommentare* 5, 1996, 273–6.

Index